D0934975

THE MUSIC OF INDIA

THE MUSIC
OF INDIA

Peggy Holroyde

Foreword
by Ravi Shankar

PRAEGER PUBLISHERS
New York • Washington

BOOKS THAT MATTER

Published in the United States of America in 1972
by Praeger Publishers, Inc.
111 Fourth Avenue, New York, N.Y. 10003

© 1972 by George Allen & Unwin Ltd.

Library of Congress Catalog Card Number : 76-158093

Printed in the United States of America

Acknowledgements

Before I could comprehend the principles of Indian music I had first to understand the workings of my own Western system. It was a young student at the Royal College of Music in London who gave many hours of her time and first set me on the road into this book, by explaining the fundamentals and then listening patiently through hour upon hour of Indian raags. That was Carol Walker. Then I went to an old friend, Donald Swann, who was kind enough to play the examples I wished to hear illustrated upon the piano; and so it went on until I found myself in the basement of the School of Oriental and African Studies in London where Nazir Jairazbhoy and John Barham took over.

To them all I am very grateful, and to those many Indian friends who have always answered my tedious but necessary questions: Prodyot Sen who has always taken patient care of all I ever needed; Rajeshwari Datta, celebrated singer of Rabindra Sangeet and now lecturer in Indian Music at S.O.A.S.; the late T. K. Jayaram Iyer; Dr Narayana Menon; Debabrata Chaudhuri; and in most recent times in Leeds, Devika Subramaniam, a young South Indian player of the veena. And long ago in the fifties there were those such as the late poet Vallathol and Rukmini Devi Arundale in Malabar and Madras respectively who gave such warmth, such philosophy and good advice.

There are also those who have suffered more by having to teach me Hindi and Urdu. R. Agrawal and D. K. Vohra worked valiantly against the overwhelming odds of a pupil who was too busy trying to harness together a host of other interests at the same time!

But there are three people to whom I owe most. The first is my long-suffering husband who never saw me for months during the hours of the night when all was quiet but for the sounds of typing and haunting raga melodies. Another is Ravi Shankar whom we had the joy first to meet in New Delhi in 1954 and who set off the first electric spark. Since then he has, even in his most preoccupied time, been generous with his help, bubbling humour and wisdom in curtailing my more foolish mistakes. And there is my son-in-law Peter MacGowan, newly arrived in the family, who, when he was a student at Durham University, made me sit down one evening with his stereo headphones and listen to three hours of concentrated group music. I could not hear myself think immediately after *that* experience but the impact sank in. A whole new

7

world of musical possibilities and intellectual stimulus opened to me – Pink Floyd, The Who, The Cream, Third Ear Band, Tyrannosaurus Rex, the Beatles of course, and now Quintessence.

I have been educated by all these people, but none of it would be down on paper without the remarkable efforts in deciphering the impossible made by Mrs C. D. Brown of Hindustan Steel in London, without Valerie Barton in Yorkshire who not only struggled with all the Indian words but imbibed a real enthusiasm for the music in the process, or lastly Kirstie Kean who retyped the entire manuscript to a deadline until her back ached. Also, I wish to thank Dr Suresh Awasthi of the Sangeet Natak Akademi in New Delhi for supplying the photographs of many musical instruments.

I would like to thank all the authors whom I have quoted, with full acknowledgements both in the text and in the Bibliography, for their generous advice and help with copyright.

To those from whom I have not heard (although every attempt has been made to contact them) and to their publishers, I hope this recognition will suffice.

8

Foreword by Ravi Shankar

Interest in Indian music has always existed in the West; I even remember it from my childhood days when I used to be in the croupe of my brother Uday, whose performances of classical Indian dancing attracted so much attention in the West from the 1930s onwards. Many people were fascinated by the music, but it was secondary to the spectacle of the dance, and classical music on its own was only appreciated or understood by a select few. There were some people who professed a knowledge of Indian music but treated it as a museum piece. I am chagrined even today to see that there are still people who categorize it in the same way as music from Java, Bali, Borneo or Africa; that is as 'ethnic' music, and – though this is found more in the USA–put it under the classification of Ethnomusicology.

This reminds me of something which happened a few years ago at a music seminar in Madras. A very learned Indian scholar of music got up and suggested that 'from here on we should term Western classical music as "ethnic music" because in India what we really consider classical music is our own'. This resentment goes to show how strongly and proud we feel about our music. I personally feel that the only two 'classical' forms of music are the 'Western' and the 'Indian' because of their roots and development which have never stopped up to date. Apart from the fact that the roots of our music are found in the religious scriptures of the Vedas which date back not less than three to four thousand years, and that it has been handed down from the guru to his disciples, they have both developed an intricate system based on strong disciplines and rules.

It is ironic to see the interest in our classical music that exists in Great Britain these days, since in all the 200 years or more of association with India, the British never, never took any interest, and in fact they even looked down on it, thinking that our vocal music was like gargling, and such things. Even the sound irritated them, and the only people during the years of British rule who took a sympathetic view were a very few music scholars who wrote books trying to interpret Indian classical music for people in the West.

The great surge of interest in Indian music really started in the middle 1950s, although it was still a very small audience to which people like myself, Ali Akbar Khan, Vilayat Khan and some other musicians tried to cater, but I found it started growing by each visit, and by 1960 or 1963 one found really very large audiences in the big concert halls of cities like London, Paris, New York, Chicago and Los Angeles. The USA was a bit more advanced in the sense that the interest shown in Indian music started much earlier and with greater zeal. All the jazz music-lovers took to Indian music very naturally, believing that it resembled jazz because of the improvization and the freedom of the artist and other such superficial characteristics. Nevertheless it was there that Indian music found its big interest.

In Europe I find that a great push was given to our music from the period of the Edinburgh Festival in 1963. Then came a big explosion through the interest taken by the fans of 'pop' musicians which really started around the end of 1965. This opened up a new interest for the younger generation and young people all over the world found a great enthusiasm for our sitar and sarod and Indian music in general; but still it was more of a fad, which continued till about 1969. From then onwards this 'fad' declined, but in its place there emerged a great number of people, mostly young but also in an older group, who had a true interest, a genuine appreciation and also to a great extent, an understanding for the music.

Although several people have written about Indian music recently, there is a continuing need to initiate people, especially if they have not had the opportunity of hearing our music in its proper setting in India. This book, written by Peggy Holroyde, whom I have known since she first came to India in 1953, has opened another vista for helping people to understand a good many things about India—not only the music, but also as it relates to our culture and heritage. What I specially like about this book is that it does not go into dogmatic assertions or deal only with the dry, theoretical aspect, but has a much more human approach. This comes out beautifully because of Peggy Holroyde's love for the country, its people, its art forms and many other facets of Indian culture. I knew, when she was in India, what great pains she took in travelling round the country to meet people, listening to all kinds of music played from Kashmir in the North to Kerala in the extreme South, experiencing it for herself and collecting information during the five years she was there. I know, also, how much care she has taken in selecting and checking her material for this book, and as a result it reveals the great love she has for the task of trying to help people understand the past and present of Indian music, as well as the enduring background of India itself.

Ravi Shankar

The Moghul Emperor Akbar asked his famous court musician Tansen: 'How much do you know of music?'
And the reply was:
'My knowledge is like a drop in a vast ocean of promise.'

Contents

Plates

Prelude

The idea of this book was born in the vestibule of the Royal Festival Hall in London after the first particularly successful concert of Indian classical music. The main auditorium was full to overflowing. That is nothing new nowadays but this was on my return from India in 1958, and I had seen 300 people turned away from hearing Pandit Ravi Shankar playing his beautiful, ivory-embossed sitar. Most of that audience had been Western. This in itself was a matter to note for me who had seen very modernized Indians on their own home territory totally alienated from much of their own artistic tradition by the indoctrination of Western-style education in their city schools and major universities.

Such music had made the vital breakthrough, but as an inveterate eavesdropper I heard the vestibules buzzing with bewilderment and confusion. My fellow-countrymen appeared to be floundering in their assessments, not knowing where to begin. I felt an urgent need, then and there, to attempt to express the inner spirit of this music in which I had lost myself and found new enrichment which will last me all my days. But it had to be done not in terms too scholarly, but in a way which the ordinary concert-goer in the West might savour the real Indian atmosphere and feel that touch of supreme enjoyment which comes with those rare moments of total identification.

Yet–if Tansen, the famous sixteenth-century musician who was one of the most sensitive and accomplished in both theory and practice, could dismiss *his* knowledge as but a drop in the ocean of promise which this music held–what then of my own limited vision both as a traveller from a far shore and as a non-playing lover of music? I believe now that these blatant disadvantages have worked to my credit in that I have painfully had to search for the understanding. Because of this I have been made to appreciate the innate problems others, equally laymen in a professional field, have as they reach through the fog of incomprehension which has for so long enveloped us in regard to the Asian arts. If I, ignoramus that I was, could journey to the shores of fulfilment across this vast ocean of promise, then others who equally despair in the initial stages of ignorance can also find a promise become tangible experience. My hope, therefore, is to be a stepping-stone, one among many, helping to make a path across these waters.

I will begin at the beginning. Having written this book and concerned myself so much with the technique of the music, it will seem a strange quirk of mind to say, 'Forget this!', but I constantly remember back to the concert my husband and I attended on a November night in 1953 to celebrate the lovely Festival of Lights for the Hindu Deepavali. It was our first concert of music–and on a most august occasion at Rashtrapati Bhavan in the presence of Dr Rajendra Prasad, the then President of India.

Dr Narayana Menon had taken us along to introduce us to the music. He could not have done a more auspicious thing, for it was an encounter so totally different and so totally aesthetic, engaging all the senses rather than existing at an isolated intellectual level, that the experience was made whole in one evening. The seal had been set from the start, dispelling in one instant of time any mental antipathy we might, like many foreigners, have undergone. We had been made aware.

The magic of the haunting and evocative tones of the shehnai played by Bismillah Khan and the gentle smoothness of the late D. V. Paluskar's voice, transformed that first encounter into a moment of real transition. These two incomparable artists were the catalysts for all our ensuing delight in the music. But we knew nothing then of the grammar, the principles, the techniques. Yet that first impression was never undermined by some of the second- and third-rate musicians we were eventually to hear.

The rememberence of that first indelible occasion when Bismillah bowed with a gracious Lucknowi 'adāb' to this august gathering and drew the elongated shadja note from his shehnai after a delicate hint of the previous note, was to stay beside me and influence me through all the years we were to spend with real happiness in India, that tragic but heart-warming land I now regard as a permanent home in the mind. The heart always speaks first in India. Perhaps that appeals to my feminine nature. Indeed the concentration of emotion in the music took my heart by storm. The head followed later.

I was lucky however. Because of the nature of my husband's post as representative of the British Broadcasting Corporation we were in intimate contact immediately with All India Radio and all its facilities. The producers and engineers there were more than helpful. Many a time I was called in at short notice and allowed to sit cross-legged in the corner of a small recording studio while famous musicians were on the air. And so gradually I had many musician friends to encourage me on this path of understanding. I was of course living within the Indian framework, an inestimable advantage over those who can only ever hear the music in concert halls in the West. I had also studied Indian Philosophy under the tutelage of Dr Radhakrishnan when he was Spalding Professor of Eastern Religions at Oxford University in 1947. The stepping-stones all fitted into a pattern that an Indian might feel was ordained. This explains why I have been so concerned to spell out in the first third of this book the background of various ways of thought in Hinduism, because without some knowledge of the mainstream of Indian thought and the atmosphere which Hindu philosophy engenders into everything Indian, even Muslim society, nothing can ever really fit together and make sense to strangers in India.

The whole temper of thinking and the very atmosphere one breathes in moving around daily among Indians, are wholly different from those of the West.

The psychological impulses that influence an Indian's outlook on life, and therefore his culture, are obviously present in the music also. Our cultures are created from the nature of our respective environments; a part of the book had therefore to concentrate on these aspects of Indian thought. For the rest, historical development and the fusion of invading Muslim civilization into a composite Indian rather than Hindu culture from the eleventh century onwards, and also the evolution of musical grammar, these together take up the remaining two-thirds of the book. I have deliberately compartmentalized the various constituents which make up the technique so that the principles which fire the movement of the music can be more easily understood, no matter how arbitrary this is when realizing the music as a whole in atmosphere and in force.

In this respect the analogy with grammar holds good. We do not enjoy a French poem or read Goethe because of the grammar. In fact, through our having to do so for formal schoolwork, much of European literature is irretrievably lost to our emotional enjoyment and appreciation.

In a production of Shakespeare we do not go hunting adverbial clauses–in fact we come to savour the essence in the beauty and construction of the writing without plodding first through the grammar. And yet, if one has studied the English language in some detail, how much higher is the level of enjoyment.

I only mention this because there are dangers in both tendencies –in over-emphasis on the grammatical rules, and in their total negligence. Wallowing in the sentiments of an art form without applying the mental disciplines never did come to much good. I can only go by my own experience in this world of Indian music because music is such a passionately individual affair and we can make of it what we bring to it personally. Having attended one UNESCO Conference of Eastern and Western music in 1958 I recall my distinct fear during some of the debates that two or three academic minds were already beginning to make of Indian and other Asian music, a museum piece. Our Western desire to have everything cut and dried–a desire born of our training in the scientific discipline of measurement and clarity–may well drain Indian music of its ebullience, joy and singing melancholy. Debate on flattened sixths and microtonal subtleties can never indicate the measure of enjoyment which the Indian musician generates both in himself and in the direct vocal response of his Indian audience. Thank God for the Indian musicians! Because of them Indian classical music is still growing and changing, less dramatically than our own perhaps; but we must disabuse ourselves of the idea some scholars hold, that this music is to be 'preserved'.

Our desire to know the mechanics is a natural and right desire. The swing of the pendulum had to come, away from the previous dismissal of Eastern music as 'sensual excitement' by the musicologists of former decades. I have seen it dismissed as such in one *World History of Music* which is still in print. In fact, this particular heavyweight volume treated Greek, Chinese, Egyptian and Indian music in a peremptory ten pages out of a 400-page book devoted mainly to European, Russian and American music. Why then call it a *World History of Music*? But such is the measure, even today when we ought to know better, of our cultural insularity, that many a 'world' assessment needs reappraisal and revision in the entire field of the arts.

Our modern tendency has swung the pendulum in natural reaction against this 'sensual' critique. At least we feel that by dissecting the grammar bit by bit, notating the shades and vibrations of the musical intervals, credence is given to the intellectual subtlety and the 'acute perception' of the Indian musician. But in so doing we are in danger of losing the essence, the secret that touches the Indian heart and mind when a voice, an instrument and a drum come together to make music.

Sensual excitement has always been regarded with some suspicion by our Anglo-Saxon minds, as precluding the intellectual standards of classical principles. But this is a warped and one-sided view which constantly creates problems – as witness Press sensationalism over a contemporary production of Schoenberg's opera *Moses and Aaron* at the Covent Garden Opera House in London. It seems that as soon as sensuality is hinted at we go overboard. Musical judgement is abandoned and we are left fluctuating between the extremes of a shaken mental seismograph.

This appears ridiculous to a true Indian who, if he has not been touched by the blight of Victorian prudery unfortunately visited upon him by the British Raj and some frustrated English memsahibs, responds warmly to sensuality within a very strict framework of mental discipline. Sensuality is not to be equated with sexuality – but even that is not to be feared.

There is no doubt that a great deal of Indian classical music is sensual, even erotic. To listen to the sarod being played is to see the glisten and sheen upon sumptuous silk. To soak in that now silent voice of the dead Bade Ghulam Ali or to be washed over by the cadences of Subbulakshmi's singing, is indeed to luxuriate in warm evenings when the heat curls around one's body like lush pashmina wool, and the smell of champak and raat-ki-rani lingers like a scented mist in the air. This is India, not some cold, forbidding northern land where grey, damp skies sap the spirit and where clothes imprison the body away from the feel of the wind and the touch of the sun.

Of course there were times even with all the advantages of living in India, when I felt intellectually lost. Only by giving myself over to the music and following where it led through intuition did anything begin to make sense as far as the head was concerned.

The pulse of India throbs in the music and the dance-drama. It is in this realm of living that India exposes herself, without self-consciousness, unlike in politics and other forms of living that most Western observers hastily latch on to in the hopes of understanding this complex and elusive people. The poetry, the stoicism in face of aching tragedy, the austere discipline of the yogi, the languishing air of over-rich beauty, the heaviness of joss-stick perfume–all these are India. The plaintive shepherd boy's voice surging across forbidding Himalayan valleys; a wandering Rajasthani minstrel intoning an hour-long mythological ballad of Shiva and Parvati and carrying with him the breath of the Middle Ages as the golden autumnal sun filters on to the cool stone verandah of a modern Delhi bungalow; the sudden ebullience of a Madras audience beating out the tremendous thudding rhythms of the South; an Orissan tribe snaking in and out of a primitive linear step with a hypnotic three-note, high-pitched chant–all these Indian people can express themselves in a naturally fulfilled way in and through the music. Here is India at her most vulnerable and exposed. But also it is her strength; so much so that we now witness young Western audiences rising to standing ovations for such austere classical vocalists as Girija Devi (who emerged the first time from Benares only in late 1970) and for two of Ravi Shankar's latest concerts in 1971, one pure Indian music, the other presenting his Concerto for Sitar in London in its premier form.

The Indian Government may strive for respect from the West in the arena of politics and technological achievement, but all the time she ignores her real, sure strength which Western political journalists pass by out of sheer ignorance. And it is towards these very strengths in music, philosophy and the arts that my own young turn in reshaping their own overpoliticized, impersonalized world. But then, in some respects Indians are their own worst enemies for they have been so brainwashed by our system of values that they search for the same equations to display for our condemnation. Neither are they a nation of proselytizers.

I, therefore, feel much gratitude towards all the wonderful Indian friends who helped me in my initial enthusiasm. Many of them were Indian musicians who at a later date were to come and play in our house in New Delhi. I was also able to travel 80 000 miles throughout India and to live in the South for some time. Everywhere, personnel of AIR guided my husband and myself to the best music and to folk-music and dance in the more isolated village communities.

I have also had the sustaining help of old friends such as Ravi Shankar who originally set me off on the first attempt in 1958 to write down what I felt, T. K. Jayaram Iyer who was conductor of the South Indian Orchestra of AIR, Prodyot Sen of the Hindustan

Steel Company in London who has so often accompanied Ravi Shankar on his tours of Europe, and Dr Narayana Menon of the Society for the Performing Arts in Bombay. For these reasons I have wished to pay a debt, and to share what I can of all that I was given. This is why in the end this book had to be written.

Leeds, 1971   P.H.

Note on transliteration

To relieve this book of too much scholastic exactitude I have written much-used terms such as 'raga' and 'tala' as they are *seen* to be pronounced, not as they should be literally written from the Hindi script of Devanagri (an entirely phonetic alphabet of characters). Nor will they be self-consciously placed in italics. Such words are becoming common currency and have been absorbed into the English language on the sleeves of even the most popular of our LP records.

One rule in pronunciation is easy to remember. Many short Sanskrit words which end in a consonant, 'kick off' at the end with a short 'uh' sound – known as visarg – after the last consonant. This is not a rule for Hindi however (which most North Indians use now for their pronunciation of musical terms). Therefore, there is confusion between Sanskrit and Hindi and their efficient reproduction in the English language. Raga, tala, sama and alapa, all transliterated from the Sanskrit, should be transliterated as raag, taal, sum and alaap from the Hindi, which is now what we usually hear. Often, however, when words are written in English the Sanskrit pattern is retained, e.g. raga, yoga, Shiva instead of raag, yōg, Shiv.

Raga is spelled in Devanagri characters as र (= a rolled 'r'), ा (= a long 'aa') and ग (= a hard 'g'). The word stands in Hindi as राग and would therefore appear to be r-aa-g with a clipped consonant at the end as in English pronunciation. But in Sanskrit there is this subtle afterthought of sound – the short inherited 'uh' – so that the English 'g' will sound as 'ga' and not as a clipped, hard 'g'. It will not be as pronounced an afterthought as the English spelling would make it.

Some Westerners will be confused when they see terms like rasa bhava written as ras bhaav (cf. heading of Chapter 2), but for the sake of consistency at the beginning I have used the transliteration in English which comes closest to the actual pronunciation in India at the present time. Afterwards I have spelled these words as the mood took me. They are now common to all our language and one hopes that we in the West will pay Asians the compliment of pronouncing their language as well as they have honoured the English language.

Chapter One

THE HINDU BACKGROUND

*'It is impossible to divorce Indian music from the whole structure
of Indian culture and philosophy.'*   DR ARNOLD BAKE

NEW TRENDS

Can we in the West ever really enjoy Indian classical music? This
is not an idle or rhetorical question. Indians themselves are still
genuinely surprised if a real and sincere interest is shown on our
part. The unexpressed question is, 'How can this be?'. There is
still the suspicion that we may be affecting an interest as a 'new
generation' Westerner who has after all been told time enough that
he should show some interest in the culture of the country he may
be visiting–but how deep does our interest go? In the light of
contemporary pop musicians taking to the sitar, can it be yet
another gimmick, temporarily in fashion?

It has to be remembered again and again that Indians have, for a
very long time, been used to the stranger from overseas coming to
live among them and showing either apathy, or worse still, active
dislike of their culture, pouring scorn on all their arts, music, dance
and sculpture.

For every Cunningham and Curzon, for every Sir Thomas
Woodruffe and Sir John Marshall (who ironically enough saved
Sanchi for all time against Indian vandals of the day), or Faubian
Bowers and William Archer to interpret her art, there have been
thousands from the West who pass through the Indian subcontinent untouched. Kincaid has quoted passages in his *Social
History of India* on British reactions at their most frank and truest
(from private letters home) in which the 'caterwauling' of the
music 'was enough to make one's hair stand on end'.

However, since political independence and the changing psychological climate among Indian artists and musicians themselves, a
refreshingly assertive quality has become noticeable in relation to
Western culture. It is an acknowledged fact throughout the newly
emerging nations that once political freedom is attained, cultural

ferment among the indigenous population reasserts itself. In fact, independence brings a subtle rediscovery of the roots of cultural identity. It is therefore all the more acute in a nation of such antiquity as India, with such a highly developed civilization as India's has been. Her national consciousness is now intensely concentrated, a very understandable characteristic which Westerners sometimes forget to take into account, especially English people who have themselves never suffered the decimating effect of alien rule in 1000 years. It is sometimes salutary as Westerners to ask ourselves what *would* have been the effect upon our culture and Christian civilization if we had lived through 300 years of Hindu rule with all its inevitable influences upon our processes of thought, education, religion and artistic expression, leaving aside our own personal psychology.

As old inferiority complexes abate so old arrogances die. Nowadays many Westerners in this generation are free and willing to take a new and more objective look at the creative spirit of other civilizations, exorcised as we are from old cultural insularities. Despite all the apparent antipathies and political convulsions which seem to pull the world further apart, there is a sense of deep currents running and swelling towards unification and wholeness, carving new channels of profound cultural significance into the rigid structures of the arts, social orders, economics, and even into the divisive and blinkered theologies of our institutionalized religions.

There is a cautious, almost unconscious, pull towards unity amid the diversity of mankind. Though this idea is politically new to the West, it is an ancient attitude within the Indian sub-continent, a quality of thought that impregnates the whole of Indian philosophy. It is the foundation-stone of the modern Indian secular state and it was the most passionate of Pandit Nehru's private themes which he endlessly and publicly expounded to his people.

Tolerance of other faiths and acceptance that there are diverse ways for diverse people towards the attainment of unity with the Divine, and the metaphysical vision that we are all fragmented parts of the whole, have given a cosmic direction to all Indian artistic and religious expression. It makes the contribution of the Indian mind to world civilization a valuable commodity at this particular historical juncture.

An Indian would find nothing alien in the thought expressed by Pierre Teilhard de Chardin that 'over the centuries an all-embracing plan seems in truth to be unfolding around us. Something is afoot in the universe, some issue is at stake, which cannot be better described than as a process of gestation and birth; the birth of the spiritual reality formed by the souls of men and by the matter which they bear along with them. Laboriously, through the medium, and by virtue of human activity, the new earth is gathering its forces, emerging and purifying itself.' This thought is astonishingly Hindu in concept.

History and art and literature and philosophy do not begin and end at the Mediterranean as a great many school and university curricula would have us believe. The younger generation tripping over our heels has to live in a world which will make them well aware that this is not so, even though their education may have done them the disservice of leaving a pattern of exclusively Western thought in their minds. Out of political and economic necessity, Asians and Africans have had to learn far more about us, than we about them.

However, at the artistic and cultural level an inevitable process of change is going on which brings us closer, certainly, to the Indian mind whether we like it or not. In the specific area of the arts rigidity of form in music and painting has, for instance, been shattered by our own protaganists: in music by Schoenberg, Stravinsky, Stockhausen, Boulez and John Cage and *musique concrète* (first proposed by Pierre Schaeffer the French composer in 1950); and in the pictorial arts by Cézanne, Picasso and Pollock, and more recently still by the School of Abstract Expressionism, and 'minimal' art. Well known musicians such as Rubbra and Holst were first in the field over a decade ago specifically to experiment with modes of music outside the Western system. Since those early days a tide appears to be flowing in from the East, most especially from India. A diverse group of musicians have therefore cared to introduce Indian themes to foreign audiences: Oliver Messiaen and Benjamin Britten (Curlew River and The Burning Fiery Furnace); the indefatigable Yehudi Menuhin who as long-time President of the Asian Music Circle in London has been most active in promoting a meeting of minds between Asian and Western musicians; Julian Bream, the classical guitar player (who has visited many parts of India and collaborated with Ali Akbar Khan, India's most

27

famous contemporary sarod player); Pierre Boulez, Larry Adler and Dave Brubeck, the jazz musician; and coming to the younger generation of popular music, George Harrison of the Beatles, who has most seriously undertaken a study of Indian philosophy as well as the music. There are many of the most intelligent and musically experimental pop groups who have turned to India also; Mike Heron and Robin Williamson complete with Eastern themes, shehnais and sitars in the Incredible String Band; Quintessence; Pink Floyd; The Who; Love; Davy Graham, the folk guitar player; Third Ear Band; and of course Indo-Jazz Fusions with John Mayer and Joe Harriott. The exiled Greek composer Mikis Theodorakis, uses sitars for his musical score of the film of Euripides' *Trojan Women* because, as he comments, Trojans were Asians. Experiments in Europe by Barney Wilen of France, Manfred Schoff of Germany and Irene Sweitzer of Switzerland are still going on; the intellectual and rhythmic reverberations are creating wholly unforeseen consequences among the young, and not only there. Films, television and radio programmes (certainly in Britain) now introduce Indian music without a hair's being turned. This would have been inconceivable even ten years ago. My husband made one of the first television programmes on Indian music in 1957; it was given a very late night showing on BBC television as being of minority interest.

Nowadays we have the familiar spectacle of kirtans being sung by young English students at the experimental art centre, the Round House, in London, to several thousand people and Hare Krishna Mantra has made the list of the top twenty pop tunes. Interest in Indian music has shown phenomenal growth in USA campuses. California has its own Kinnara Music School, pioneered by Pandit Ravi Shankar who also appeared at the definitive Woodstock Festival. Indian musicians of all kinds and calibres spend three or four months teaching in and touring America, and American students by the score can be seen boarding Bombay planes in dhotis and kurtas, carrying sitars and sarods and tablas. One may pour scorn on such antics, many older people regarding them as trendy occupations. However, in the last few years, instead of proving ephemeral the interest shows every sign of growing in depth and spreading through the whole classical field. The Edinburgh Festival has brought Ravi Shankar, Ali Akbar, Vilayat Khan, Bismillah Khan and Palghat Mani Iyer, the great South Indian mridangam player, to European audiences. Other younger players such as Ashish Khan, the sarod player, and Debabrata Chaudhuri have successfully aroused attention throughout Europe and America. Subbulakshmi (dubbed the Indian Callas) has sell-out audiences wherever she goes, whether in America, the UK, France, Germany or Italy. Nazakat and Salamat Ali, Pakistan's leading vocalists, leave a wake of responding young people transported by the soft touch and astonishing range of their voices.

A few years ago audiences would not have known what a raag was. Who knows what fusions the future may hold? Indeed, who does when Ravi Shankar has in 1971 composed four ragas – Khamaj, Sindhi Bhairavi, Adāna and Raag Mānj Khamāj – to be linked as a Concerto for Sitar with the London Symphony Orchestra playing with him under the direction of Andre Previn.

Who indeed would have thought at the end of the war that the staid city of Bath in the west of England would, within a few years, find itself playing host to the thrumming resonances of South Indian veenas and the commanding percussion of the magnificent mridangam – sounds that ricocheted off the fluted columns of that most august of Guildhalls with its memories of portly eighteenth-century kings, dainty minuets and the baroque mannerisms of dandies such as Beau Brummel. I doubt if the streets of Bath, secure in their own harmonies of golden stone and yellow-green light, have ever before been subjected to this bubbling rush of Malayalam, nor the fine shades of fragmented tones which Indian musicians can conjure into such full resonant sounds, floating and wallowing like the large, lazy turtles in the waters of their holy city of Brindaban. This India in Bath was one of those cultural frictions that sets off chemical reactions of which Yehudi Menuhin is so especially and sensitively aware.

Speaking at a UNESCO Conference on Eastern and Western systems which was held in Paris in 1958, he said then that the need of our time was to get under each other's skin, to understand the part of truth that is in each individual. 'The leaves of the tree have their own life but as the leaves of the tree are a part of the whole so we also are part of a unity.' This again speaks to the theme which motivates all Indian thought.

The old, constricted view of the occidental musician that *real* music only exists in the West, is no longer true. But it is no use our being emotional and rushing into a sense of oneness with the rest of humanity without understanding the fundamentals of our differences and misunderstandings. The heart has to be harnessed to the mind. A musician such as Bismillah Khan, with his shehnai, can appeal straight to the heart and to our emotions because of his distilled discipline. All the sad-sweet atmosphere of the hills of India, the pathos and melancholy, like the northern colouring of a Grieg piano concerto, inextricably mixed with the surprising gaiety of India and as syncopated as a Bach air, speak plainly enough in his renditions to anyone. But an even more agonizing sense of beauty, as acute as it is ever felt in India's tragic and beautiful land, can come by the tough intellectual knowledge of what Indian music is about.

The process of educating our ears to accept alien principles of sound has been long, hard work. Pandit Ravi Shankar deserves our thanks during years when he was much criticized in his homeland for having become 'too Westernized', when in the fifties he spearheaded a concentrated movement of Indian musicians to the West. I remember concerts in those days when our audiences were slow to respond numerically or appreciatively. But he has done a lasting service to India by his perseverance and steadiness in withstanding criticism from his own countrymen, so breaking through our subconscious inhibitions, our ignorance and misconceptions.

Does this mean then that music is becoming truly international, with a common language that communicates directly across national and cultural boundaries, or that it can be assimilated instinctively if you happen to have an ear for music? I think not. As one who was totally ignorant of the music but was pulled instinctively by force of emotion across the boundaries before even learning the mechanics, I still feel too much is taken for granted in the explanation of the music by the Indian performer and that neither of our two traditions has recognized sufficiently the force of the differences which our respective traditions and cultures drive between us.

Certainly, Ravi Shankar has expressed concern that many of our classical musicians are so entrenched in their principles that they judge every other kind of music by their own ingrained Western yardsticks. Few still dare to take the universality of view that Menuhin achieves.

Among young students there may be more natural empathy for India's music due to the cultural shift in present-day attitudes, but confusion abounds for the ordinary concert-goer who has come out of curiosity or because of a prevalence of Asian friends (and one has to remember the overnight transformation of Britain into a multi-racial society with concentrated Asian settlement and its eventual concomitant influence on school text books and curriculums).

The average music-lover, being no musicologist, and therefore wary of all the frightening technicalities that bespatter the pages of books written about musical systems, will possibly wonder what hit him. There is indeed for this reason alone a compelling need for interpretation of this new musical language.

Did that singer really 'gargle'? What was that evocative melody that made such a lingering sense of the musical scale in the slow introduction but which seemed to disappear in a cacophony of repetitive sound towards the climax? How could that fantastic percussion ever be differentiated, broken down into its component parts? Why do we sense a magnetic pull in the long passages of seemingly unbroken sound despite the fact that the music seems to flow irresistibly onwards without recognizable shape, rhythmic form or tangible pause? Constant listening (and there are many long-playing records now available), some support along the way and the desire for understanding can brush away the bewilderment until the melody becomes recognizable and the listener finds himself singing as an harmonic accompaniment the refrain from the Skye Boat Song against the melodic line of Raga Lajwanti! It can be done.

The irony is that to the trained musician, Indian music is no longer as strange as it was. More consonance can be recognized and the melody is more acceptable than some of the most recent tonal experiments which are being carried on by *avant-garde* musicians such as John Cage and others in the United States and by Nono, Berio, Peter Maxwell-Davies, Penderecki and Xenakis in Europe.

The traditional diatonic scales (the major and the minor scales as opposed to the chromatic scale which runs consecutively through the twelve tones of the piano keyboard octave) and the fixed system of harmonics which has been in use since the tempered scale evolved centuries ago, are now deliberately being shattered by Stockhausen, and others, since Schoenberg and Stravinsky startled the musical world with their unorthodoxes. Chordal harmonies are thrown overboard. The result is a far more angular dissonance—a 'thin-ness' of sound, an assault upon the ear—than any Indian raag could purvey. The assault on our conventional expectations of musical sound gathered momentum with 'serialization' (the process of using the twelve-tone scale in serial order or tone-rows of melodic sequence chosen in certain arbitrary orders or used up in simultaneous chords before a new row of notes may be started). In *avant-garde* free-chance improvisations, random gatherings of sound from musicians in experimental combination create an indeterminacy like the throwing of dice (specifically used by John Cage) and an increasing fragmentation—an acoustic phenomena in fact—with silence as part of the musical interval used in composition. The final *coup de grâce* has been dealt by electronic 'happenings'—high-frequency oscillations and tape-jugglings, such as those undertaken, admittedly with controlled mathematical principles by Cage and Lejaren Hiller in the Experimental Music Studio and the Department of Computer Science of the University of Illinois, Urbana, in America (Nonesuch Recording Stereo L 71224, Polydor Records, London), and Le Groupe de Récherches Musicales du Service de la Récherche de la R.T.F. (French disque BAM LD 070(M), 133 Boulevard Raspail, Paris VIe).

Some of these electronically controlled sounds, *in extremis*, leave the ear with the distinct impression of a flock of Canadian geese landing with a flutter of wings and much honking in the midst of a Paris traffic jam! If our ears can encompass this then Indian music is lyricism of a high order in contrast.

At another level in so-called pop music, rapidly expanding its frontiers into experimentation with full-scale, classically orthodox orchestras (Malcolm Arnold, for instance, and Deep Purple in London in 1970), the popularity of the guitar, echo-chambers and folk-melodies has introduced all kinds of grace notes, slurrings and overlapping sounds to young audiences. When the Rolling Stones, the Yardbirds and the Beatles take to the sitar, Indian music has arrived, even if it is not exactly in the manner its dedicated exponents would wish or have imagined! But in the process our ears have become accustomed almost unwittingly to these almost imperceptible changes, even if the mind has not.

It is the mind that is the stumbling-block and many an older music-lover may equate both Indian music and the new atonal experiments and write them both off as a seeming anarchy of sound. But if Indian music is listened to without preconceived ideas and without the expectancy which our own harmonies and modulations have created in us, then its own well ordered framework of discipline and its pure melody (embellished with spasms of intricate improvisation and a rudimentary counterpoint of a kind between melody and percussion) will work their own magic.

One has to be a realist however. True understanding comes after much hard work. We may try to cast away our inhibitions and our inbuilt concepts but still there will be certain immediate difficulties to slow down our process of absorbing the full impact and measure of the music, for knowledge of the arts presupposes some familiarity with their sources of inspiration in religion and civilization. Art has always had roots in and reflected the innermost beliefs of societies. This is even more true now in Asia than in the West where pictorial art has become international and unrepresentative of spiritual civilization, being more influenced in the last ten years by the upward surge of scientific technology. This may be a more accurate reflection of our secular civilization than Christian themes now are. But this could not be said to be true of Asia where there is still an embracing and individual piety and humility before God.

We can only become aware of the inward exploration of Indian music if we comprehend the metaphysical urges that are so part and parcel of the thinking of each individual Asian. These urges gave rise to the principles of the music many thousands of years ago, and have remained consistent, coherent and contemporary for a longer stretch of time here than anywhere else in the world, except China.

Interestingly enough, and ironically, the musician who creates greatest controversy in the West, Karl Stockhausen, showed himself to be more psychologically in tune with this search when he acknowledged recently his own mysticism in relation to the new Age of Aquarius. He is quoted as saying that as a result of this 'we are fast moving into a spiritual era and must concentrate on the intuitive and the suprarational ... The music is a vessel, a vehicle which people can get tuned into and discover their inner selves.'

THE NATURE OF REALITY
Western Reassessment and the Hindu View

Ever since the development of psychology and molecular biology and the growth in knowledge of physics and neurology, the horizon of our intellect has been stretched. The inner mechanics of the mind, of electrical impulse and atomic particles, has broken down what seemed so stable on the surface of the material world of tangible matter. Things are no longer what they seem superficially to be. Thus our own exploration beyond the finite limits which we have had to acknowledge in past centuries into the intangible and previously inaccessible areas of mind and molecular matter, has brought us perhaps more in communion with the ultimate concern of the Indian mind than at any other moment in history.

The concern of India's religious thinkers (philosophy never having become an entirely academic discipline cut off from individual spiritual action and motivation in this world) with maya dominates Indian thought. Maya is the concept of illusion, false reality. The immediately recognizable material world is questioned on the validity of its realness. Humanity takes it for real, not realizing the opaqueness our ignorance gives to the outer form. 'Real' reality is within the essence of a thing rather than in its outer shell, just as the molecular structure of life, unseen, is the prime cause of the visible outershell.

At last we can meet therefore, as science begins to enlarge our own concepts of the universe and liberates us from the confines of organized religions which have paradoxically divided us as human beings rather than unified us into a comprehensive whole mankind. We meet where the new truths of astrophysics embrace us all within a much greater and more mysterious miracle of creative energy, overwhelming in the majesty and orderliness with which it begins to unfold the inherent laws (the dharma to a Hindu) that govern macrocosmic galaxies as well as microcosmic cells.

Certainly at the level of the pictorial arts, our artists are wrestling continually now with the presentation of these abstract truths which are increasingly being thrust into the forefront of our minds. They are attempting also to break up the kernel of existence to portray the impalpable energy that sparks off reality in the molecular forms which we see as solid matter. One can almost sense the forbidding nature of outer space and the amorphous nature of exploding gas and galactic dust in Mark Rothko's sombre last paintings bequeathed to the Tate Gallery in London; and the late Morris Louis (1912–62) who experimented with the rainbow hues of dyes, and Jackson Pollock who surely is one of the symbols of our space-age culture, discard the concrete in visual terms in order to concentrate the intensity of vision on the mobile world of creative reality. In the very process of exploration–the activity of searching inwards to find the structure of reality–such artists are clearly on the same track that Indian musicians have been on during all these centuries in their intensive exploration of abstract sound. The certain and particular notes of each raag are examined in every conceivable way to get at the secrets of the 'inner feel' of the structure of each raag.

The Indian musician has also discarded the solid, the representational, narrative in order to concentrate his efforts on the inner search into the nature of sentiment, in the true sense of the word. This is called ras or rasa (pronounced 'russ').

But paradoxically his methods are exactly opposite to those of our modern artists with their revolt against form, grammar and the long-accepted rules of draughtsmanship on canvas.

Within a very strict discipline, i.e. the framework of a raag, which would correspond to a strict use of draughtsmanship in the composition of a painting, the Indian musician will use the specific tools of his trade, the grammar in fact of gamaka or grace note, portamentos and talas or rhythmic cycles, to release the mind in this very concentration upon these concrete exactitudes.

Here again is a paradox in the meeting of opposites. In trying to comprehend the vast formlessness of the cosmos with such specific technique, the mind is explored and undergoes a process of 'becoming one' with the real reality beyond the tangible. This process Yehudi Menuhin has well understood when he comments on the hypnotic, trance-like effect that such concentration upon the finer points of the music has on the psyche. It *is* as though one is transported beyond the tangible reality into an amorphous, cosmic reality, where mystic, saint, poet, artist and musician meet on common ground.

Music-lovers who come fresh to their first Indian concert are often puzzled by this process and put it down to boredom or the monotony of the music. But this again is nothing new to Indian processes of thought. It happens within the disciplines of yoga, in the dance with its repetitive techniques, in the pada yatra pilgrimages on foot with all their prolonged and attendant hardships, in the Hindu preoccupation with moksha–the liberation I have just mentioned from the outer forms of this world and the prison-house of maya, false reality. Western painter and Indian musician are becoming one in the same haunting pursuit.

The Indian takes this process perhaps one step further because his search is accepted as being in the nature of the religious. Reaching this point, Hinduism teaches that liberation (moksha) brings peace of mind–shanti.

The French writer Madeleine Biardeau gets nearer to the truth of this strange (to us) chameleon interchange that is continually occurring in Indian philosophy and which can even be experienced by the more prosaic foreigner if he is willing to attune himself to the Indian atmosphere. She writes that, as well as being 'a personal loving God in the form of Krishna in the *Bhagavad Gita*, divinity is at the same time referred to in the *Bhagavad Purana* and in many other texts as supremely impassive–none other than the cosmos itself.

'The God of Indian devotion–bhakti–who responds to the same eternal needs of the human heart as exist anywhere else, never detaches himself wholly from this immanence in the world. He is personal and endowed with feelings only in the eyes of popular piety; to thought he reveals himself both far beyond and within at the same time; the universe is his manifestation rather than his creation, he reveals it as much as he hides it; and each man is in himself in some sort a manifestation of God.'

New thinking, inspired by our own relentless scientific drive into outer space and our mental lurch beyond the confines of a terrestrial planet, is certainly at work in our literature and drama. Art has already been affected; in the process it has indeed become international. But music for us still trails within the confines of the tempered keyboard, Schoenberg notwithstanding. The majority of our audiences still tend to take a cloistered view of all those systems of music that exist beyond these familiar confines. As a consequence, it is still harder for a Japanese musician or an Indian vocalist to reach a point of communion with his fellow practitioner in the West than a Japanese artist or an Indian sculptor will with *his* own counterpart.

Ordinary laymen still seem to be locked within the sounds which are familiar, and a majority of classical musicians also hold fast to their precepts of harmonization and modulation. They are much more hidebound in regard to new development than are Western painters of kinetic art. Therefore it is even more difficult in terms of music for the person who is virgin to the whole experience to come to a concert of unknown music, and, in listening, for him to enjoy what he hears. When two or three Indian musicians bow low in namesteh or namashkar greeting and take their places to play, as they sit cross-legged in spotless white clothes on the carpet, their shoes left at the edges of the durree in respect for the occasion (all music having originated in sacramental worship and instruments still being venerated in puja ceremonies, certainly in South India at Saraswati Puja) a very real challenge is thrown out to the uninitiated among us. The musicians take up their gleaming instruments and skin-tight drums. But what do we know of their background, their culture, the *raison d'être* that gave shape to what they are about to play? There is bound to be confusion at first because we all tend to judge any artistic experience by the standards of taste and criticism we already possess–standards evolved over many years within our own environment and conditioned by the familiar. We understand what we know.

Emotional expression springs from the personal philosophy of an artist. The living roots transmit the sap of adrenalin upwards. This is the creative impulse. And one always has to remember that the roots go down so deep because of the force of time and un-broken continuity of growth in the Indian subcontinent, which reaches way back to the hoary beginnings of Vedic worship after the Aryan settlement. Chant and music were conceived of then as mediums for expressing the inward yearning of a man's very breath (=naad or vital power, as defined by that great scholar of Indian thought, Sir John Woodroffe) and therefore his soul. This was symbolized in the Sanskrit word 'praña' which will be dis-cussed later; this was the actual breath of a human being expelled outwards through the vocal chords until it merged with the other part of his individual soul or atman–the outward entity or great Atman–in the very air of the universe.

No one who wishes to go beyond the cursory understanding of this music can therefore readily ignore the gigantic matrix of Hindu thought, in which framework all the Indian arts not only *did* flourish but still do.

HINDU PHILOSOPHY

The sparkling energy of India lies in Hinduism. Without the framework of Hindu belief India would fall apart–even today in both modern political terms (which embrace sixty million Muslims and numerous other religions) and economic terms. Without Hinduism (in undogmatic and tolerant form) India is not herself. 'It is impossible', Dr Arnold Bake, the late Dutch scholar of Indian music, has written in *The New Oxford History of Music*, 'to divorce Indian music from the whole structure of Indian culture and philosophy with which it is interwoven in a number of ways from the earliest times of which we have records.'

At least 1500 years before the first Muslim invasion of India, Hinduism had established its codes, customs, systems and philosophies. The first Muslims, sons of Turkish slaves who had been freed and risen to power, entered present Pakistan around the eleventh century. Even during 700 years of Muslim rule Hinduism remained active as a living philosophy although custom and social tradition became fossilized due to defence mechanisms set up by Muslim proselytizing and physical attack at the temple level.

After the initial full development of Hindu thought—from the early animistic beliefs of the Aryans, through the formalizing and codified ritual of the Brahmins, to the abstruse metaphysics of the *Upanishads* and the later reaction these created, towards a warm, mythologically based, religious concept of the world of gods and goddesses in the vast range of the two epics *Ramayana* and *Mahabharat*—there was no further need to essay change.

All thought in later centuries traced its inspiration back to this solid bed-rock. The truths remain constant and the Indian still sees no reason for the frantic search of the Western mind always to remain discontent with what is. *Hamlet*, the play, remains constant, but so dynamic is the charge of Shakespeare's genius, that each age sees *Hamlet* in its own light and with its own perspective. In the same way Hindu principles of the fundamental philosophy remain constant, but each age emphasizes one or the other quality depending on the changing need of that age. Because there is no dogma or theology, no hierarchy or church-body, Hindu thought has remained flexible and responsive to new needs. It is only the old words given a new interpretation.

In the same way again the scale of a raag remains constant, but the individual artist approaches it with his own insight. Truth remains constant indeed, but its facets are many-sided.

Perhaps because every quality of life is highly charged in the tropical burgeoning of India's climate, even the truth has expanded beyond our grasp. Those of us from the West do indeed find

Hinduism hard to contain in our intellectually analysing minds. We like things cut and dried, precise and logical, and Hindu thought, ritual and belief refuse to conform to this need. The compass of Hinduism touches life at all its points of confusion, messiness and paradox. Truth is seen in opposites and multireflections. Its ultimate concern with the human soul caused it to admit the inexplicable, to acknowledge the imperceptible vagaries of the human mind, to recognize the impreciseness of reality and the illogicality of some creative processes, long before the sciences of psychoanalysis, biophysics and biochemistry began to reflect on the untruth of our own preciseness and philosophy's obsession with linguistic semantics. Logic is not the nature of life–even cell-structures carrying in their construction an inherent law (dharma again) of symmetry in positive and negative balance, occasionally revert to an unaccountable asymmetry.

Fortunately our own reassessment is mounting as scientific discoveries force our minds to accept that the human condition is irrational–paradoxically at one moment definable, at another moment fluid and unattainable by measurement, just as solid matter has now proved to be, with the discovery of the neutrino particle, neither here nor there.

'It is not this–it is not that'–neti, neti, declare the *Upanishads* on the nature of reality. It even defied the Hindus for clarity of analysis and only by a negative description could the truth be achieved. In speaking positively one only distorted the truth. This is the final paradox which they fully recognized.

Writing on Indian aesthetic theory and practice, Kapila Vatsya-yan, one of India's talented and articulate women educationists, has commented on this constant urge to unify the opposite impulses of human life. For one thing, the Indian layman 'does not believe that life ended with death. It was on account of this belief (which the traditional Indian even today shares with his fore-fathers) that the drama of climax could not be conceived of in this country. Life was a varied manifestation of the end and death was a mere passing . . . Even the apparent contradictions and ironies of life were only different manifestations of a greater unifying power. The greatness of the human being lay thus according to the Indian, in holding contradictions or apparent contradictions together. The counterpoising of opposites or of two completely contrasting forces in order to arrive at a third force was a conception which was known to him but which did not become the central principle of his life. He thus did not believe in conflict as a central principle . . . He was indeed looking at life as a conglomeration of different moods and aspects which were after all the different forms of the detached one . . . The aesthetician and the art-creator both accepted these assumptions. To them also life was a series of happenings through which *detachment was to be achieved in the very process of playing one's part as an involved but not an emotionally attached person.*'

Personal v. Co-operative Salvation

Fundamentally each Hindu is preoccupied with his own personal salvation, which is comprehended as ultimate union with whatever God is – Brahm (or Brahman as it is sometimes written) the Supreme Neuter, scientific in principle embracing as it does the concept of a thinking energy, the true active creative law of the universe.

The emphasis, therefore, throughout Hindu development has been on concern more with individual rather than corporate welfare; logically the emphasis is right. If all the components of a machine are working fluently to the order of their intrinsic laws, then the machine in its wholeness is efficient. The parts are essential to the whole. This concept is ever to the forefront of an Indian's mind and has been indelibly stamped upon his subconscious mind during at least forty-five centuries of uninterrupted development.

There has, of course, been the other strand: the emphasis on concern for a wider society beyond the individual and his immediate family, but it has never been so concentratedly developed as the individual search for moksha or liberation. Similarly, in the raag all the strands of the music are concentrated upon the liberation point of the sum (sama), the ultimate, emphatic joining-together.

I have often wondered if this predominant characteristic of individual searching towards release rather than corporate Christian worship, is not the reason for the continual reiteration of the personal, contemplative qualities of the music, as against our own 'corporate' music synthesizing a great many conflicting components into an orchestral whole. So often in concerts I have felt, through the searching genius of a musician exploring the alaap, the swelling introspection, piercing ever inwards into the very core of one's inner spirit until the music culminates in an explosion out of the contemplative into identification with the source of creative energy.

Westerners are primarily concerned with life in this tangible world which we consider real because we believe we have only one life to live here – with then perhaps the touch of immortality. What we do here is therefore important. This can hardly be said to be true of Indians! To the Hindu, time stretches in the spatial sense. The day in the life of Brahma is measured symbolically in astronomical figures: some Hindu scriptural text give it as 4320 million years to be cosmologically exact. Brahma lives for 100 years, and then in the dying process recreates the world of universes again. In complete destruction comes the redemption. A new avatar or reincarnation is born as redeemer to lead mankind from the Kalyuga, the dark and evil age into which, incidentally, we now have been born.

This is the fourth stage in the life of the Brahma and has to reach completion before that avatar can lead us into yet another recreation of a golden age at the beginning of another life in Brahma. And somewhere, finally, through actions (karma) which develop the individual soul of time, comes absorption into the Brahm, the ultimate Neuter far beyond the male personification.

Time is cyclical but moving forwards, like a series of overlapping circles, and therefore without beginning or end. Hence this particular fractional existence in the world of today takes on a quite different perspective. The tangible world seems no longer to have such compelling importance. Urgency evaporates like the heat which throbs at the horizon's edge in an Indian summer when the thermometer reaches 120 degrees in the shade. Another reality begins to shape in the mind, and I speak not from a woolly-minded theoretical point of view but from sharp experience! The spirit curls inwards away from the merciless onslaught of the sun and one tries desperately hard to forget body and concentrate upon forgetfulness.

A tangible thing is. At the same time it is not. In terms of matter for instance, a graceful sitar is obviously an instrument made of wood, metal frets, carved ivory and hollowed gourds. That is tangible reality. At the same time it is more than the sum of its parts. It is also the particular sound that it creates. That is an intangible reality. Beyond this at a further reach it can be depicted as a molecular design by the physicist, a composition of atoms.

Hindus have wrestled all through the long centuries with the complexities of these metaphysical problems. Reality and maya, the great illusion of this outer husk of life, are in constant antagonism. Illusion–maya–is something from which Hindus must eventually escape to moksha or mukti–liberation. This has had its own effect on artistic concepts and principles and undoubtedly has influenced that tremendous pull inwards that is so often felt as one listens hour after hour to the music floating gently upon the heavy air of an Indian night. As one lives through it one longs for its final climactic liberation.

The Modern Concept of Shiva

Being and non-being is a concept that has at last come again into the forefront of our own minds as we plunge into outer space. It is a modern postulate, a dilemma with which our own astrophysicists also wrestle. As we try theoretically to search into the truths about creation and the apparent anomaly of new particles coming into existence from nothing and the void of outer space, we meet Hinduism at the core of the dialectic. From the furthermost receding edges of space to the innermost nucleic acids we come together again on common ground, in front of the bronze statue of the dancing Shiva, the Nataraja, Lord of the Dance, the third god of the Trinity with Brahma and Vishnu.

Within this image is embodied a truth that is as relevant to our own scientific and technological age as it ever was to that first artist who fashioned the Nataraja into a symbolic equation of energy–the elemental creative energy which sparks into life and dies away just as the primordial gases of outer space explode into young stars while dying galaxies atrophy.

Dance is so closely allied to music in India, interlocked as it is organically with the taal (tala) or beat of the music. At the same time it is a vehicle for the sensuously yearning padams or love lyrics addressed to God which in turn enrich the statuesque positions of this sculptural dance form. But dance has, in Indian metaphysics, come also to symbolize the state of rhythmic energy which is the source of the creative instinct in this world. Shiva, Lord of the Dance, whose temple at Chidambaram, south of Madras, is one whole sculptural glory to this art of movement and the rhythmic energy of the universe, represents the scientific principle of birth and destruction–this ebb and flow, the elemental, creative and dying-away process which we now begin to see in our comprehension of space. Shiva also is seen as Akarsh–ether.

In the temple at Chidambaram there is a shrine in his honour which is entirely empty in order to symbolize this aspect of his quality as Akarsh. It is as if the Indian had known these abstract concepts all the time. The algebraic equation of physics is unified by a single force into this one compelling image, this god ringed with the fire of destruction, sublimely balanced on one foot above the demon evil of Ego.

Shiva stands poised. Ganges the goddess of the river of salvation peeps out from his locks of hair; the half-crescent moon indicates the lunar phases of time; the skulls around his neck are associated with the Shiva of the Terrible Aspect–the emaciated ascetic who frequents the funeral pyres, the Shiva who presides over the living and the dying, the extinction and rebirth of successive generations of mankind; the serpents symbolize the measure of time by years and the coiled energy of the nervous system, the kundalni, known as the vagus to our own neurologists. Shiva in his character of time orders the astronomical regulations as well as the fluctuations, the rise and the fall, the continuum of immortality. His trident symbolizes the triple figure that so fascinates the Hindu mind: the Trimurti, trinity of creation, preservation and destruction; the triple theory of action circumscribed by sukarm (=right action), suvachan (=right speech [mind]) and suvichar (=right thought [spirit]). It also embodies the idea of the three-pronged punishment of law (spiritual, subtle, physical); the three modes of worship (religious ritual and ceremony, philosophy, and the metaphysical on a higher place); and the three subtle arteries of the body which influence all yoga systems.

One hand is raised gesturing: Fear Not. The other, gracefully pointing downwards, says: For I am here. In another of his four hands he holds the wasp-waisted dumru, the little drum heard even now in the streets of the big cities rapping out the simple thythms for monkeys to dance to for the tourists who visit this land. Here is the symbol of this rhythm of creation: 'Thy hand holding the sacred drum has made and ordered the heavens and the earth and the other worlds and innumerable souls.'

Somehow it seems so familiar, so unstrange, so part of this world where of a sudden we are having to come to terms with a new comprehension of those immutable laws that silently govern all that exists, and where reality is measured in terms of the millionth part of an atom but also flows out to the overwhelming dimensions of expanding universe upon universe where planetary ideas of earth-time are wholly irrelevant. Shiva has become to be a quite unique symbol of the nuclear age, an ageless, artistic vision of a constant, scientific principle.

Because Indian society has, like the Chinese, been a unitary one where science and religion have never really been in conflict, there has been no basic split as has happened within our own Christian background. Our own antagonism between the two disciplines of theology and science has created chaos in our thinking and a curious dichotomy during the past two centuries. In India I found a thankful release from our restricted vision of the creation of God: Shiva within his bronze frame, mirrors the scientific truths that surround us, the spark, the explosion, the expansion and gathering of forces, the ultimate retraction. These patterns and shapes and all their entities are totally reflected in the music and dance forms of India, yet another instance of the magnetic hold which the unitary principle of their belief has on Indian minds. Every aspect of their culture does in fact reflect their philosophy to a concentrated degree.

The interweaving and expanding shape of the raag is the very essence of this gathering-and-retracting process. A mournful slither of tones announces the creation; a continual playing around a full note with grace notes clustering like constellations, explodes into long elastic lines of melodic tones; then there is a sudden pull, a retraction to the leading note or a dominating note heard again and again, bringing the ear back to the drone which continually holds these notes as a recurring theme.

This supplies the steadying process of creation, a fountainhead for further effulgent displays of shimmering sound scattered out in ordered disarray like *feu d'artifice*. And yet all such ornamentations are anchored rigidly within the specified notes of a raag scale. A unified design is maintained throughout, no matter how anarchic the creative process may superficially seem to be.

This creates a compulsive hypnotic effect. The listener sinks deeper and deeper into himself, almost in meditation. The result is profoundly emotional. This is part of the fabric of India where everything is permeated by this timelessness and this intensity of serious thought.

The essence of the philosophy, the interminable days of searing heat, the burnt-down plains of the North stretching to the hazy edge of land in the distance where nothing is clearly discernible, the torpor of Bengal in the monsoon, the sublime disregard by the worldly but ascetic Madrasi for what we should consider the necessities of life, the driving urge to curl inwards against the onslaught of environment and hostile space, all these influences leave the same imprint.

The author of *The Story of Indian Music* speaks of this aim to create the conditions of a temporary oblivion. Mr Goswami says: 'The suspense created by climaxes in music distracts the listener's attention from the physical world and leads the mind to the super-sensory plane.'

The result is something different from the aesthetic experience we feel when moved by the creative demands of our own music. To Mr Goswami, writing as an Indian, the aesthetic sense 'which is contemplation, is also an inward expression . . . Indian art and music do not deal especially with individual transient emotions . . . in it one hardly meets the joys and sorrows of an individual life expressed so effectively in Western music'.

The listener is in fact led 'to live his life along the progression of the rise and fall, deviation and resolution of tones which constitutes the melody, *an abstract and spaceless theme singing through time* [my italics] capable of carrying the listeners' attention more poignantly and intimately and *objectifying his will*'.

This is called sādhna, the supreme act of ego surrender, of merging individual identity into the object worshipped. In enlarging the explanation of how the feel of the music, the rasawadhana, affects an Indian he goes on to put it into words that only an Indian can, because this is what he feels is important in the experience.

'The impressions or ideas received from the outer world after exciting, clashing or corresponding with the experience or experiences stored within are synthesized [a word put to evergreen use in India] by the force of the contemplative spirit, which is a cognitive force, otherwise called intuition . . . Expression is the actuality of intuition and representation its visible and audible form.'

This is very important. A raag as an elaboration of a set theme can be dead or alive depending on the inward quality and sensibility of the artist performing. The performer is, after all, not only an executant musician as we know him; he is also, simultaneously, a composer. This is very different therefore from the Western concept of interpretation and presentation of 'composed' music. already set down in notation. In Indian music where only the basic framework of a certain scale is delineated and notated, the great body of the raag which enlarges upon this skeletal backbone is created each time and on the spot by the performing artist. The Indian musician is therefore not retelling what has already been composed. He is spontaneously expressing an inner feeling of his own, drawn from a multitude of personal resources, very long training and musical discipline. The audience then find themselves 'in direct confrontation with an artist in the heat of creation'.

This immediacy of Indian music is the key to its religious implications and its amazing effect on audience participation. The listener, the subject, through mental concentration of such a force, becomes compacted into the object–the notes heard, i.e. the music. It is the wholeness of yoga, which in fact is what music has always been regarded as being. The spiral moves from the musician inwards to the climax of the music and outwards to the audience who listens, so taking hold of each listener and working inwards again to the musician.

The development is not linear as in a symphony but swirling and whirling as galaxies of sound in progression. Of course in a sense there is movement along a line of the melody because that melody is governed by the principles of a linear succession of single notes, each in a relation of certain intervals to the others. But each note of the progression of the ascending and descending scale of a raag can become the starting-point for a chandelier of sparkling ornamentation. There is no progression along a line of narrative or along an extrovert and dramatic development as in, for instance, Beethoven's Pastoral Symphony. The search for the Indian musician is ever inwards in an attempt to restate the general through the particular, the overall raas or distilled spiritual mood, in the intricate and skilled differentiation of thousands of fragmentary intervals.

The consequence of all this is a peculiarly haunting, lyric mysticism in the classical music which showers out, glides, swirls, zig-zags in escalating jumps, and slurs in beautiful arabesques like the dying falls of a graceful ballerina. The intensity establishes itself so unmistakably in the ear in concrete terms by the repetitious and emphatic beat of the sum in the taal and the *perpetuum mobile* of the drone instrument in the background.

The mechanics of the mesmerizing music which the vocalist or instrumentalist uses to create suspense and tension in the audience, run parallel to similar techniques in yoga. The end in view is the same in both disciplines: the extraction of mind from self.

The very concentration of the mind on the infinitesimal expands the mind to a liberation beyond all the confines of its limited actuality. The listener lying under the tropic stars (always that much more brilliant in the intense, dark-blue sky of Asia) concentrating for perhaps six to eight hours in a timeless Indian concert, overwhelmed by the balm of humid air and the perfume of a thousand jasmine garlands tied around black chignons of hair, can and does lose feelings of self.

Contemplation v. Action

Philosophically then there is this impetus towards and emphasis on concern with inner self. This is not to be mistaken for egoism. Nor is it to be misinterpreted in the image of the world-withdrawn hermit, although of course there are the visual extremes of this tendency at the popular temple level in the strange self-flagellating saddhus (popularly envisaged in the West as faqirs on their beds of nails). This is temple-level Hinduism encrusted by the barnacles of over forty-five centuries of man-made development (including principles of caste) and village superstition.

The true Hindu does not compartmentalize life and in early Hindu teaching the four stages of life bound a man's life into a whole: the stage of the student for learning (brahmacharya); of the householder (grihasta) for loving, bearing children, taking property and amassing wealth; of the retiring thinker in a forest retreat (vanaprasth); and of the sannyasi, forsaking all possessions and emotional entanglement to concentrate upon contemplation of God. Therefore in the ideal development of the individual life of each Hindu, action and contemplation, self-gratification and inner self-discipline have been evenly balanced. There is little conflict between the material and the intangible, and in the process of seeking spiritual enlightenment and personal release into an enlarging world of real self-knowledge, the arts were regarded as important means towards achieving this 'self-realization' so important to the Hindu. 'Self-realization' means God-realization. In ancient times Yajnavalkya, the famous law-giver, wrote:

> Vinavadanatatvajrah Srutijati visāradah
> Talajnyaschaprayasena Moksha margam nigāchhăti

'One who knows the principles of playing the veena; one who is an expert in jati, and has the mastery of sruti and tala attains to moksha without any effort.'

Thyāgarāja, the famous eighteenth-century saint/musician of South India, declared in his *Sripapriya* that music is yoga: 'Music which is composed of the seven svaras is a treasure for the great tapasvins (ascetics) who have cooled the tapatraya (the world of involvement). Moksha is impossible for one who has no music in him.'

Hindu philosophy, which so encompasses all things Indian, influenced totally–quite totally–all the principles of aesthetics upon which the arts were founded, so long ago that one forgets the physical impact of such a long, unbroken thread of continuous tradition. It is there, an influence as inevitably self-sustaining and re-creative as the order of daytime and night-time, sunlight and moonshine. Such a total comprehensiveness makes everything whole. Thoughts, art, music, logic, drama and poetry may not have clearly defined, logically analysed boundaries or stepping-stones of intellectual movement forwards, but the impetus towards a defined central point is there all the same in the subconscious of all Indians. One has to remember that it is not for nothing that the Indian conceived zero for all of us. The early Aryans also conceived of non-being becoming manifest–no matter whether as the nucleus of a cell, as a molecule or an atom, creation has to begin at a point–in space and time as that spark of matter which springs from intangible energy. Hence the peculiarly potent use of the bindu or round point both in Hindu rituals and as a yantra or symbolic or magical 'diagram' in yogic meditation. If one considers what might be the visual symbol for the West, a line depicting progression laterally might be most appropriate. At least it would define our sense of time and mortality.

Our Western principles of aesthetics were based upon Aristotelean concepts of balance and force in Greek philosophy; Christian religious thought came later and often was in conflict, especially with regard to dance and drama. But those aesthetic principles of India find sustenance within this larger embrace of the religious rationale of Hinduism—at one level utterly identified with the rarified upper reaches of metaphysical speculation and at the same time merged, as negative is to photographic print, with the basic religious ritual of popular puja or worship where an exploding population of gods and goddesses, each and all personifications of the infinite aspects of God, exists at the level of devotional bhakti worship. Secular, artistic and spiritual are all one within the Indian context, where the banal and the sublime can exist side by side in a way countenanced nowhere else in the world. Indians are the ultimate anarchists. Complexity becomes simplicity to the Indian because this is the very composition of human life. A Hindu does not see his pantheon of deities as separate entities—categories of divinity even—but rather as symbols of the multifaceted aspects of an overwhelming unitary truth. All this is somewhat disturbing to a Western mind seeking clarity rather than diffuseness, a Mozart quintet rather than an Indian raag.

In the music and dance we soon become very aware of this world alive with gods and goddesses. Much of the imagery used in the poetry is concentrated on their loves and lives, and they attend music and dance performances as benevolent and controlling spirits. The Hindu is also a realist *par excellence*. The duality of human nature in the biological sense has long been recognized and male and female deities are seen as one unity, equal but differing as human beings. In fact, on temple walls androgynous figures of the Deity—half-male, half-female—are forcible reminders of how harmonized the Hindu view of life is.

Gentleness, tenderness, the ethics of ahimsa or non-violence, are as freely and naturally accepted in the male as aggression and blood lust are in Kali, the Dark Goddess, and in the female. This is much nearer modern psychological study and discovery than we have been willing to admit in our culture where male and female components remain in uneasy balance and, more often than not, in jagged conflict. For this reason it does not seem strange to an Indian to think of the foundation-rock of his music, the raags, in terms of male raags and female raaginis. In fact they have been depicted as such, with their corresponding qualities, in charming miniature paintings of the Moghul period.

One image that may well appear at concerts or on concert programmes is that of Saraswati, consort of Brahma, carrying the veena (the original multi-stringed instrument of India) as goddess of the creative arts. It is at this point that the abstract concept of metaphysical philosophy and ordinary people's needs of a living religion, meet.

The Ramayan and the Mahabharat

In exhuberant contrast to the austere disciplines which developed through the speculative hymns of the Vedic books (2500 BC) and the abstruse, intellectual questioning of the *Upanishads* (800 BC) (a Sanskrit word meaning 'sitting near to God' as a pupil or shishya does while listening to his guru), devotional worship at a personal religious level has always found expression in India through music and dance.

The bursting revelation of the heart has centred on the lives and loves of this pantheon of deities. The two great epics are the source of all these legendary tales, but the religious mythology of the *Ramayan* and the *Mahabharat* (c. 9–500 BC, written down in 2nd–3rd centuries AD) is projected in terms of spiritual philosophy as well.

Lyrical mysticism in everyday life is still a common phenomenon in this land. As one travels around the massive landmass of India the itinerant saint/musician is still to be encountered. In his ballads and with a simple, stringed accompaniment such as the ektara he will be expounding a living musical philosophy under the garb of specific stories of Krishna and Radha, Shiva and Parvati, Vishnu and Lakshmi, all in their respective personifications identified with the great universal source of energy.

Such gentle songs I have heard in Benares where two or three devotees have gathered together to sing praises to Rama, or Narayan, or Hari, or Isvara, or Gurudeva–all personal or abstract names of the *one* God. The joyous intoning radiates into the burning air in worship to Him–or rather–It. The praises of gods and goddesses are sung by lonely hermits in mountain caves. They are carried through the bazaar lanes and back streets of modern suburbs by wandering balladeers, the Bauls in Bengal, troupes of musicians in South India, even the lone, blind, Muslim musician I had occasion to experience one morning as I sat down with my Hindi teacher on a lawn in Delhi's new Diplomatic Enclave.

In his tremulous voice he sang first of Krishna and his loves in personal terms; then the song moved forwards to a coda concerning universal love of God. Here again was this common culture born from the two great rivers of Hindu and Muslim belief that has made India such a remarkable secular state amid all this religion. This was India speaking, neither Hindu, nor Muslim, but a blend of both.

> Oh man! give up all the worldly affairs and fix your attention on God.
> Oh man, in this short life what can you do?
> What did Alexander the Great take with him when he died?
> Both his hands were empty, stretching out of the shroud.

This belief in a personal, loving God, combined with a metaphysical view of creation on a cosmic scale, swells through the music also of the composer/saints such as Thyāgarāja, Swati Tirunal, Dikshitar and Shyam Shastri—names so familiar in South India, not only to the musicians who play their compositions with an almost medieval single-mindedness, but also to the multitudes who worship in the majestic temples of the South and who throng to the music concerts in a sense of devotional expectation. Music and dance are living forms of worship to the really integrated South Indian. In this part of the subcontinent, music was never separated from its religious context in the actual temple; all the great composers were devotees of God in the same way that one might speak of Bach and his own passionate intensity of worship.

Hindu Unity

To get to the root of anything in India therefore and then to try and judge it in terms of our own ways of scientifically analytical thought, is to get nowhere. Nor is political history in the conventional sense a good guideline to trace the cultural development of India. We cannot judge the body of Indian thought even by these empirical standards; somewhere, imperceptible to us, the current of thought has flowed on through the immense, unreachable masses of Indians who live beyond our Western comprehension. Hinduism has remained in constant, replenished usage throughout this tremendous stretch of time, impervious to outside influence, as onward-flowing as the imperturbable Ganges itself.

Not even Moghul invasions and Muslim supremacy for 700 years, nor the arrival of the British, Dutch, French and Portuguese with their own civilization and standards, penetrated into the impervious core of this steadfast faith. Hindu thought took and absorbed according to its own will, folding itself inwards at the sense of approaching danger like some gigantic sea-anemone drawing up all its tentacles, only to stretch outwards and flourish when the danger was past.

One continues to hope that this will remain so, that modern Indians will realize that this is their enviable strength despite all their understandable yearnings for the material advantages of technology which they have seen give power and monopoly of advantage to the Western world. But their quality of synthesis, of intelligent absorption, may still save them from the sterility of urban life and the monotonous obsession with quantity and things, rather than with quality and life-perspective.

It is only modern political systems imbibed from the West that have created the bitter infighting, schisms and internal divisions concentrated on the wielding of personal power and prestige. Indians have never suffered the antagonisms of religious schisms internally nor been shaken by heretical battles. Doctrinal squabbles are nonexistent in that there has never been a 'revealed truth'– once and for all–like that which, in an historical sense, Moses, Christ and Mohammed provided for the Semitic faiths. Each Indian man and woman expresses an individual belief in intimate communion with his personal view of God on the lonely and isolated path back to union with perfection. Music is one vehicle to attain this end, whatever the term by which one wishes to designate the metaphysical idea of Brahm.

If one cared to analyse India in all her complexities and statements of truth a library of fat volumes would be necessary. This book is only one attempt to reach through to the essential spirit which in good time grows on one through the music of India, and which in turn illumines and sparkles in the richly embroidered melodies that come to haunt both heart and mind. This is the key to the treasure of the inner self, the use of heart and mind in conjunction to arrive at an intuitive truth.

In my own discovery of India I came to understand one thing: not to be afraid of emotion. Somehow in our own development, philosophy has become intellectualized and the idea of rationality has bred scepticism of anything to do with the emotional impulses of the heart. Consequently, it appears to me, especially as a woman, that we lead damagingly fragmented lives. On the other hand, the Indian thinker, whichever his religious philosophy, even in his most lucidly intellectual moments has retained all aspects of his life as channelled to the one purpose of coming to know himself better in reaching forwards to self-realization. This is liberation, moksha. Perhaps this is why there has been such interest recently, especially among young people in the West, about the meditative processes of Indian mysticism, as they seek to 'liberate' themselves (in Laing's words).

Within the Hindu framework of reference every aspect and activity of human life has been analysed to an astonishing and sometimes ludicrous degree (as any reading of the *Kama Sutra* will show), but at the same time the fragments are welded together into a gigantic urge towards unity–wholeness of mind through the medium of a warm heart. This in itself is important to the whole understanding of the music.

Chapter Two

RAS BHAAV: The Feel of the Music

'An abstract and spaceless theme singing through time.' O. GOSWAMI

All Indian classical music is concerned with the development of a single melodic line, its rising and descending scale structure, its exposition through reiteration which is continually amplifying itself–so expressing the many-faceted aspects of the flashing prism of each single note in relation to the next–and finally the linking together of this linear development within the density of complex syncopation, the rigid taal or rhythmic framework that climaxes the unfolding of any raag.

This structure, the skeletal essence of all the historical development and expression of aesthetic principle, makes as heavy demands intellectually as does Western classical music.

Only the points of emphasis are differently placed. We have to jettison ideas of symphonic enlargement, of solo sonatas and concertos embedded in massive orchestral richness and diversity of harmonic consonance (or, increasingly in modern music, of dissonance).

When a newcomer hears a concert of Indian music for the first time, what then is the initial impact? 'I was off at another level of existence, lifted outside of myself.' 'I felt extraordinarily at peace with myself and everything around me.' 'I did not want to come back to earth and felt very irritable when everyone started clapping.' 'It was like being pulled to a point of release, floating way out again and then being pulled back once more.' These are remarks that have been made. They reflect the impact of this essence, the ras (literally 'juice') which is distilled in such devotional and emotional intensity in Indian culture–not only in music, but in all the visual arts as well–to such an extent that even the barriers between our diverse cultural backgrounds and, more particularly, between our grammatical principles of sound structure, are dispelled in the immediacy of the emotional response. How is this? What is there in this aesthetic relish (a more just term for ras) which enables it to create an upsurge of emotion (the bhava or bhaav), more muted than an Indian response perhaps, even if we are not yet aware of the destination to which it is leading us.

Is the emotional response to be trusted so readily? This is our predicament. Our cultural conditioning has been a mistrust of sentiment – and rightly so in some contexts – but for the Indian, the word 'sentiment' does not carry the same undertones as it does for us in current English parlance. The *Oxford English Dictionary* classifies sentiment, 'whence sentimentality', as 'a tendency to be swayed by feeling rather than by reason, emotional weakness, mawkish tenderness or the display of it', the derivation being surprisingly from the obsolete word 'mawk', meaning maggot! An Indian, on the other hand, marks sentimentality in its true meaning of sensibility, not as a maudlin sloppiness of heart. Ras is in fact sublimated emotion, directed by, or rather harnessed to, clear processes of thought. Music is, as I have already said, an acknowledged form of yoga.

Within the framework of Indian music, the raag and taal, there are very specific principles of engineering, strictly in accord with the same theories and processes of yoga. Ravi Shankar has written: 'I think that the most accurate definition (of raag) is that it is a scientific, subtle, precise and aesthetic melodic form with its ascending and descending movement which consists of either a full octave or a series of six or seven notes.'

The same four definitions could be applied to any description of the entire philosophy of yoga and the bodily disciplines which are its means of achievement. The word 'scientific' is crucial. Many Westerners have told me that *on first hearing* they find Indian music to be lacking in form and the highlights of contrasting melodic elements; in effect, they feel it as a monotonous monochrome in sound colour. The absence of modulation and harmonics arouses a sense of loss in our conditioned hearing processes; the density of the mass, almost on a miniature scale compared with a symphonic structure, gives the impression of a great body of sound, swaying to and fro, in ebb and flow, like a sea in a gigantic saucer subject to tidal pulls.

If the listener continues his acquaintance he will find that he has been using the wrong signposts. Western principles have to be entirely reorientated (literally as well as metaphorically speaking) to new sets of principles equally valid in the context of their cultural environment and philosophical view of life.

55

A raag expresses more than just musical statements; it is the means whereby Indian musicians conjure up the inner world that moves their beings.

A raag is the basic structure of all Indian music. Even popular 'filmee' music can trace its tenuous links back to the deep roots of traditional raag systems. The vertebrae are the tones in serial line, heard strictly in relation to each other, progressing upwards in one defined order and stepping down the scale often in a slightly modified form or shape, with flexible intervals between them, not tempered or fixed as in the Western keyboard.

At the beginning of the raag, in the slow introductory alaap (the prelude in slow, free time), an exploratory definition of both this arohana, as it is called (rising scale notes), and the descending avarohana is given. The descending line is the one always to be 'watched' mentally, it being more important in the development of the melody with its characteristic groupings so prominently displayed. It is also used for tuning purposes. This is one example, Raag Khamaj:

The melodic line of this evening raag of romantic flavour not only has a change in the 7th note in the descent, it being diminished or flattened, but also includes the 2nd note, which was omitted in the arohana ascent. Throughout the exposition whenever the musician is singing or playing an ascending group of notes he has to adhere to this strict principle of sound for this particular raag, and to make the same precise differentiation in the downward phrases. I have simplified this matter to an extreme. In practice, this aspect of musicianship is much more complex in the density of the music, in its 'volume-filled form', as Ravi Shankar has so aptly described the mental impact of the music, 'which moves in smooth united motions, including within its curves definite units of musical form'.

Of course, in one instance this differentiation between ascent and descent is taken note of in our own system: in the change between the harmonic minor and the melodic minor scales. We dislike certain gaps in intervals, such as that between upper C and B♭ coming down the scale. The ascending B♭ reverts back to B♮ in the melodic minor scale. All this is much more exaggerated in Indian music where accidentals are introduced because in the Indian sense of an untempered scale they are not so termed, there being no major or minor scales. All the time one has to keep in mind a full chromatic scale, where deliberate dissonance occurs as a natural chiaruscuro for the Indian musician (and audience). Our ears have been trained to expect consonance from our scales and the chordal depths that arise from our harmonic principles.

Even in this introductory explanation of the fundamentals of Indian music, necessarily cursory at this point, it has to be emphatically stated that Indian music is, however, not just a raag. Although a raag is the basic element of composition, it is not the composition itself. The whole ethos of the music spills out beyond the actual mechanics of the raag, beyond the development through a series of movements, beyond the compass of the musician as performer, into the wider realm of an activated audience, responding, enlarging the impact, enhancing the impetus towards a spiritual absorption one into the other, until all the component parts merge into an experience beyond the purely musical.

The alaap and the three other sections of the raag defined later – the jor, jhalla and gat – represent the mechanical stages in the enlargement of these certain notes, their intervals and interrelationships, but other deeper processes are at work also.

Briefly, the alaap creates the momentum forwards in the exposition of the particular phrases of specified notes; inflections by grace or gamaka are introduced, and ornamentations fill out the whole process until rhythmic pulse establishes itself in the jor. The listener begins to feel at this point the even flow of a river coursing across the regular interruption of inflowing streams. The drone strings with their persistent, even strikings amid the melodic and sympathetic strings, build up a readily held pattern in the ear until the jhalla is reached. Now the improvisations on the fixed patterns and phrases extend in depth of both octave and treatment. The density of the mass intensifies, the musician now bringing in triple and quadruple strikings on the drone strings with rapid tempo, while at the same time composing instantaneously the intricate cross-weavings, veritable cat's cradles, of melodic lines. The gat exposes a further deepening of the strata of sound with the new texture of percussive resonance. Recurring rhythmic cycles, now even, now uneven, reinforce these melodic syncopations. Taal and raag complement each other, so extending the main themes of the alaap, returning again and again to emphasize them almost lovingly, eventually coming to rest in the completion of each cycle of beat, on certain terminal notes with characteristic flourishes, and so repeating these cadenzas in a prescribed mathematical formula.

The whole development, layer upon layer, extending linear-wise through the one melodic line of that original simple scale, is a geometry of tone-structure, into which the exponent player/composer breathes inspired life from the very first moment of invocation (in its true religious sense) when the alaap conjures up the prevailing personality and mood ascribed to the raga in question. It is as though a philosophical way of life is transformed into a poetry of sound. And so–according to the ancient realities of India summed up by her religious sages or rishis, teaching gurus and aesthetic theorists–it is.

THE PHILOSOPHY OF PURE SOUND

Certain ancient Indian philosophical concepts about the nature of sound itself held that the fundamental emotions of mankind–the nine moods or nava rasa–crystallized in definite combinations and permutations of notes and in very fine shades of sound that surrounded these full, round tones. These fundamental pure notes were seen to be–eventually in technical terms–the octave scale.

Particular sounds still hold to this day especial overtones for the psyche of devout Hindus. The sound 'OM' (ॐ), pronounced 'a-u-m', rings out like the tolling of a cathedral bell along the stone steps where people bathe in their millions in the Ganges as it flows serenely by the Benares ghats, a sound coming from the lips of devotees praying for deliverance from the tribulations of this reincarnation.

Such an onomatopoeic sound syllable represents to a Hindu the most basic metaphysical idea of all, the inward-dwelling immanent God. God, it has been said, 'is the most comprehensive of man's ideas'. To do Him justice and to conceive of a sound that expressed the sense of God within one–'Thou Art That, You are within Him'–the earliest theorists could only express what the body made possible in its most comprehensive way. This is the syllable 'aum'; it is released from the innermost reaches of the breathing system, starting as it does in the root sound 'ah', passes from the lowest part of the diaphragm through the throat without touching any part of the palate or tongue, narrows down to 'oo' to roll through the mouth and is cut off finally by the lips in the closed sound of 'mm'. The guttural 'ah', the labal 'oo' and the nasal 'mm' are the physical limits, according to Hindu theorists, to all the possibilities of basic articulation.

This pregnant sound (ओ३म्), which has the potency of magic power to the Hindu, is the least particularized of all sound, according to their theory, and from it as the original root sound there has been built up a whole system of conceptual sound which combines philosophy, religious belief, ritual musical theory and aesthetics.

'The intoned formula is the pivot of the whole structure of Vedic offerings and sacrifice,' Dr Bake has written. 'It is the power of words enunciated with the correct intonation, that determines the efficacy of the rites; a mistake may destroy everything. The priests claim that by their activity they not only uphold the order of human society, but maintain the stability of the universe. By means of well conducted ceremonies they have compelling power over the gods themselves. The instrument that conveys that power is the word.'

With such a background to their religious worship and the use of music in connection with this worship, one can now see how compelling is the rationale behind the use of vocal music–even to this day. Another word as equally evocative to a Hindu is the word 'ram' (or 'rama'), pronounced 'raam'. Raam Naam Satya Hai . . . (The Name of God is Truth) is chanted fervently in religious ceremonies, the long-drawn-out vowel possessing particular connotations to the Indian vocalist when expressing his devotions and love for God.

The sol-fa notes of Indian music, the shuddha scale, of the straightforward octave, incorporate the same elongated or half-open vowel sounds in their abbreviated syllables: sa, reh, ga, ma, pa, dha, ni, sa. When the throat is at its most relaxed (as when the doctor requests a patient to say 'aah'), Indian metaphysical reasoning says that the soul is at its most expressive point. Even to this day the listener will be able to pick out this frequent sound, the 'ga-ma-pa', (or sargam as it is called) in the syllabic singing which is so often used by Indian vocalists in the almost mathematical formula of the raag. Actual words, lyrics as we know them, are not often used alone to convey the emotional content of the melody, except of course in popular music. Pure sound, this syllablic sound, can function in the same way and to the same ends as specific words. The nature of this sound has a trance-like effect which I shall mention again when dealing with the mechanics of the music principles, but anyone who cares to chant 'OM' or release the sound 'aah' for a long time, can see what is entailed. The hypnotic effect is well known to the yogic expert who wishes to wipe his mind blank of all its 'telephone-exchange' flitterings to and fro.

Here again a concept of music principle is closely allied with a profound spiritual awareness fundamental to the Hindu view of life in the body, in fact the very breath of life itself – Prāña.

Dr Bake has best explained it in his essay 'The Music of India': 'In music – the Sanskrit term samgita includes vocal music, instrumental music and dance – vocal music is considered to be pure sound, sound *per se*, in contrast to instrumental music which is described as a manifestation of sound. Dance, the third component of the triad, is dependent on both vocal and instrumental music so that music as a whole is dependent upon sound.' On the physical plane the entire human society is dependent on sound, as he explains through this reasoning: ' . . . by sound the letter is formed, by letters the syllables, by syllables the word, by words this daily life. Hence this human world is dependent on sound.'

One immediately recognizes the same Biblical connotations: 'In the beginning was the Word; and the Word was made God.'

Prāña

Dr Bake goes on: 'The metaphysical explanations are principally concerned with vocal sound, as being primarily in nature. This . . . was produced by the gradual upsurge of the prāña or life breath.

'In its course the prāña passes different mystical centres of power, bearing the name of cakras (circles) . . . Two of these cakras have special importance from the musical point of view, namely the anahatacakra situated in the heart, and the visuddhacakra in the throat. The sound alluded to so far is only the ahatanada (struck or manifested sound) which cannot exist without its ideal counterpart anahatanada (unstruck or unmanifested sound). It is this dual nature of sound which brings it right into the centre of religious-philosophical speculations because the unmanifested sound, the anahatanada, is identified with the creative principle of the universe in its transcendental form of Shiva himself, as well as in its immanent form as the syllable "OM" which is said to reside in the heart. . . .

'So it remained for the individual to find the right way to realize the connection between the latter aspect of the unmanifested sound and the manifested sound, in order to be brought into direct contact with the divine principle of the universe itself, which *amounted to the desired liberation* [my italics]. The obvious means to this end was music, and preferably vocal music, which by its own nature was pure sound itself.'

Thyāgarāja in one of his spiritual treatise, the *Mokshamugalada*, questioned whether there could ever be moksha or liberation of the individual human soul from the trammels that inhibit its full realization without knowledge of music which he declared was based on bhakti, personal devotional worship. To him the sapta svara (seven notes) emanated from the prañava, the unifying state born from prāna (breath) and agni (fire). Merely liking the sound of the veena was useless unless one understood the implications of religious disciplinary worship of the god Shiva, symbolising creative energy.

This 'unifying philosophical approach' (in Dr Bake's words) forces the Indian to see all things whole. All aspects of life are interrelated, to an extent such that many Westerners find exhausting, overwhelming and downright maddening. There is no escape from the total embrace.

In other matters also the interrelationship works for the Indian. Mr Goswami has mentioned in his recent book, *The Story of Indian Music*, the fundamental connection between sex energy and music. This has, of course, always been freely acknowledged in Hindu treatise. 'Many of the concepts and techniques of Indian music', he writes, 'are often found associated with tantras and yoga shastras (books of codes and laws). The source of music according to the *Yoga Shastra* is nada, which consists of na (which means praña or life breath) and da (which means agni or fire). The conception of nada is inseparably connected with the kundalni or the spiral energy (vagus) which when awakened starts from the mulādhara (basic plexus)[1] and reaches the crown of the head. It is identified with kamakala or sex energy in the *Tantras*.'

[1] In Sanskrit, mul = the origin, basic root, and adhar = foundation.

Writing in another connection about the attributes of Shiva, Alain Danielou has this to say of the serpent coiled around the phallus of Shiva: 'This is taken to represent the spiral, which is the symbol of the cycles of time; but the main meaning attached to the serpent is to represent the basic dormant energy, akin to sexual power, which is coiled at the base of the spinal cord and which is the support of the yogi in his attempt to conquer the higher worlds during his inward journey. This energy, source of all spiritual conquests, is called kundalnī (the coiled), the serpent power.'[1]

This coiled energy of the vagus nervous system is not to be mistaken for sexual energy itself. It is in fact the reservoir for all the bodily and mental energies, and sexual energy is just one part of the whole life energy which is to be used in different ways in different situations.

Our own Western psychologists and physiologists now recognize the vagus nervous system as central to the expression of our own personalities, but the Indians take it one step further and inextricably link it with their complex theories of the entire yogic system of bodily and mental discipline. It is asserted in India that yogis who have reached the ultimate in spiritual discipline and are approaching samadhi or self-liberation, can draw the semen up to the solar plexus through the spinal column. One famous musician has declared this to me of his own spiritual guru. This is not a negation of sexuality as we might be inclined to regard it, but a harnessing of its powers through mental discipline to a more comprehensive vitality in the total bodily entity.

Western scientists may well deny this as anatomically impossible. However, the point which it is relevant and vital for us to note is not physiological, but psychological, the fact that it is *believed* to be so with consequent far-reaching influences on the Indian subconsciousness. This is where Hindu India functions so often and with such powerful consequences. It is a force which constantly alarms Westerners. Nothing is what it appears to be, nothing is scientifically clear or measurable, and so often those who search become bitterly disillusioned. Truth is like the mercury globule. Incapable of being pinned down, it wriggles free. And certainly in the intangible area of yoga and the forces harnessed there, we are only just beginning to focus in the West on the impalpable strength and influence of the psychosomatic.

[1] 'The Image of Shiva', *Hindu Polytheism*, p. 217.

In India, then, it comes with no surprise that the physical aspects of yoga are inextricably linked with intangible elements of breathing philosophy and physical expellation of sound—nada Brahma.

Saman Music

This philosophy of musical sound (literally meaning the sound of Brahma) emerged into a coherent liturgical form as the beginnings of Indian music, the saman chant of the Vedic hymns. The Aryans sang their elementary plainsong to the greater glory of the five elements, their animistic principles of Godly energy: the sun, the air, fire, water and ether (energy), the elements without which humanity cannot maintain life itself.

The rules of this liturgical music were established by memory and handed on from father to son until set down and recorded permanently in book-form in the *Saam-veda*, one of the four Vedic books and the one devoted to the ritual music accompanying the distinctive Aryan fire sacrifice.

Saman music established the sacramental nature of the early singing which took place along with the drinking of the soma juice (named after the plant) which was offered up as in the ritual of our present day communion to symbolize and to bring about a merging with the Divine.

Deshi Music

As in other civilizations there was a parallel musical stream running alongside the liturgical one. This was ordinary folk-music, deshi music, the word 'desh' meaning country in Hindi.

The historians think the Aryans incorporated this from the folk-melodies of the pre-Aryan tribes of India, some of whom may have been of Neolithic or Dravidian origin. These nomadic tribes and settled communities moved southwards away from the Aryan invasions, thus giving, according to some Indian theorists, a special quality to the South Indian music, now known as Carnatic music, or music of the Karnatakam.

Again, no two historians seem to agree on what exactly happened, but this is perhaps the most logical surmise since the facial structures and languages of the South are undoubtedly different, and Carnatic music itself makes a totally different emotional impact on the outsider even though the principles are not all that different in execution from those of Northern Hindustani music. What one is hearing therefore in Carnatic music, may be nearer the sound of the original music of India before constant invasion in the North brought innumerable outside influences (most especially Muslim ones from Persia and upper Asia) to change the flavour and add virility, flexibility and experimentation in the more individual approach of Hindustani music.

The combination of sacred and secular in both regions transformed the earliest music into something a little less forbidding in its priestly conventions and less remote from the peasant population. The earliest prayers and songs had been only mere accompaniments to the ritual dance which was far more important in the Vedic forms of worship. But this new music, more sophisticated in form, drawn from both the magical and awesome world of worship and the more uninhibited melodies of folk-dancing and harvesting, became known as marga sangest. 'Marga' in Sanskrit means 'the path' and, by implication, the way to truth through meditation.

Marga Music

Authorities can trace no exact markings along clearly defined historical paths in the early Indian landscape and often no two authorities agree upon the path. But it does appear that over centuries of settlement the Aryans evolved a remarkably mature civilization and during this period the art forms of dance and music were closely examined and rules of technique and content began to be established. These were later to influence the whole course of the expanding artistic imagination in India. The earliest texts refer both to the classical music (marga) and the folk-music (deshi).

'The former,' says Professor Muherji, whose small book on Indian music was written for an English friend and so cuts through all the complexities of musicology, 'being associated with rituals, was careful of voice production, accuracy of pronunciation and the chant-like movement of the songs.'

Indians assert with no sense of incongruity that this marga music of the early rural Aryan civilization transformed itself into 'celestial gandharva music', music that is sung 'by the celestial musicians or by those who know the theory of sacred music which has come to them through the beginningless tradition, and which is the sure means of attaining liberation'. In the Indian mind, shift and interplay occur between the secular and the divine. It functions in a live and provocative way, even among the most urbanized and modern, so that they still consult astrologers, walk in a world peopled by very real gods and goddesses, and mix formal earth-time history with a mythology beyond the planetary. The *Sangeet Ratnakara*, an important treatise on music written in the thirteenth century, asserts that music is 'composed in accordance with the cosmic law of which physical harmony is but a reflection', and is identified with the gandharvas, celestial musicians who like flying angels grace the warm, cream-stone walls around the friezes of Indian temples, or elsewhere in the glory of the Ajanta caves tempt with seductress sensuality the boddhisatvas and Buddhist monks who sit there, serene in everlasting contemplation.

Because of the very nature of the Hindu belief that music in its origins was mythologically created by Brahma, there is always the ready acceptance of the divine inspiration of the music and the spiritual nature of its content–even though it may well be, and increasingly is, a secular form of entertainment in modern India. But scratch the surface of any of the South Indians participating in it, for instance, and you will revert back with disconcerting immediacy to this acceptance of the interplay between religious myth and historical fact. Imperishable antiquity asserts itself immediately and even the most modern Indian finds within him qualities struggling against new-fangled scepticisms acquired while in contact with Western education. Invariably his roots assert their stabilizing influence and these cold rationalities recede!

Long before the Christian era the systemization of Indian music was being laid down. Not only were definite laws of theory and practice being codified but also an appreciation of what music could do to the human mind was unfolding.

In music these concentrated rasas, flavourings of mood which were formulated into a theory of music known as nava rasa, the nine highly-charged emotions aroused their corresponding emotions in the listener. This principle of nava rasa evolved from the experimental playing of combinations of tones vibrating at length on the earliest instrument to show any real versatility, the swaradhyae veena.

Nava Rasa and Rasawadhana

These nine moods or aesthetic relishes, so to speak, were categorized as love (which includes eroticism quite naturally), heroism, disgust, anger, mirth, terror, pity, wonder and, eventually, tranquillity (shaant)—peace, which summed up all the others in a comprehensive rasa. The Brahminical codifiers of four thousand years ago had arrived at similar conclusions as the Greeks. Certain scales and tones produced visible and predictable emotions.

The refined art of realizing the flavour or rasa of a melody is as cultivated as wine-tasting is to a European connoisseur, and yet much more subtle. The mind is involved. Its intricate processes and caverns of discovery, as we ourselves are well aware, are much more difficult to delve into and realize in the full sense of that word, than are the body's. Even today at Indian concerts, rasawadhana, the capacity for tasting the flavour of a raga, is as cultivated an art as ever it was. Dr Narayana Menon, until recently Director-General of All India Radio and now Director of the Centre for the Performing Arts in Bombay, and himself a veena player, has pointed out many times in the critiques he writes on music (being conversant with both Western and Indian systems) that in India 'the spectacle of a silent, immobile audience, holding its breath until the last phrase to applaud a fine performance, is unknown in traditional circles where the cultivated part of the audience often punctures improvisation with nods of assent and little eulogistic phrases'.

Emotion is important to Indian worship. The knowledge of psychology in those early theorists was remarkable considering the lack of scientific precepts as we know them today. They were as equally aware of the power of the subconscious as is contemporary psychoanalysis. To them, therefore, music was not only an aesthetic pleasure, an art of great beauty; it was in the nature of a joyous and solemn religious discipline as well. In this respect all artistic expression in India is impelled towards the same end, and classical dance was itself the culmination of all desire for union with the divine, as was sexual love, yogic discipline of the most arduous kind, temple sculpture and the thrusting of the temple spire (trichur) of the North Indian temple towards the pliability of space above. Unlike the West where theological doctrines and orthodox puritanism conflicted with full-blooded sensual expression in art, in Indian the division never arose. The Greek Dionysus

(Krishna, the flute-playing god of ravishing delight) never was discarded. Neither was Hindu thought ever afraid to face up to the challenge of the body (epitomized in the phallic lingam or the womb-like yoni) and its natural senses, which are accepted as part of creation – in fact, as the vital instruments of all creation.

Within this impressive continuity of civilization, art and worship are really synonymous. Only a minute fraction of her most modern artists and sculptures has broken away from this prevailing framework. Hardly a musician or dancer to my knowledge has cut that umbilical cord which brings them sustenance from centuries of dedicated worship. Temporarily they may 'Westernize', but I have known personally those who were written off a decade ago by fellow Indians (always disturbingly hypercritical of each other), who return to puja, to acceptance of astrological portents, to private yoga and meditation, to an awareness that what they find in visiting the West is far from the ultimate answer in arriving at personal tranquillity of 'self-realization'.

Dr Narayana Menon has summed it up as an Indian: ' . . . music is an instrument in the realization of God. A song is a yantra, an apparatus of worship, to achieve identical consciousness in worshipper and deity. Some of the texts were very explicit and went so far as to say: "By clearly expressing the rasa, and enabling men to taste thereof, it gives them the wisdom of Brahman." '

As far as this identification goes, it has to be emphasized again that the concept of vocal music in India implies something much more basic than our own sung music. A song in the West is now secular and separate from our devotional natures, if we have any to express. Even our religious hymns, cantatas or masses are not as totally involving of our personalities as vocal music is of the Indian devotee; the actual vocalization *is* an act of worship, identifying the singer with God through the song, and through the emission of pure sound from lung and larynx.

In the learning of such an art of rasawadhana, a deep dedication at the guru level takes place, with a worshipful attitude between pupil and teacher and a marked respect towards age and tradition which even the British can no longer match. This is accompanied by long hours of physical practice, yoga, and the harrowing effort of acquiring by heart the technical knowledge which cannot be left to the tangible world of notation. And then at the end of the day comes the dedication of obedience to God and the touching of the guru's feet.

I myself was never more moved and impressed by this quality of dedication than on my visit to the poet Vallothol's school of dance and music at the Kalā Mandalam at Chirutiruthi in Malabar, where each dancer left the hall at the end of hours of gruelling massage *under* the oiled sliding feet of yet another teacher, and of rigorous practice (beginning at dawn) learning the tala or beat of the dance; as each one left he touched his feet in a full bow before the symbolic lamp of Shiva, Lord of the Dance. Even in the tedious hours of training and rehearsal the yantra or act of worship must be complete.

And so it is for the musician also whose garlanded god accompanies him into the dressing-room backstage, even in a London theatre or an American college-hall, and the musician I have in mind here happens to be a Muslim by birth!

One has to keep on reiterating the dangers of generalization about a people as multiple and diverse as the Indians. This is even more true in the amorphous region where culture and civilization are concerned. But worship and devotion follow a natural turn of mind in Asia, where populations still carry with them the broad sweep of rural piety and a healthy sense of belonging to the soil in a way that our increasingly urbanized societies can never again feel. They are not divorced from nature, and the ebb and flow of the seasons are marked by their own music and festivals like Dussehra and Holi, and Basant. Raags were created for the seasons, and still the audience responds to the 'feel' of such raags as Basant, the name given to the spring festival when the yellow sasson or mustard seed is aflame in the hedgeless fields of the Punjab. There is Hindola (Mālkauns in the North), a gay and lilting melody of the South Carnatic, redolent of springtime when the hindolas (creaking wooden swings) are slowly curving back and forth under the immense boughs of the banyan and keekar trees. Professor Mukherji has rightly commented that association is an old virtue for the Indian listener.

The music is the very specific expression of these intangible qualities that have grown out of the continuum of Hindu philosophy and from the later synthesis with Muslim religious thought, especially as expressed in the mystic poetry of Sufism.

The pulse, the subtle heartbeat, of India is focused here. There are no sharp edges, nothing concise, no definition to hold on to in our limited state of comprehension. Where in fact is the discipline? This is the point at which nearly everything in India, from the philosophy to the arts and down to the social customs, misleads.

There appears to be no backbone, but so many excrescences, so much involuted thinking. The very fact that the raag is expandable according to the inventiveness of the performer and that a concert has no real beginning and no necessary end, proves the point even in the execution of the music. Or so we think.

To us it twangs on and on, the dissonances incapable of being ordered in our ears into any harmonized semblance whatsoever. There is no depth of orchestration, or so it seems. There is no visible conductor to bring order and form out of the fluidity of sound. There is no conciseness in the note, no clarity of, say, the pianoforte keys, even with pedal resonances. There are no chordal harmonies.

A sarod string is plucked and held; a dozen microtones assail the ear in an elastic surge forwards and are then pulled back again to some fundamental peg from which they are suspended in space. Again this process happens; the tones linger but escape identification, leaving only a memory like the diaphanous imagery of a Shelley or a Keats.

A nerve end is touched, but there is no certainty that our responses are the right and proper ones. Our unsureness is further sharpened by the actual physical conditions of the music, much of which in a tropical climate takes place amid huge audiences the size of those at recent pop festivals in the West. To an Indian swallowed in such a gigantic mass, communion as well as individual liberation are tantamount. And here the quality of climate takes over, a quality which no indoor concert can ever reproduce. Suddenly, lying on carpets under the immensity of an Indian night, the phenomenal infinity of space has a very real, physical impact. I have sometimes been overcome by the loneliness, as a shooting-star fell in green flight, reminding me of light-years pulsating in those unseen deep recesses beyond the farthest, flashing star. It is on these rare occasions that the Greek philosopher's flight of the alone to the Alone becomes more than a literary phrase learnt in the textbooks of philosophy courses. Time is cyclical but progressing within the cycle; immortality is not only in the future but of the past also, curving around universe upon universe, melting everything at the edges until there is no beginning and no end—only a liberation *in* life lived within each individual personality and a liberation *from* the false reality of outer forms. This the music portrays in its constant return to what has been. But to say this is to give the impression of an incontrollable amorphous mass. Yet discipline there is. It is not overt, and made clear by outstanding clarity or notated scores. It is in the head, as taut and manipulated as a schooner's ropes stretched to hold full sail. That is why one single raag within its own specific framework of scale and taal (rhythmic cycle) can be expanded in long passages of improvisation, inwardly analysed, by individual performers, expressed in many different moods depending on the musician and his own personal view of beauty and conflict, love and sorrow.

The text sung in the most classical form of a song, dhrupad, is laden with a wistful loneliness: 'A man may mutter the Vedas, invoke Brahma, Shiva and the serpent of time, study the words of the sages Narada and Vyasa, the transcendent remains ever beyond his reach.'

People therefore do not march to this music. The impetus is to sink one's self into a still and limpid pool of quietude, 'the individual soaring mind', as Yehudi Menuhin has defined it, finding 'its own redemption in the infinite but within the lonely pattern and within a very tight control.'

A prismatic radiance of tones conducts the mind along the full length of mathematical permutations in the changing shape of the chosen notes, but the heart as well as the intellect, also feels an insistent tug. A seductive breath of lyricism reinforces the hard clarity of musicianship. The wallowing resonances of each restatement of the raag's especial 'feel' pull at the very fibres of one's sexuality, partly because plaintive melancholy of unrequited love suffuses many raags. (This is a favourite Indian literary theme where love seldom seems to reach a happy consummation—although Indians would say that in the West it ends before it begins!) At the same time, running parallel with the emotional impact of ras, there is always the irresistible pull, the heavy grandeur of the worshipful—the evening raags of eroticism counterbalanced by the meditative quality of morning raags such as Bhairav, Asavari, and Bhatiyar. The Hindus have always been mindful of the need to release the adrenalin 'charge' to the surface of the mind, purging it by a culmination or yoking of sensual and spiritual.

The tension is always being renewed, the ropes tautened with each pull on the line, as instrumentalist or vocalist, percussion player and drone combine and fuse, link and cross, stating a phrase and echoing it. One after the other takes it up, places it again before the ear and examines it in yet another way, stretching each fibre of rope that little bit tighter, until heart, mind and spirit blend in tension in a way that is difficult to explain. But the catharsis is complete.

The principles are Aristotelean. Emotions, no matter in what mood created by the raag, are purified as in a crucible of heat. This again is the function of ras bhaav, the release, as Mr Goswami says, of the emotions into a state 'completely unrelated to desire or the fulfilment of desire'. This is the language of the *Bhagavad Gita*. It is the essence of yoga. And in Sanskrit the curtailment of passionate impulse is contained in the one word 'sthitpragnya' (=steady-minded, 'gyan' meaning knowledge), suggesting the absolute steadfastness of wisdom, unassailable discipline at the heart of enjoyment—a suggestion of detachment and equanimity born of the idea so close to the Biblical one: Be ye in the world, but not of the world.

It is difficult, no doubt, for us to comprehend the whole fabric which lies behind this sense of detachment. It is entirely alien to much that motivates us today in a century and civilization which cultivates all that which is implied in that wholly American phrase 'the pursuit of happiness', a phrase which has come to mean self-gratification in very mundane terms. Happiness to the Hindu has always been elevated to a transcendental experience. This would not have appeared strange to our own Christian mystics, who also identified happiness with detachment bred of personal discipline and directed an apparent anarchy of feeling into the harmony of a purposeful framework which made everything whole. This sums up the form of the Indian raag where apparent anarchy of sound will, on analysis, be seen to comprise infinite gradations of space and form as surely disciplined as the Parthenon of the Greeks and the fugues of Bach.

Chapter Three

HISTORICAL DEVELOPMENT
and the Growth
of Aesthetic Principles

Not all is good that bears an ancient name,
Nor need we every modern poem blame;
Wise men approve the good, or new, or old;
The foolish critic follows where he's told.
Kalidas, Malavikagnimitra 1.i.2
Trans. ARTHUR RYDER

A person can go to a concert in London or New York. It will not matter one iota if that person is totally ignorant of a Greek mode nor has ever heard of Lydian and Dorian scales. They were part of a history in which a great cleavage occurred towards the end of the sixteenth century when the scales we now use – diatonic major and minor scales – were fixed, supposedly, for all time. Now, of course, the reaction is gaining ground against the arbitrary nature of this finality. But because of the unitary nature of Indian history and culture, the impulse is always there to remain true to tradition. Because the physical act of learning, the pedagogy, has been handed on by word of mouth over centuries rather than written down – which would have exposed it to more examination, comparison and experiment – there have been few major changes in Indian musical tradition since it became properly established between the third and tenth centuries AD.

It is as well to remember this because it illustrates the force of tradition in and the static nature of Indian art forms. The long arm of memory is still at work, even today, creating problems and tensions not encountered by contemporary Western musicians. They are not held in thrall at all by orthodoxies or inherited traditions. As creative people they are entirely free to order form out of chaos. An Indian musician nowadays has much to contend with if he steps outside the ordered path. The two predominant aspects of art and worship in India are the music and the dance together, and the sculpture which froze them into stone on the sun-bleached temple walls of India. They began with ritual worship and were adjuncts to the full expression of devotion to the gods who were eventually housed within the temple.

As I mentioned in the previous chapter, these creative arts are popularly believed to have been brought down from the mythological heavens and taught to men by the gods, Shiva being the archetypal master interpreter. The fact that this is historically unproven is of no importance. What moves the spirit of India is not the letter of actuality but the intuition of that poetic truth which is always incandescent in Indian minds. It is enough that it is popularly accepted as having come about at the edge of recorded time when gods and men merged and walked the earth together.

Therefore, the names of the deities Brahma and Shiva, and of Bharata (the most famous sage of antiquity), will be quoted again and again as the progenitors of all the codified rules upon which the principles of artistic development must rest. This happens in quite real terms. I have talked to educated Indian musicians who could not care less in the face of evidence put forward by Indian historians that these names may only stand in for generalized professional theorizers who, at one time or another, enunciated certain principles. Brahma may have been many a priest, Shiva a holy person, Manu a lawyer, Bharata an art teacher, and there may have been many in these walks of life who were given these nomenclatures as titles indicating their calling rather than as first names as we would think of them. In Sanskrit, the original words have philosophical (i.e. spiritual) meaning. 'Bharata' in fact means 'to be' or 'being maintained'.

As an attempt, I suppose, to acquire some anchorage in the whirling void with which the nature of his abstract philosophy tends to encompass his thoughts, the Hindu especially, throughout all the development of his culture, has busied himself with codifying and analysing the mechanics of principles down to the most minute and, one sometimes suspects, most obsessive mania for detail. These have been formulated and learnt by heart in the thousands of stanzas which constitute the shastras, still actively in use in the hands of hundreds of musical gurus who carry on this vital verbal tradition.

NARADA MUNI (THE SAGE)

At the earliest period in the formulation of thought when epics such as the *Mahabharata* were coming into existence in pre-Christian times, there were already theorists who had sorted out the fundamentals of music and begun the process of codifying. One such was Narada; he is said to be the first to identify the Vedic notes with those of the more simple and popular folk- or deshi music which had been developing naturally within the peasant population, unconcerned as it was with the theoretical. There were other musicologists of the same name who are difficult to place chronologically; and even around this Narada who existed in historic times, mythology has closed its hand and elevated him to a mendicant's life in heaven where he spends his time playing on his veena!

Even when we come to an epoch much closer to our own there is still the scholastic difficulty of placing an exact date upon the most famous of all their musical theoreticians: Bharata Muni.

BHARATA

It is this man who has given his name to the Bible of Indian dance, the *Bharata Natya Shastra*, a treatise which has been dated variously by Sanskrit scholars as having been set down between the second century BC and the fourth century AD. By this time the notes of the scale, the measures known as talas, and certain compositions in the elementary evolution of the raga had been established. The flute and the veena had acquired popularity in an increasingly sophisticated society which had by this time made many contacts with Greek civilization through incursions made into the subcontinent by not only Alexander the Great (who had come to Taxila, now in Pakistan, in 326 BC), but also by sea-farers from Arabia and overland traders.

During this massive period of history since the first Aryan settlements, a period of about 2500 years, much of which ran parallel with Greek civilization (Pythagoras himself is said to have worked out the musical system of Grecian modes in the sixth century BC), numerous unknown theoreticians had begun to refine the music to suit the tastes of very cultivated people. A society that could during this period throw up a man of the calibre of

Ashoka, for instance–he being one of India's most rightfully celebrated emperors, who spread enlightenment through the philosophy of ahimsa or non-violence wherever he went–is not to be scoffed at.

Musical instruments had already been mentioned in the *Upanishads* (*c.* 600 BC) and in the *Mahabharat* (*c.* 500 BC–AD 200). In the *Ramayan,* the other long, mythological and philosophical poem, the mridangam and the veena are mentioned. A contemporary of Buddha, Vats Raj Udhyan, the King of Kaushambhi, was and is still known as the master of veena. Kalidasa (*c.* AD 400), the Indian Shakespeare whose drama *Shakuntalla* is as famous in India as *Hamlet* is in Britain, frequently referred to music and used the imagery of music in his verses. Bharata in fact used the word 'kutupa' for instrumental ensemble, implying thereby some degree of sophistication in working out arrangements between instruments. By Bharata's time the form of the scales and their diminutive intervals, the shrutis, had been worked out and the fact had also been established that certain combinations of notes (jatis) were more expressive of moods which grew out of the atmosphere of certain climatic seasons (the monsoons for instance). This was the embryo gestating. At a much later date this idea evolved into ragas such as Megha or Malhar, ragas of the season, when the rains come, when much work has to be done on the land, and lovers are thus prevented from meeting overmuch–hence ragas of yearning passion.

Bhava

Bharata carried on the most intensive investigation into bhava, the state of mind with which Hindus are primarily concerned in all their philosophy, as being different from outward behaviour and moral attitudes. Bhava is the word used for the inner psychic processes which motivate all human behaviour and which are expressed in all artistic creativity. It is the outcome of a highly refined mood or spiritual relish, which is created by the active artist and with which the participant spectator is also identified. 'Bhaav' in Sanskrit (=what makes something become) actually means the process of becoming, being or occurring, as distinct from 'bhav' which is the actual birth, production or origin. It therefore indicates an active identification with creative energy, culminating in a dignified climax of the basic emotions aroused and arrived at by slow degrees and varying processes. Bhava is intrinsic to the whole theory of Indian aesthetics in all the fields of art. Especially in Indian music this has crystallized into a wholeness by the *sentiment* expressed emotionally, thoughtfully and with supreme technical musicianship.

'Brahma bhavehn jagat bhavatee', it is said in Sanskrit. From the utter bliss of Brahma, the universe comes into existence. In exactly the same way the artist in fact can be identified with Brahma. Such a concept was what Bharata was evolving over 1500 years ago.

NARADA AND MATANGA

The next landmarks are the treatises of Narada (not to be confused with the earlier sage already mentioned) and Matanga of about the seventh century AD. These are the *Sangita Makaranda* and the *Brihadeshi* (a comprehensive account of deshi music) of late Buddhist times. Some authorities put the writing of the *Sangita Makaranda* as early as AD 400. Lately, scholars have begun to question the validity of any dates set against Bharata Narada or Matanga, asserting that those given in recent histories are incorrect and that the dates may be earlier than hitherto agreed. In these two works the raga was first defined, called so specifically and different types designated as different genders – male, female or neuter – depending on whether they were like the primary colours or were derivative, allied or in some way related, perhaps through a certain ordering of notes for instance.

Narada also codified the shrutis or microtones which cause such controversy nowadays among theoreticians of Indian music. He acknowledged their existence by giving them twenty-two names, some of which are now in use as girls' names, i.e. Kanta and Shanta. One shruti, madhyam (the fourth), which can never be flattened, was called ugra (formidable), an epithet given to the god Shiva. Two, sa (the first) and pancham (the fifth), were acknowledged as static. The idea of komal or flattened notes was conceived.

Ranja

The word 'raga' is said to have derived from the Sanskrit root word 'ranja' meaning 'to please' or 'to colour' (in the sense of colouring a mood) and indicating delight or appreciation. There are of course other derivations for the word 'raga' which will be explained later. By this time the raga as we now know it was in its embryonic form. The values of the duration of notes, the ascending scale of the melody, the differing but related descending scale, and the movement forwards in the raga from slow to quickening tempo – all these characteristics were being clarified and regulated.

Varna

Matanga defined the raga as 'a combination of notes, illustrated by melodic movements, varna,[1] which is capable of producing pleasant sensations.'

Never fewer than five notes were incorporated in these elementary ragas. Development of the form was extended by this idea of varnas, variations of melodic form which could be derived from one particular group of notes of a chosen melodic line. At this point the skeleton of the raga was growing flesh.

Theoretically these early musicologists were reaching towards a strong and unmistakable emotional pull in the music, far more concentrated than in our own and distilled like a tiny phial of heady perfume into a few full tones and their shadings in the complementary graces, clustering like miniature fire-flies between the peaks of full tones.

TAMILNAD CODIFICATIONS

Even more concrete were the specific notations of the South Indian ruler King Gunasena of Tamilnad, who had engraved on stone his entire codification of various ragas. Five centuries later Bharata's *Natya Shastra* was engraved on stone *in its entirety* in the spacious temple of Chidambaram. Here also the 108 poses of the classic dance form, Bharata Natyan, are enumerated in superb stone sculpture and under each is carved the appropriate verse from the treatise.

SARANGADEVA (1210-47)

It was Sarangadeva who next produced a treatise of worth in the

[1] Sometimes pronounced or written barna, depending on the region of India and the ambiguity of the letter 'v' in Indian phonetics.

thirteenth century. This was the *Sangeet Ratnakara*. Here again, even in Chaucerian times, its author was acknowledging his predecessors in chronological lists beginning with the Lord Shiva, Brahma, Bharata and Durga Shakti, the female goddess of earth power worshipped most commonly in Bengal; mythology and history were inextricably merged.

By this time the Afghan invasions were steadily augmenting themselves throughout North India. Influences were coming from Persian and Arabian melodies, and grace and embellishments were being added to enrich the indigenous themes and musical forms in use. But during this time the South remained comparatively untouched. Sarangadeva lived in the Deccan, lower Central India, when the Maratha empire stretched right down to the Cauvery River, so he must have been aware of the stream of music from both North and South and must have tried to give a common basis to them both.

He certainly dealt with the shrutis again, eliminating some, and since that day and age their usage has gradually diminished so that only the most important ones are now used.

He classified ragas in groups according to the seasons and times of day, i.e. dawn, middle of the day, early evening, deep night (a phrase evocative of this country at that marvellous time when the ink-black sky seems to throb with intense absoluteness of colour amid the shimmering stars) and late night. The force of the feeling aroused by these melodies and the technique of playing them in different ways according to the temperament and gifts of the individual, began to be explored in depth.

Length of duration, a quivering use of the note, the way it is approached from either direction or curled around and embraced by grace, create the essence of a raga. The notes may be almost identical in two entirely separate ragas but they may be attacked sharply or played tenderly (this is often the musical direction for evening ragas of sringara or erotic emotion) or very softly or stridently with a sudden crescendo.

'No principle of classification will help a listener unless he attends to the special way in which a note is used, singly or in combination.' I cannot refrain from quoting Professor D. P. Mukherji again because, of all Indians, he comes closest to helping the hapless stranger who does not know quite where to start. 'A semi or one-third note, say of reh (ray or the second note of the scale) is used in various ragas. In fact sometimes it is the whole scale of notes which is similar (in various ragas). The thing is to weigh their emphasis, to distribute the notes lovingly or rudely, vertically or in a wave-like manner. The minor reh of Todi Raga is not the minor reh of Purbi Raga, the komal (flat) ga (the third note of a scale) of Kafi Raga is not the komal ga of Kanada Raga. An expert shows it clearly. Playing fast, he utilizes the next note, no doubt, but his voice or his finger must know how to rest and dwell on the exact measure stipulated by custom or treatise for that raga.'

As there was never any real notation in Indian music and the ragas and their styles of singing were handed down from father to son, uncle to nephew, guru to shishya, in very tight circles akin to the clannish guild systems of medieval Europe, constant changes took place in the ornamentation on the basic notes at the same time as the tradition was kept intact. There could be no burning of the books to destroy the links in the chain as happened in Europe. Ragas were therefore combined and interrelated but with fierce precision and discipline of technique, to be played with infinite skill, just as today a master musician can play a raga-mala or necklace of ragas and show his skill in weaving related scales into one another, particularizing the special motifs and figures and phrasings, yet still keeping their individual identities clear for the listener, as separate pearls in the necklace.

An elderly South Indian friend in New Delhi happened to be the conductor of the South Indian Vadya Vrinda, a group of instruments being used experimentally in orchestration for All Indian Radio. He often allowed me to go and sit in on rehearsals and in the breaks from work would treat me to his South Indian humour, his sanity in the midst of my musical confusion, and to a genuine desire to clear the air when I was most in need.

'My dear lady,' T. K. Jayaram Iyer would say as he chewed and adjusted his betel nut, 'let me tell you a little more of our long history for I am from the South, from Tanjore, and that is the home of our music. Now in the *Sangeet Ratnakara* (the Gem in the Ocean it is called, ratan being a pearl and kar that which makes a thing), Sarangadeva listed nearly 280 melodies. Again in 1620, *Venkatamakhi* wrote: "I challenge the three-eyed god, Lord Shiva, to create one more melody than the 72 I have systematized." He listed the 72 primary scales or melas and the 500 moulds or ragas and the bhava or spirit which could be created from these.'

There seemed to be no limits to the mathematical permutations which could be worked on those 72 primary scales. And if the ones quoted are not enough Mr Crossley-Holland, in his section dealing with non-Western music in the *Pelican History of Music*, mentions 11 991 ragas said to be possible among ancient Tamils!

'Ah! But you want to take no notice of this, my dear lady. What is mathematically possible and what the heart can speak are two different things,' T.K. would emphasize. 'We are concerned with the soul of music, whether it speaks of the heart's longing for the love of a woman or of a god, of sadness or anger, the joy of the rains, or the great serenity when we have come to rest.'

The inherent potency of each note is therefore all-important. Along with this special concern for the approach to a given note, Sarangadeva also began to classify the types of instruments which were coming to be used: sushir were the wind instruments to be played solo; anaddha were the skin-covered drums to accompany the dance; ghana were the striking instruments or cymbals so often used in the South today for both singing or dance; and tata the stringed instruments to accompany the human voice, vocal music being far more dominant and important in India than instrumental (which incidentally we hear more often, partly because it is more acceptable to our ears).

JAYADEVA

At the same time, about the twelfth and thirteenth centuries, Jayadeva, court poet to the King of Bengal (1179–1205), was composing in Bengal the incomparable verses of the *Gita Govinda*, a poem which was to express bhakti or devotional love of God in the most sensuous and erotic Sanskrit. Yet this was held in total check by the nature of the love expressed. This was based as it still is on the recurring theme of Hindu lyricism (and for that matter Muslim mystic poetry), a yearning for union with the Divine symbolized by love at the human level, the ecstasy of which is the only one known to the average man and woman. Remarkably apposite imagery can be expressed in this way in terms going beyond the devotional mysticism of most of the Christian saints, being closer in temperament to the 'Song of Solomon'. In fact the *Gita Govinda* is an allegory of the soul's striving to escape the allurements of the sense in order to find serenity in mystical union with God. Radha's outpourings of love to Krishna who acts as protagonist are the passionate expressions of love of God by all men devoted to return to Him.

Jayadeva was the first composer to mention in what tala, or beat and rhythm, the song should be sung, tala which was to become the controlling factor in vocal music–sangeet music–giving vertebrae to the tenuous melodic line.

MUSLIM INVASIONS

The intensity of love for God expressed in such erotic poetry must have been the psychological reaction of the Hindu mind to the traumatic experience that the land of Hindustan was suffering during this period–a watershed indeed of Indian history.

Almost contemporaneous with the Norman conquest of England, there were similar convulsive invasions of North India by the first waves of Muslims to come from Asia Minor. These marauding exercises were different in kind as well as degree from the incursions of the later Moghuls who settled in India and identified themselves with an ordered society of many races and religions.

The early invasions were damaging to the whole fabric of the northern area of the subcontinent (comprising present-day West Pakistan and the whole Gangetic basin). Armies swept in for conquest or rapid enrichment in the form of immediate loot (a word we anglicized from Hindi and Urdu), abduction of women and mass conversions to Islam by fire and the sword. This is still part of the racial memory of Hindu and Buddhist Indians, balanced fortunately by the more rational minds who do recognize the differences and the later involvement of Moghul society in a common culture.

The nature of Islam is no less fierce than Christianity in its proselytizing phases; Hinduism in reaction to this dramatic impact underwent a period of emotional expression and identification with a personal, loving God, during what is termed Bhakti Yuga, the age of devotion.

As Ravi Shankar once explained to me, the Vaishnav cult (followers of Vishnu and, through his many avatars or reincarnations, Krishna and Rama as preserving forces coming into the world at times of darkness and peril, to save mankind) swept through India as a great wave, a wave of reaffirmation in Hindu belief, led by great saints such as Shri Chaitanya' Sri Rup Goswamy in Brindaban, and Tulsidas, Surdas and Meera. In addition, most of these were musicians, setting their poems to melodies themselves. Ravi Shankar writes about this period of vital and powerful emotionalism: '... an average Hindu's conception of God and religion is different from anywhere else! To him his Krishna, Gopal, Rama, Mother Kali, Shiva, Ganesh, Subramanyam (Kartikeya), Saraswathi or Hauman is very near and dear to him, as intimate as a living human being. The intensity of this "feeling" his God in and around him makes it so very human! This is what we find in the songs from Jayadev, Chandidas Vridyapati, Tulsidas, Surdas, Kabir, Dadu Tukaram, Narsibhagat or Thyāgarāja. Along with sections of highest philosophy, wisdom and Bhakti, one finds parts so full of eroticism and sensuality, the same as in paintings and carvings in the temples.'

Hinduism is not all asceticism and life denial, as is often popularly supposed, and yet one never has to mistake this other force for a titillation of the senses as we know erotica. Using words as emotive as these always leads to unnecessary misconceptions, and certainly Hinduism has been much maligned by careless use of this word. The religious ecstasy of true erotic emotion is well known to Western psychology: when fully released towards identification beyond the limited individual personality, its forces are illuminating in the truest sense. This accounts for the vibrancy and perennial qualities of these melodies in which are embedded such gems of poetic and religious feeling as Jayadeva so vividly expressed.

But not all was dark in this land shaken by the intermittent destructive forces of conquering invaders. Like Christianity, Islam also has its constructive, peaceful qualities and Muslims born to creative principles.

In the development of secular classical music one such Muslim stands out.

Khusru (or Khusro) (b. 1254)

Hazrat Amir Khusru, born in the reign of the last Pathan king, Allandin Khilji, was a Turkish disciple of Sheikh Nizamuddin in Delhi. He introduced the qawali style of devotional songs so popular with Muslims in India and Pakistan today. Lengthy passages up and down the melodic line, sung in fast tempo with well punctuated choruses carrying the theme of the song in abstract words taken from phrases of Persian mystic poetry, give qawali-singing its easily recognizable identity.

Khusru himself was again one of those creative Indians born into Hindu and Muslim society, who invariably contribute to this composite flowering of culture which gives such breadth and vision to the Indian mind. His ancestors were Turks but he called himself a Hindu Turk and was fluent in Hindi as well as Persian. Whatever had fallen under the dead hand of formalism during century upon century of theorizing was released from these strictures by his own imaginative sense of discovery. Such was his genuis that he became known as a shrutidar (derived from the word 'shruti'), and the legends about him still maintain that he could reproduce any melody and elaboration of it after hearing it once only.

He worked on the three-stringed tritantri veena until it became the modified sitar, the Persian word 'sehtar' meaning the same thing. He brought into being new ragas such as Kafi, Zilaph and Sarfarda, and composite ones such as Yaman, popular even to this day. With the coming of the Muslims and their Persian musical influences there was a conscious attempt to adapt the Hindu bhajan or hymn to the more elegant style from the North. Secular music became more agile and under the busying hands of Amir Khusru and his more ambitious instruments, all kinds of experiments which would nowadays set the purists' hair on end, became possible. Now, of course, history has sanctioned these derivative melodies evolved from Persian airs and tones. They were consequently absorbed into the Hindu body of serious thought and philosophic artistic endeavour, adding elegance and lightness as a characteristic Muslim contribution.

From this period onwards, great changes came about in the artistic and social life of India. For several centuries the authoritarianism and militant attitudes of the Muslims from Asia Minor clashed with the more tolerant philosophy of Hinduism at one level, but with the rigid social codes and obscurantism of Hindu ritual at another level. Hinduism was placed on the defensive and became less inclined to outward reform and change. Atrophy set in at temple level. The period was one of wind and storm, pressure and tension. But then there were other currents running at a deeper level in society to counteract the violence and the upheaval.

The seed was germinating towards a tremendous flowering of culture. During much of the period from the first to the ninth centuries when Buddhism flourished and many Hindus were converted to its clean-cut asceticism and straightforward beliefs, a certain austerity and puritanism had seeped into the Indian spirit even though there were pockets of regionalism where Hindu kings encouraged a burst of baroque artistic endeavour, such as at Khajuraho. Even then the Buddhist temperament could not quench entirely that effusive love of life that the Indian has, and the cool inner walls of the Ajanta caves near Aurangabad radiate the life-giving warmth of those Buddhist monks who must have painted the tempera murals of a society alive with the champagne-effervescence of good living. Here beside the glorious equanimity of the boddhisattva throng the seductive, gossamer-clad and lissom beauties of that age with their dark skins and pearl-bedecked hair. Some even hold wine-glasses in their hands as their eyes watch the courtly warriors and hunters in the deer-chase, and among them also they carry the old swaradhae veena to enchant the crowded courts. There they stay, imprisoned for all time in the shadowy caverns of Ajanta.

The iconoclastic attitude of the Afghan, Pathan and Turkish invaders which, holding that the representation of God or Prophet in human form is a blasphemy, caused them to treat the images of Hindu gods and goddesses they saw upon the temple walls with pathological destruction, began to give way to other forces and constructive aesthetic principles. Mahmud of Ghazni had popularly been known in tenth-century India as the Idol-breaker; faces were disfigured on temple sculptures, noses knocked off and the melon-heavy breasts of full-bosomed apsaras or flying goddesses smashed.

Only in the South did Hindu culture remain free from the stresses and conflicts of two cultures so temperamentally different from each other as Islam and Hinduism. The Karnatakam remained uninfluenced because the alien forces never physically touched this part of the country. South Indian music, properly known as Carnatic, and South Indian dance, survived therefore in more-or-less pure form, inheriting much of the older musical traditions when they were at the formative stage. This is why Carnatic music of today is recognizable even to the outsider as being different in shape, sound and form, from the Hindustani music, although of course similar enough to be recognizable as Indian rather than regional music. What has happened is that the original scales and their usage have been more faithfully adhered to than in the North, and the names kept that existed before all the reassessments and reorganization that took place as later theoreticians and musicians came to clear away the undergrowth that nearly strangled Northern music in later centuries. This is why ragas of North and South use different nomenclatures for the same raga. The style of singing also differs, not in the grammar of the system, but in the use of the vocal chords–in which there is almost as great a difference as between Indian music in general and Western.

Hindustani music has quite obviously been open to influences from all over the high hinterland of Asia Minor, Arabia, Mesopotamia, Slavic Russia, Tibet and China. This had its own positive and progressive impact and even today many of the important musicians of Hindustani music are Muslim and their vocalists in no way think it incongruous or heretical to be singing hymns and love lyrics in praise of Hindu deities. The Krishna/Radha themes and the Shiva cycle of legends have over the long centuries become the rock-bed of Indian, not Hindu, art, and it has been said rightly indeed by a Hindu writer that some of the most devout songs to Hindu deities have been actually composed by Muslims in the classical medieval music of dhrupad. 'Even the specifically religious songs of the Muslims, e.g. Kawali, Soz, are also cast in exactly the same mould, which India evolved during the Muslim period as one product in joint endeavour.' So writes Professor D. P. Mukherji.

The miracle of the Indian genius is that from the very birth of its Hindu culture in the early Vedic period it has–because of its inclusive attitude to other beliefs–been able to absorb over century upon century, during 4000 years of *continuous* growth, elements from all the races and cultures which have migrated across Europe and Asia to that downward-pointing triangle which is the Indian subcontinent.

Hindu culture has taken in Aryans, Persians under Darius, Phoenicians, Greeks under Alexander, white Jews and black Jews, Huns, Mongols, Scythians, Parthians, Chinese, Muslim slave kings of Turkey and Moghuls from Afghanistan, and, finally, in the last 500 years, Portuguese, Dutch, French and British.

Synthesis is indeed the Indian genius.

Nor has this been one-way traffic. Ancient Indian music must have influenced those lands of the Middle East in turn because, even in the time of Alexander, there was exchange of ideas and art between Greece and India. The great conqueror himself is said to have returned from India with a group of her musicians. Modes played on the lyre and the flute in Greece must have been very similar to those played on the early bansari (flute) and veena in India.

What Hindustani music has lost in purity of development – and this is a point of view from South India only, where the people's integrity in all manifestations of Hindu life is matched only by their chauvinistic pride in representing the true, unadulterated Hindu Indian – the music has made up in delicacy of enrichment and diversity from all these other sources. For instance, the veena which used to be the common instrument of Indian music was superseded by the sitar, sarod and sarangi in the North, instruments not played at all by South Indian musicians. There the veena remains the classical instrument *par excellence*.

MOGHUL ERA

Babur

The Moghul era began in 1517 with Babur, fifth in descent from Tamburlane. The first act after Babur had fought his way from Afghanistan through to Delhi, was to lay out a water-garden in the Persian style. This is symptomatic of Moghul rule, when an enlightened interest was shown in Hindu music and art, if not in dance, which has always existed in Hindu culture as a high and sacred form of art and worship to God. It has always evolved *within* the temple as an aesthetic and lyrical act of worship in its true representation. Chaitanya, the great South Indian saint/philosopher, danced the kirtans and Mirabhai, a mystic, herself danced in kirtana (forms of devotional hymns).

But Islam looks on dance as suspect. In the opulent courts of the Moghuls the Indian dance forms were, ironically, extracted from the worshipful level of the temple and turned into secular and sensual forms of entertainment and delight. In this way it could be said that Muslim influence hindered and warped the natural development of the North Indian dance forms, but not those of classical Bharata Natyam and Kathakali in the South. Kathak became a specialized form of rhythmic dance with fantastic feats of control in the fast movements of footwork. The word 'Kathak' comes from the Hindi word 'Katha', a holy story. Kathaks were the people who had always existed to tell these religious stories in mimed dance form.

Babur was not only a soldier-statesman; he was also a poet and man of letters and he set the tone for the whole great period that followed.

Akbar (1566–1607)

The new and welcome enlightenment came to fruition in the Moghul emperor Akbar whose expansive universality influenced so many aspects of Indian development. Under his benevolent domain an extraordinary process of synthesis occurred between Hindu and Muslim cultures, exemplified in the Emperor's personal life by his taking a Hindu wife and by his giving every kind of encouragement to Hindu painters and musicians and royal patronage without any communal kind of bar. This interaction between Hindu and Muslim has, despite all that we have seen in modern political terms, brought real benefits to India and been a source of creative inspiration. Some of the most lyrical and intellectually satisfying poetry is Muslim. Grace and rhythm was brought to architecture. Individuality was infused into the playing of the raga and, in addition, the Muslims added a necessary and irreverent humour to all things weighed down by the more serious Hindu temperament–Malabar with its bubbling laughter being wholly excepted however.

Here in this middle period of Moghul rule in the fifteenth and sixteenth centuries the culmination of an Indian renaissance burst forth and fused the two cultures, so that to the outsider the two, even at this distance, seemed to be completely integrated. In music, poetry and art the images of the gods, the songs sung in praise of them, the pictures illustrating the ragas, the forms of music and art whether given by Muslim or Hindu, were identical. India was again united as it had been under Ashoka, so many long centuries before.

Two great civilizations, both with a strong tradition and well defined aesthetic sense, though the diverse outcome of very different religious and social histories, came to exist alongside each other; accepting within the humility of spirit of this great man a meeting-point in the contemplative aspect of the divine.

They flowed together into the mainstream of Indian life and

created a truly expansive burst of artistic expression in painting, music and architecture. Nearly every single Moghul emperor was a music-lover, barring Aurengzeb who took his hatred of Hindu culture to a maniacal degree of xenophobia–a disaster for India, himself and his family, his father being murdered at his own instigation.

As a result of all this patronage and awareness of the artist as a necessary and important contributor to the needs of Indian society, there was a rapid development in techniques and in the instruments capable of reflecting this aesthetic upsurge. The kabuli rabab from Afghanistan, for instance, had already evolved into the sarod; with such a sophisticated instrument with its 25 strings, 15 of which are for sympathetic resonance, further exploration of sound was possible. From all this, new forms of classical singing grew which are the inspiration and aspiration of gatherings of classical musicians even today. Cross-fertilization, patronage and technical knowledge raised music to its highest water-mark.

New melodies were inspired; there was also a more flexible attitude to the strict rules about playing a raga. New forms of secular singing such as group vocalizing and the chanting of poetry *ex tempore* in mushairas (a social, religious and musical activity all rolled into one, unique to the Muslim tradition) had already been experimented with.

As elsewhere in all similar historical periods, when the waters rise and the imagination of a people is caught on the tidal wave, quite naturally great men and artists seem to be born. Either it is because they themselves bring about that period of full flowering by their exceptional activities, or because the unparalleled volume and density of ideas and new technical processes challenges men in like manner to aspire to new heights – and then genius emerges.

Tansen (1506–89)

So it was under Akbar in the sixteenth century. Tansen was born. This genius of music is spoken of by both contemporary musicians and laymen as though he lives today, and the tamarind tree at Gwalior beside his grave is still an object of pilgrimage. To chew its leaves is said to bring about gifts of voice similar to those possessed by this great man. (To my chagrin the legend failed to work on me.) What had been the forerunner in Khusru now erupted into com-

plete fulfilment in Tansen. The coping-stone was laid on the classical edifice. With that certain endowment intrinsic to greatness – an
instinctive ability to absorb all the old without casting it aside in
haste or rebellion, and so to transform it naturally and with the
even flow and potent force of time, just as the withered husk throws
out the green spring shoots in the fullness of natural growth –
Tansen reshaped Indian music of the North. Abul Fazl, an historian
of the court at the time, wrote of Tansen that he was the greatest
singer to be born 'in the last 1000 years'.

Although there seemed to be abundant life in music at the folk
level and many styles were shaping under the new ideas born of
Muslim influence and experimentation, classical music was
bounded by all the archaic rules and the dead hand of Hindu tradition which had for the time being lost its natural inspiration for
growth.

Tansen is the personification of the synthesis of Hindu and
Muslim cultures. He was in fact a Hindu Brahmin, despite his
Muslim name of Ata Mohammed Khan. He was born Ramtanu to
Mukund Pande under the blessing of a Muslim saint, Mohammed
Ghaus, who later became his benefactor and near whose mausoleum
at Gwalior Tansen is now buried.

The title Tansen[1] was conferred on him later on in his life by the
Emperor Akbar when Ramtanu was called from the court at
Gwalior as his fame grew to become one of the Nava Ratna or nine
jewels in the splendour of the Agra court.

It was predicted by the fakir saint Ghaus that he would become
famous, and as a boy he was able, so the legend goes, to imitate
sounds with uncanny gifts. Such ability was said to cause the rains
to fall when he sang Raga Malhar, fire to flame at the sound of the
Raga Deepak, and trees to quiver as though the wind had rustled
through them. This brings to mind the capacity of Orpheus to do
similar feats in ancient Greece.

The most quoted story about Tansen is that of his guarding a
park which had been broken into many times by vandals. He took it
upon himself to play the ventriloquist and he became the tiger's
voice. Once too often he roared in imitation of this beast, this time
scaring a group of disciples of the famous yogi and teacher, Swami

---

[1] According to some Indians the word derives from its component syllables.
तान सेन = taan = run of notes, and sen = army, implying 'conqueror of
taans'. Others suggest the original syllable was chehn = peace.

Haridas. When the holy man discovered a ten-year-old boy to be the culprit, a boy with such a strange gift to imitate sound so realistically, he went in search of his father and took the boy to Brindaban. This is the still thriving temple city near Mathura in Uttar Pradesh, made famous by the blue-skinned god Krishna. Tansen studied here in the temple for ten years and then went on to Gwalior to join the court of the Dowager Rani. He married a Hindu girl, Hussaini, whose Muslim name arose from her father's having embraced Islam.

There were four sons, all of whom became musicians in their own right, and one daughter, Saraswati, who became a leading veena player. Emperor Akbar brought about her marriage to a royal prince who also held Hindu and Muslim names. He too was an accomplished musician and also a pupil of the yogi Haridas.

As can be seen, this was a tightly interwoven family of master musicians from whom two gharanas or music schools evolved. One gharana derived inspiration from Tansen's side of the family, specializing in the rabab (not to be confused with the kabuli rabab from Afghanistan which was eventually transformed into the modern sarod). From his daughter's side another gharana, known as Beenkars, concentrated on the development of the proper Indian veena. There are descendants of this notable family still living, including Ustad Dabir Khan of Calcutta, whom Bengalis eulogize for the greatness of the days when no other veena player could match his musicianship. Nearly all the sarod and sitar players of today have derived their techniques and inspiration from these two guild schools.

One of the most useful services Tansen performed was a sorting-out of the tangled skein of ragas and raginis that had grown in mass over the centuries. With the fine toothcomb of his perceptive ear he discarded many that were loosely framed or overlapped, pruning some 4000 down to a manageable 400.

So it was that he shaped the old dignified form of religious singing with its weighty modes and stanzas and abstract syllabic sounds into a freshness and liveliness of form again. The sweet and mellifluous melodies of the folk-music joined forces with the polished and intricate grammar of the classical. The old clay was shaped, and dhrupad music evolved to its fullness.

Dhrupad

Dhruva pada had been the vehicle for the singing of the raga in Hindu vocal art. It was as if a Shakespearian sonnet had been used and adapted to new improvisation by whichever singer came to expound it. From the tenth century onwards, dhruva pada (Dhruva=Truth or God; pada=a fixed line or text) had acquired the accretions of very formal ornamentation linked to a certain pre-scribed melodic form. It had become a static art form, kept alive behind the protection and sanctity of the Hindu temples during the dark period of about 200 years since Khusru, by the Goswamis. Swami Haridas belonged to this tradition of the temple city of Vrindaban, not far from Delhi. It was however Raja Man Singh Toman of Gwalior (who died in the late fifteenth century) who revitalized dhrupad singing and brought it into prominence by organizing seminars, conferences and a school or gharana under his patronage.

He set a pattern, bringing this form of music, a sung prayer or hymn of very serious import, out of the temple precinct and into the secular world of the performing arts. He encouraged famous singers such as Nayak Dhondu and Bakshu. This freeing of spirit and aesthetic principle was carried further forwards by Swami Haridas as an exponent of the Gwalior Gharana, and his own pupil, Tansen. It was in the court of the widow of Raja Man Singh, the Dowager Queen Mrignayani (also a disciple of Swami Haridas) that Tansen matured his music; from here he went as court musician to the Raja Ram Singh of Rewa who was a great connoisseur and patron of the arts. From here the Emperor Akbar summoned him to the court at Agra.

The dhruva pada consisted of two or four sentences in the language of Brij bhāshā expressing emotions of sublime love, with repetitions of final syllables or groups of syllables which, to an Indian who knows this devotional shorthand, conveyed different meanings of religious overtones. This is similar to the evocative force of such a mystic symbol as the word 'aum' and its resonating sound.

The musical principles behind this demanded that the musician returned again and again to these fixed melodic feet or 'lines' of the text with the formality of classical architecture, embroidering them with austere and lofty variations upon the same theme. The rigour of discipline is as severe as in yoga, a strength imparted to Tansen by his guru, Swami Haridas; but combined with the sensual, richly-emblazoned mysticism with which he had been imbued by his spiritual mentor and guide, Mohammed Ghaus, it surrounded him with a Miltonic grandeur and that certain soaring glory that our own sixteenth-century metaphysical poet Thomas Trahearne knew with poetic Christian vision: 'You never enjoy the world aright, till the sea floweth in your veins, till you are clothed with the heavens, and crowned with the stars.'

Every force within him seemed to combine in praise of the Lord God, whether He was the impersonal Narayana, Hari, Ramnarayan, Shiva or Allah. So passionate was he in all his singing; all his joy and unconscious compass bearings were turned towards God in whatever shape or avatar He cared to show himself to the whole wide-ranging world of men.

This was India at work again. A new humanism enriched ordinary life, coinciding with the great spring-tide that was flooding Europe at this time – in the Renaissance and the Elizabethan age when Christian and pagan themes, religious belief and philosophical humanism jointly created a new statement of the human condition in Western civilization.

Antique saman music had thus moved stage by stage from the obfusc solemnity of Vedic hymns to the more formalized but enlarged form of Raga Samgeeti (the Sanskrit now being anglicized and abbreviated into Sangeet).

In the social wasteland of the period between Chandra Gupta II in the fourth century and Harsha in the seventh (the two most outstanding rulers) and in the long interval before Akbar claimed the Peacock Throne of the great Moghuls in the North, North India seems to have lain under a heavy torpor, starved of imagination and the technical knowhow which is always a prerequisite of any inspirational advance in the arts. Only Khusru and another saint/musician, Baija Bavro (a contemporary of Tansen and also taught by Haridas) had carried the development of music forwards to some extent. Using the traditional form of the dhruva pada hymns or quatrains and their shorthand syllables used in Indian vocalizing –syllables such as 'tum', 'dar', 'dani'–and combining them with certain words from the Persian which also had abstract connotations, he created a style of singing known as tarana.

Tarana is best expounded today by such vocalists as Ustad

Nisar Hussain Khan and Pandit Rao Pattavardhan, but one of its
more unorthodox exponents in the last half-century was the remarkable Khansahib Abdul Karim Khan who took its form and
fashioned his own style out of it. Fortunately the old recordings of
his singing are now on long-playing records. He died at the age of
seventy-three in 1937.

Baiji Bavro had also elaborated on the idea of a poet's singing a
'fixed text', reforming on the old basis of singing long stories which
were well known, and around which the musicians improvised by
selecting only certain potent words and musical themes. It is said
by some authorities that this originated the Raga Alapana singing,
so characteristic of dhrupad-singing.

By Moghul times Sanskrit was under pressure and the advent
of Urdu[1] words with the Persian invasions changed the name of
this type of devotional singing from dhruva pada to dhrupad.
Tansen worked on the form as it had been transmitted to him and
created a new shape as formal and stylized as a Grecian ode yet
capable of conveying thoughts and emotions as devout and moving
as the Bach B minor Mass.

Dhrupad is full of dignity and majesty of emotion, singing the
praise of God and kings: ' . . . its verbal and emotional dignity is
conveyed by slow elephantine movements and with the utmost
economy of flourishes and decorations (alamkars).' This is D. P.
Mukherji's summing up of it as an Indian.

'To this day', Alain Danielou as a Frenchman writes, 'it represents the most severe and noble style in Indian vocal art.
Vocalizations as practised in the kyhal and the lighter variations of
the thumri are not permitted here. In the dhrupad the expression,
the significance, of the mode, or the raga, is fully conveyed. A
prelude introduces the mode and the poem is followed by the
theme of the song. The verses of the poem or its words can be
repeated several times, and some verses can come back again like a
refrain.'

Dhrupad-singing is accompanied only by the tampura (the
drone-like instrument of gleaming wood and gourd which has four
strings played by continually passing the fingers over the strings in
a crab-like motion) and the resonance of the pakhāwaj drum, the
Northern equivalent of the mridangam or one-piece drum (unlike

---

[1] The Persian word 'urd' (pronounced 'oord', not 'ūrd') = tent; 'Urdu'
= the language of the tented people.

the tabla with its two separate components). 'Between the resonance of the tampura and the thunder of the pakhāwaj', D. P. Mukherji goes on to comment, 'the voice of the dhrupad singer must needs be open, steady and deep to secure the necessary grandeur.'

Nowadays there are not so many vocalists who are able to execute such exacting standards of singing. Neither technique nor the grammar of the music is enough. That touch of a Bach in all his mysterious glory has to come over as well. The treatment is essentially masculine and virile, often sung in a bass pitch with a sweep and dignity which also appears visually as well in the curious figurations made with the hands as the singer marks the phrases and describes the rhythm and flow of the thematic development, like a conductor shaping the music in the air for both himself and his accompanists to follow.

The classical severity and the slow rolling wash of the waves in the grandeur of this mood enables each note to be defined individually and emphatically reiterated. Notes are not slurred nor lost by merging, as in most other forms of singing. Few ornamental flourishes are allowed with grace notes, or trills or sliding falls in fast tempo. The pace moves forwards with the stately manner of a royal procession, with few variations in the talas chosen.

The composition which follows after a short alaap or introduction is fixed in four parts, like the movements or varnas of the raga system.

The first is called sthayi. This is the statement of melody or theme. Its elaboration is worked around the lower four notes of the tetrachord (the two sections into which an octave can be divided – a lower four and an upper four notes) and the four notes next down in the octave below. Their combinations and interactions can be carried forwards using such condensed sounds as 'hari', 'raam', 'om' as pegs from which to hang the elaborations.

The next part is the antara, the second subject, which takes the movement of the raga forwards into the ascent of the higher octave to touch the upper sa. This marks out the antara. There is a considerable amount of carry-over into this from the sthayi, and dedicatory phrases such as 'Ananta Hari Narayana', best translated in our own terms as 'the peace of God passeth all understanding', are introduced. Similar devotional phrases are stated in the raga chosen and move in measured progression through the ascent and descent of the notes, often changing to abbreviations of these sacred and devotional words. They are indeed a bridge in sound structure between sense words and abstract sound, from the 'Aum–Ananta Hari Aum–Narayana', to the 'Anarita', to the broken syllables: ne, te, ri, ra, na, num, tum. A musical shorthand is carried by the reiterations of melodic motifs and the listener can pick up the monosyllabic sounds: a...na...ri...num... tum..., which enable the vocalist to elaborate in mathematical terms upon the full notes of the raga. This also provides a fascinating shuttle between vocal and instrumental music following the tradition of Swami Haridas, Tansen, the Rababiyars and the Beenkars and those who stemmed from these schools, using the rabab and the been.[1]

Such worshipful thoughts may be expressed in lines such as this:

> Ra .. jata .... Chou .... ndra ... la . la ... ta
> Tre .... lo . cha . na . tripura ..... ri
> Gao .... nga . dha .. ra .. na . a . ra
> Dhou ... gi . na ... ra .. ra ...... ja . ta ...
> .... O . Ha . ra . aa ... O . Ha . ra . aa . aa .....

The whole of the composer's thoughts are turned to the Lord Shiva whose attributes and qualities he will enumerate as the song progresses.

> Shankar, the benign, on whose head shines the moon,
>
> The three-eyed one, the killer of the demon Tripura.
>
> The carrier of the Ganges and he who assumes the form of a woman in one half of his body (adhana-isvara),
>
> The wearer of the tiger's hide, who besmears his body with ashes ...
>
> Oh Hara, the great Hara, who is known as Shankar the benign God, the dweller of the Kailash mountain.

Rhythmic drum-beat is added in this section.

---

[1] In fact the 'num, tum' singing which is the second part of Raag Ālāpāna (where the element of rhythm is added to the peaceful, leisurely elaboration of the alaap) is a direct influence of the rhythmic jod section played on the instruments rabab and been. Ravi Shankar has pointed out that many believe the four banis or styles of dhrupad (gobar or gowhār, dāgar, nowhār and khandār) are from the influence of these instruments, the places where they were brought into vogue by some ancient and famous musicians.

The third part is the sanchari or development containing phrases from the first two parts but greatly expanded and in a quickening tempo. A traditional stanza can be taken here also, a lyrical verse in a highly romanticized tradition, perhaps about the god Krishna and his many amorous exploits incorporated with a loving devotion to God.

The final section of dhrupad is the abhoga, the coda or the summing-up of all that has gone before. This is raga rendered in its purest form, both because of its regal classicism and because India places vocal music at the apex of its musical attainment, the voice being used in this context especially as an instrument.

The mechanics are as rigid as in any Western composition. The vocalist is on his mettle. The methods are intellectual, but within the stern confines the singer is still free to range over long passages of improvisation depending on his skill, the pitch of his voice, his ability to span several octaves and his musical memory; this last will recall from his subconscious mind after a decade of training, all manner of variations in the permutations of notes and the approaches to a given note.

This is the art of Leonardo da Vinci who knew every nerve and muscle of the human frame in anatomical detail. It is Michelangelo as architect rather than as painter of the Sistine Chapel. It is Bach at the organ rather than Chopin skipping merrily through his Etudes. Periods of artistic creativity however run dry towards the end of their historical sweep through the centuries.

Nowadays dhrupad is considered too much of a good thing for modern audiences and there are only a few exponents, such as the Daggar brothers (who recently visited Europe and one of whom is now dead), who can put fire and passion into so cool and classical a form. In their natural habitat they may take perhaps one hour and a half to get into 'good voice'—meaning appropriate mood and its reflection at proper pitch—before a concert of dhrupad is properly under way.

The heights had been scaled with Tansen. Three centuries followed during which Indian culture broke up at the end of Moghul rule and there came the British Raj. Other styles of singing such as darbari (from the Urdu word 'durbar'=court) and the fast-moving khyal (also spelled khayal, the Urdu word for imaginative thought) which held sway at the most popular level, became the fashion of the age. Both have been carried on from one musical guild to another down the long line of ancestry to this century.

Khayal

Khayal-singing is very popular in North India nowadays and is essentially a Hindu-Muslim syncretic art form. The very mention of the word brings to my mind a velvet-soft sensuousness, an evocation to love, an abstract lyric which, unlike opera, is not carried in the words but in the music, with eloquent vocalizing in mathematical permutations of musical syllables.

Sometimes this vocalizing can become a little too ostentatious if the singer gets carried away with his technical display in the quickening tempo. Increasingly, the modern generation of Indians begins to show impatience with these verbal gymnastics. Sparks of sound–trills, fast glissandos and graphic oscillations–all add to the skeleton of the syllables and the few words chosen as pegs from which hangs all this decoration. Occasionally one feels mentally breathless after such a *tour de force*. This is my own personal re-action, but some Indians regard the khayal as too austere for modern tastes and turn to the thumri to deal with the more roman-tic themes of all-consuming love.

Thumri

As the Moghul period moved in all its fulsome abundance into its baroque period, stretching its patrician rule down into the ancient hills of the South, thumri style of singing evolved from the more austere forms of dhrupad and khayal. Typical sentiments of a thumri song run thus: 'Darling, why did you not come? I could not sleep last night for the longing for you.'

Although the Moghuls were connoisseurs in their liking for the refinements of life they were wholly democratic in their social codes and customs, being free from the restrictive ideas of Hindu caste. It may be for this reason that even the ordinary people enjoyed some of the richness of the culture. India has not always been flailed by poverty and the despairing problems one has come to take for granted as being the village condition of life in recent years. So it was possible for classical music to loosen up and borrow from the stream of ordinary folk-music and create the thumri form of vocalizing. Sweet and evocative melodies,

97

sometimes but not always in quicker tempo than khayals, sometimes heavily ornamented with flourishes of fast-moving plummeting notes, made the thumri style more free in form than the khayal which still has to adhere to strict classical rules of movement and a tighter discipline. Thumri can freely express its sensuality in the spirit and richness of the music by means of seductive, smooth tones, which float in golden sound like some imagined magic carpet unsupported in the air.

Grace, delicacy and balance had now been added like the sinuous tracery of flowers which Moghul architects conjured into their harmoniously proportioned mosques and courtly halls of meeting and durbar. The Diwan-i-Khas of the Red Fort in Delhi is one such. This was a time of arabesques and rich costume and leisure to savour the glories and fineness of all this artistic exuberance. The lintels and architraves of the Hindu mandirs or temples, solid with their classical proportions, depth of thought and seriousness of purpose, were elevated as upon invisible hands into sheer splendour of curve, as in the domed mausoleum of the Taj Mahal and others that sprang so dramatically from the flat monotony of the North Indian plains.

European rule established foreign powers who were not basically interested in the indigenous culture. Neglect now settled on the music, dance and sculpture like a heavy dust-sheet. This time the foreign ruler was not willing to merge and synthesize with Hinduism. Consequently Hindu life closed in on itself again and atrophied. The outer forms remained and the traditions were handed down through families strongly possessive of their intimate knowledge of these crafts, but dhrupad had lost its motive force.

The personal Hindu disciplines of yoga and pranayama (breath control) which even Tansen and other Muslim musicians had embraced, sank into neglect with the decay of society at the base of the pyramid. 'The deep fountain of spiritual and mystic richness within, which dhrupad devotional singing gave rise to in a fine musician, became dry and technical' writes Ravi Shankar, 'whereas khayal and thumri thrived on an extrovert, physical, sensual inspiration, and so gained more popularity.'

Decline in Development

At the turn of the last century, musical theorists such as Pandit

1 Sitar

2 Sarod

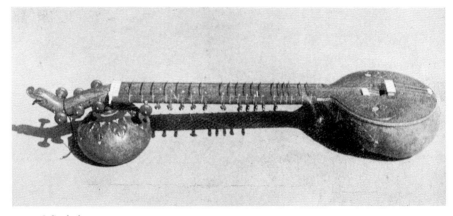

3 Surbahar

4 Sarangi

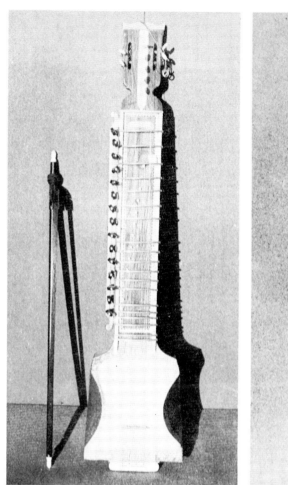 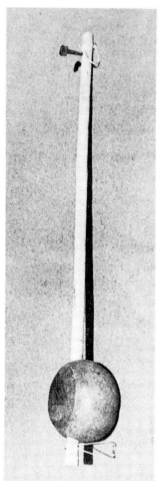

5 Dilruba

6 Ektara

7 Veena

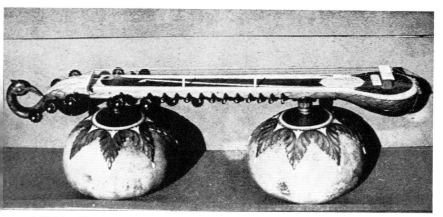

8 Vichitra Veena

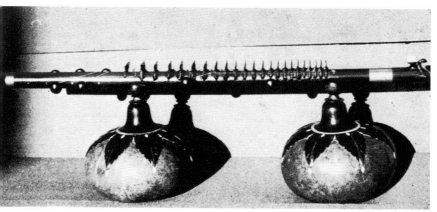

9 Been (North)

10 *Right:*
Tampura

11 *Far right:*
Rabab

12 Santoor

13 Shehnai

14 Nadaswaram

Bhatkhande, worked on re-classifying the ragas and did further authoritative research into the primary and derivative ones in his *Hindustani Sangitach: Paddhati*; the great singer Pandit Vishnu Digamber Paluskar founded the first music schools all over India; and odd pockets of musicians still played under royal patronage in certain princely states left intact by the British. But on the whole the neglect of the fountain of creativity which bubbles at the source of Hinduism was complete. Alien educational systems and the setting up of Western-type universities, no matter how beneficial to and productive of intellectual attainment, served only to create further alienation and confusion in the culture amongst a great many of the educated, and ultimately dispossessed them of their own traditions, from which influences they are only just re-arighting themselves. Not all of them were of the genius of Tagore or Vivekananda, able to absorb ideas from the new world of imported Western thought and to transform what was good into a restatement of old Indian truths in yet another metamorphosis–variations on an infinite theme.

Bengal and Tagore

One region however did record a capacity to absorb and transform. This was Bengal. In the end, when the new liberal ideas and the political theories had percolated sufficiently, a sudden energy came over this prolific region of India, throwing up a versatile array of intellectuals, artists, statesmen, musicians, poets and saints. Ram Mohan Roy, numerous Tagores, Aurobindo, Ramakrishna and Vivekananda, Bankim Chander Chatterji, Thakur and Tekchand were but a few of the more famous of this renaissance. Perhaps this was because Bengal, having played enforced host to the British since East India Company days, had had time to absorb and carry on the process of harmonizing the disparate elements which over and over arouse this continent from deceptive lethargy, just when the stranger thinks that all life has ebbed from her gnarled and prehistoric frame.

This emergence of new inspiration sustained and inspired the Bengali musicians who have always followed the cult of intense worship of God. This is bhakti, already described as a personal passionate devotion akin to the ecstasy of human love at its fullest that Christian and Muslim mystics have also expressed in poetic

99

form. Bengalis being people of highly charged emotion anyway, and of mercurial temperament, are capable of the most exquisite thoughts and sensual expressions of love and beauty distilled into spiritual awareness – as well as of the most questionable Tantric pursuits of worship which at one time became perverted into thuggee and were the natural and obverse side of this coin, one which any psychiatrist would explain as being the complement of such volatile character and intensity of emotional expression.

It is in Bengal too that the traveller can encounter the wandering mendicants known as bauls (pronounced 'baa-uls') who walk from village to village like the balladeers of old – not as cranks or charlatans but with an ascetic sincerity – to sing (often in a moralizing double entendre) some of the loveliest melodies of India in praise of the One. The bauls have had a long tradition in this region and still can be seen and heard in the villages, living chroniclers who carry with them the immediacy of Hindu mythology, so much so in fact that they have now been put to use in village uplift schemes to sing of birth control and improvement of crops – all grist to the Village Block Development mill!

To the humble people who listen worshipfully, their impassioned love of the Divine implies a complete identification in mystic terms, and always there is the familiar theme of tayage shanti – the sense of renunciation which brings happiness and an enjoyment not so different from the Christian sense of grace.

'You do not know', the baul will sing, 'that you have opened a shop and six thieves (shara-ripu – the arrows of passion) are stealing away the goods.'

> Ploughman,
> are you out of your wits
> not to take care
> of your own land?
>
> A squadron of six birds
> is picking at the rice
> grown golden and ripe
> in the field of your limbs.
>
> Farming the splendid
> measured land
> of this human body

you raised the crop
the devotion to God.
But passions eat at it
like sparrows.

The fence of consciousness
is down to dust
leaving open gaps.
Cattle clamber up
and feast on your harvest.[1]

Those thieves are madh–pride of possession or conceit (pronounced 'mandh'; = ahankar in Sanskrit)–from which all the
other sins originate:

matsarya–caprice or envy (pronounced 'marts-sharya'; lrsha)
moha–love of self which is illusion (a-gyān)
mudra–money and greed (lobh)
moithun–lust for the flesh (kaam)
mānksh–anger (krodh)

It is always at this level that the village Indian is transformed
from the desolation of his material life to another inner reality
where music and belief and morality are totally merged.

It was the same with Tagore's artistic genius. He used the same
yeast of music, poetry, and philosophy, which run as a singular and
perpetual ferment in the deep body of Indian culture. This quality
of Tagore culminated in *Rabindra Sangeet*, his own personal statement in music of this continuing exploration of the Indian classical
system.

There can be no more emotional an experience than sitting in a
vast Calcutta crowd at a Ramakrishna meeting-house and swaying,
responding, murmuring in approval with these emotional Bengalis
while the joyous cadences of Tagore's singing words drift into the
humid air. Here are poems of such gentle beauty, searching for
God along the highway and in the golden flicker of leaves and grass
in the sparkling sunlight, yearning in the heart for the long-lost
lover, and expressing an optimism which is also characteristic of
those gay and sumptuously disciplined kirtans of the South composed by Swati Tirunal and Thyāgarāja. This is vocalizing very

[1] Sung by a modern baul, Jaduburdu, and translated by D. B. Bhattacharya.

different from the austere product of the dhrupad tradition, lilting melodies in which the words are redolent with sensuous meaning and much closer to our song tradition. Tagore said of himself that he could be called a baul. He composed more than 2500 pieces of music, many of which stirred up opposition by their new melodies and unfamiliar patterns. But no great artist can ever remain fettered by orthodoxy. Professor Mukherji has said: 'Tagore did a thing which all great revolutionaries do. He dipped into the springs which well out of the soil . . . In his early days Tagore had met stern opposition from the classicists. They alleged that he was making music soft and loosening its discipline by departing from the set pattern.' This is a familiar accusation today against all those younger musicians who are trying to bring new freshness to music; they will have to discover the same ironic truth for themselves – that only a 'dead romantic is a living classic'.

'He did receive training in the classical style,' D. P. Mukherji has however pointed out, 'although he never submitted to its senseless disciplines. The mark of the classical style is all over his compositions – their dhrupadic structure of four stanzas of which the first and third, the second and the fourth have similar movements, their avoidance of decorative phrases, the dignity of their composition and the close alliance between words and notes are typically classical. But he was not the man to remain content with being true to type. He tried a few Western melodies, and though a few of them are more than adaptations, he has never been happy with them. But the second period of his musical development saw the blending of ragas by the sheer pressure of the specific mood of each poem.'

This continual urge towards innovation, towards restating old themes in new patterns and motifs and in phrases outside the long-accepted orthodox forms, is something that is often forgotten when Indians themselves criticize contemporary experimenters of the North.

One area of India, however, has remained extraordinarily inviolable. Perhaps nowhere else in the world can the same homogeneity be found in music, running uninterrupted as it has for such a long and consistent period of time – almost fifteen centuries from the time of the Pallava kings of the sixth, seventh and eighth centuries when there was great creativity in devotional music. This is South India.

CARNATIC MUSIC OF THE SOUTH

The South, that downward-pointing triangle of India, although of course an integral part of the same historical process, has for various political and geographical reasons retained a certain unimpeded tranquillity of purpose. It suffered little from the disrupting invasions of the North; it also survived British rule psychologically, since the British Raj was centred first in Calcutta and then in Delhi. South Indians have come through unscathed in their fundamental Indian-ness. In the field of music one senses the same quality. Change there has been. No art form stands still, otherwise it dies a natural death from mediocrity. But coherence continued to come from the temple and the dance where Hindu culture still remains in its original form in the South. For instance, in Kerala no Indian is allowed within the temple precincts unless he is wearing the dhoti and the sacred thread. Western trousers are out, even though the highest-born in the land might be wearing them. Traditions are encrusted in the Karnatakam and the whole region carries with it effortlessly a confident integrity into all aspects of its life, and a marked identity of its own.

For this reason it is more conservative in outlook and its musicians reflect the same natural tendency towards permanence of tradition. I was told in South India of certain musical inscriptions that are now coming to light and being edited at the Academy of Fine Arts in Mysore, which prove beyond doubt that a system of absolute notation existed in South India as early as the seventh century. At this time few ragas or jatis – patterns of scales – as they were then called (not to be confused with jati-tala or the percussive rhythms of South Indian Carnatic music today) existed, but the strength of verbal tradition is so great that even at this early date the regional influence of Dravidian culture was marking out Carnatic music to be different in emphasis from that of the North. Form has been placed before personality in the austerity of this classicism of the South, so that the individual musicianship encouraged by the different traditions of the Muslim religion in the North has not made such a mark here. We are therefore closer to original forms and sound when listening to Carnatic music; less experimentation has been undertaken by the individual artists – or in fact been allowed by musical audiences. It is still admitted in North India that Southern audiences are the most discriminating

103

because even the man in the street knows more about his music and the principles that give it force than, say, a Bombay-wallah or a Punjabi.

This of course has social reasons behind it. Music in the South, unlike Moghul court music and the traditions that grew from this physical and political environment, has never been separated from its devotional context. Even today as the traveller moves around the South, he is forced to remark on a notable difference in life style. Much of the social life and culture is still an adjunct of the temple. Families can be seen in their thousands paying their daily respect in these magnificent cathedrals of heavy stone to the gods and goddesses whose sanctuaries are alive with activity from pre-dawn hours until late at night. There is no locking of the door, no specified service, no accepted time of 'going to church'. The entire day is allocated to that. I myself stood in the dark shadows of the great Meenakshi temple at Madurai for four hours and watched the dawn creep through its stately columns, while hundreds came to worship at 5.0 a.m. as the God and Goddess were taken for their morning bath. The strident nadaswarama, a long South Indian instrument, and liquid veenas accompanied them. In another sanctuary, three flute players acknowledged the dawn with a breath of melody as tentative and fragile as the pale-pink morning light.

Worship and music seem to be a very integral part of the South Indians' daily existence, and the temple becomes the market-place of our county towns where community and bustle and common interest draw the crowds. But this meeting-place is inextricably bound up with the service of higher things. It is understandable then to see how temples became the repositories of all that mirrored this search for spiritual grace, especially in the joy and moving beauty of music and dance. The North Indian, having had to suffer so many social upheavals, did have the advantages of enriching his culture by cross-pollenation, but he also had to carry indelible marks of its consequent insecurities. Melancholy and pathos are evident in Hindustani music to a degree not encountered in the Carnatic tradition.

The South Indian is noticeably less troubled in spirit; his humour is more jovial, allied as it is to his marked intellectual capacities and his muscular and sure Hindu faith. Dr Arnold Bake has said that, generally speaking, the classifications as well as the system of South India as a whole are more logical and bespeak a more mathematical intellect than the pronouncedly emotional Northern traditions. A South Indian wears no chip on his shoulder. But he moves not. He knows he is superior. Therefore logic implies that there is no need to change such an immutable order of life which grants him this innate view of his own superiority. In this respect the British met their match! Arrogance met with like arrogance. For this reason the South Indian took freely to the use of English and perfected it as his own, feeling no psychological inferiority in so doing – in fact he now defends it as a useful commodity against the Hindi-speaking drive of the Northern politician.

Although of course to an outsider Carnatic and Hindustani music appear to have a great deal in common, which sets them apart from other systems of music, to a resident of India the differences are more apparent. They reflect these historical and social differences. To me the Carnatic treatment of the raag seemed always to be that much more circumspect, as though the individual musician could not be allowed to wander through the melodic line of the alapana (alaap) with too much personal interpretation – for that was not the essential thing and encouraged emotional rather than devotional emphasis. Of course much *is* similar in the two systems. Only nomenclature marks the difference between ragas and between the basic forms of statement; the four sections of movement forward are there: the level asthayi, featuring the predominant note (pallavi in Carnatic music); the antara movement into the higher part of the octave when the introduction of a secondary important note occurs (anupallavi); and the mixture of the two, sanchari (charanam); and again the pallavi as coda or summing up in the abhoga.

The alapana or introductory melodic scale is really given short shrift. There is little chance of a reflective exposition in which perhaps eighty per cent of the playing will be improvisory. In the South Indian kriti the length of its exposition can be as long as in a North Indian dhrupad composition, but most of it will be pre-composed, allowing for improvisation only in the ornamentation. In the Hindustani system the pre-existing 'fixed piece' which is precomposed is short, and the improvisation, the free passages of 'instantaneous composition' correspondingly long.

The main meat is in the balance between percussion and melody. The South is indeed marked out musically by its astounding range of drums, a fact which rightly attributes it to the title of 'home of the dance'. There can be no other region in the world which has brought to such a perfection, because of its being the necessary adjunct to the dance forms of Bharata Natyam and Kathakali, the intricacy, the dexterity and the mathematics of the drum language called mnemonics.

The marvel is that the South Indian musician treats such an erudite and intellectual art form with unusual gaiety, as though the immense depths of his belief and its absolute sureness gives him rare and impressive gift of sublime optimism. To me the Carnatic treatment of the raag always gives this impression of a dancing Bach. It is more outward-going, more readily acceptable to the Westerner, despite its intellectual and mathematical demands. Its precision has the clarity of a Mozart string quartet and its swinging syncopation is unmistakable. One's feet automatically itch and the body is pulled into the swaying beat. The overall laya which marks out the sweep of the rhythm is as beckoning and infectious as the greatest classical jazz. This may appear to be heresy to a South Indian vidwan, a knowledgeable teacher or guru, but the rhythms are an undeniable syncopation towards which the Westerner feels a natural magnetic pull.

For some unknown reason, which no-one has been able satisfactorily to explain, the timbre of South Indian voices seems to me to be less harsh to Western ears than that of North Indian voices. Vocalists like Subbulakshmi, D. K. Pattammal, Semmangudi Srinavasa Iyer, Balasubramanyam and the greatest of all, so recently dead, Ariyakudi Ramanuja Iyengar, give an impression of a softer quality than do the exhibitionist contortions of Northern singers, other than the great ones like Bade Ghulam Ali, Ameer Khan and Keserbai. There seems to be less straining after effect, although this is only my opinion and there may be those who as musicologists may wholeheartedly disagree. All I know is that both my husband and I were immediately involved in Carnatic music and enjoyed its challenges from the very first of our encounters with it. This was not so with a great area of Hindustani music, other than that played by the masters whom we were fortunate to hear in our first few months of living in New Delhi. It took a long time and many private as well as public concerts for us to begin to understand even the elementary grammar of the North Indian vocalist. With instrumental music it is a very different matter, as

Western audiences know from their immediate response to the sitar, flute, shehnai, sarod, sarangi or veena. In the Carnatic system the emphasis is so markedly upon the percussion. This necessitates different mechanics. The slow, medium and fast tempos of vilambit, madya and drut are not compartmentalized as in the North. Different tempos are intermixed. Kritis are sung in all tempos but without the long monosyllabic passages of the alamkaras or ornamentations, the groups of notes fused into melodic figures of ascending, descending and spiralling graphs of sound, which so often repulse the outsider in his initial acquaintance with Northern music, because at this stage these may sound like sterile abstractions without emotional or mental implications.

Notes appear to be held for a much longer duration by the Carnatic vocalist and the 'argument' with the drum player is carried on with such an outward and gay abandon that first impressions come to mind of a prevailing exuberance bubbling up in all the forms of art in which they enlarge their interior selves. The lingering bitter-sweet taste of the human condition belongs to the flat, dun-coloured Northern plains.

An exciting fusion exists within the music of the Karnatakam between these two levels of the percussive and the melodic lines. Both seem absolutely essential to each other, whereas in Hindustani music the singer or the instrumentalist can carry the raga in the melody alone. But in the South rhythms of the most elaborate kind, such as we hear very rarely in the West, are the expected partner of the poetry and the melody. The insistent beat is there, whether struck by the drummer or called out in syllabic mnemonics by the nattuvanar or music teacher; it is there in the vigour and sensuousness of the love poems, in the padams of Bharata Natyam dance, in the virility of the Kathakali dance-dramas of Malabar, dramas which engage emotions of a bloodthirsty kind. To the strident clamour of the chenda drum, erotic Malayalam poetry and stylized dance of the most martially disciplined kind are blended with the music. But the beat of drum and feet remain supreme.

One especial morning in South India haunts me still. I drove in the half-blue light of a summer dawn along the red, earthen roads of Malabar to Chirutiruthi to the Kathakali dance school of the poet Vallathol, then a spry eighty-year-old. Along the sweeping curves of the river where the soft, pink rays of the early sun flecked the surface like peach blossoms, not a sound stirred–but then across the dense undergrowth came the rhythmic slap of bare feet and a high wall of monotonous chanting thrummed in the still air.

It was 4.30 a.m. Where the flickering oil deva lamps burned, a flow of brown bodies moved in unison, sideways and forwards and back again they leapt and slid in the basic dance step of Kathakali. These dancers looked like young gods, their bodies shining in the gathering sunlight like burnished wood. Already they had been practising their rolling-eye exercises for two hours, and some were now undergoing foot massage as they lay on the ground in joint-cracking yogic positions. Two men between two poles slid backwards and forwards along their oiled bodies, walking and feeling into every muscle with their sensitive feet as though these were another set of finely carved hands moulding the clay cast of a medieval bronze.

The musicians were beginning to warm up in a large, bamboo hall under the fierce eyes of the nattuvanar, who presided with a tamarind stick which he brought down on a block of wood with the precision and the crack of a whip. He successfully drowned out the poetic song of the two vocalists, the two drum players and the man who clashed the cymbals. To the ultimate discipline of this rhythm the music is totally subordinated. In fact there is nothing but incredulity when a virtuoso performer of the calibre of Palghat Mani Iyer takes the stage. Western rhythm is left standing. Such mastery and fluency are seldom heard in the West except when the great tabalchi Alla Rakha from the North accompanies Pandit Ravi Shankar. But when Palghat Mani Iyer runs his fingers over the mridangam, the double-sided South Indian drum, even the gentle lyricism of the saint/musician Thyāgarāja is heard swaying to the dominating rhythm of the jati-talas and the great speaking drum.

Even nowadays when dance performances have moved from the temple into the secular world outside, music is still a constant background to South Indian devotions and wandering minstrels, like the Bengali bauls, are often to be seen along the crowded country road and in the remotest villages of South India. In fact, this is more often where they are to be found than in the centres of urbanized life. They always have their drum.

All the great composers of the Carnatic were devout Hindus. The verses they composed had *meaning* in the literal sense, and in the Western sense. In this way was created a great body of songs differing from the syllabic-shorthand singing of the North and

corresponding more to our own mystic poetry and religious oratorios. It is as though Bach's sparkling cantatas were being played
the day long as people moved in an ever-flowing tide through the
great mandapas of the South, such are these joyous litanies in their
outpouring love and tender compassions for God.

The tradition began under the Pallava kings with two yogis or
saints who composed psalms to the Lord Shiva and Vishnu,
Jñana-sambandha (c. AD 600–30) and Periyalvar (c. AD 850). This
was the age of great psalmists known as alvars (still revered in the
South) whose Tamil invocations to the Lord, reincarnated as Rama,
Krishna or Vishnu, are still sung in South Indian classical concerts
today. Devotional inspiration was carried forwards by Jayadeva's
glorification of Krishna, and yet another famous musician/saint of
the South, Purandaradasa (1480–1564), an early contemporary of
Tansen in the North, composed thousands of songs in a variety of
styles to the Lord Vishnu.

The devotional tradition culminated in the flowering of four
geniuses in the eighteenth and nineteenth centuries.

*Thyāgarāja (1767–1847), Dikshitar (1775–1835), Shastri (1762–
1827) and Tirunal (1813–47)*

Thyāgarāja, and his contemporaries – Dikshitar, Shyam Shastri and
Swati Tirunal – were not only musicians and composers; they were
also religious yogis, and scholars or vidwans. They were devotees in
the way that Thomas Trahearne, Newman, and William Blake
were also; and even the equally devout Jesuit priest Roberto di
Nobili who settled in Madurai could admit nothing but respect and
admiration for the whole-heartedness of their religious philosophy,
their discipline and their asceticism, all of which rested with the
ease of a mantle upon their brows. It is said of Thyāgarāja that
Narada, the rishi of pre-Christian times, appeared to him during
one of his yogic meditations, because of the stature of his musicianship. To this day it is their kritis which are sung in concerts.
Hardly a modern composition exists because of their domination
over the music.

NORTH *v*. SOUTH INDIAN MUSIC

The differences from the North Indian are in degree, not in kind.

For the Northerner it must be said that he has pride of creativity on his side in being able to sift, absorb, reinterpret and transmute all the conflicting influences that have meandered through the wide plains of history into the very source of his being, whereas the Southerner, having escaped the rough handling of history, retains an equilibrium not given to flux.

Both can decry the other's qualities, and they do! A long-established Punjabi vocalist, Dalip Chandra Vedi, who was the same age as Bade Ghulam Ali (a famous Muslim Hindustani singer, now dead after suffering grievous paralysis) and as equally individualistic, has been quoted on his reflective views of Carnatic music. He himself, always ready to bring experimentation into his rendering of North Indian ragas, visited South India to stimulate his mind with the theories and presentations of South Indian ragas.

But it seems that he was unmoved. When asked what he thought of the music he said that he did not care for it: 'First it lacks originality. There is no regard for the vadi, samvadi (the main notes in the raga): their method of shaking the voice is anathema to us.' And repulsing the suggestion that the rhythms of the South were 'attractive features' he stated that Indian music 'strives mainly to express peace. It symbolizes the concentration of a lone man, for which the elaboration of notes is primarily suitable. Rhythm distracts.'

For this reason he objects to the trend towards rhythm and the battle of rhythm which is so common a feature of the closing phases of a raga concert in the North nowadays: 'Raag rang (emotional content in song) has disappeared and raag jang (the duel of rhythms) has come in,' he deplores with obvious disgust for these Southern influences.

Yet this is one of the freedoms of Hindustani music which is conversely its strength–the capacity to experiment without such psychological restrictions as the Southerner feels. As a result of his own transformation under outside cultural influences the Northerner has expanded the themes of his musical imagination and his knowledge of the transcendental, and gives the individual a chance to escape the confining framework of the Hindu background.

On the other hand, the South Indian seems–to me anyway as someone outside this framework–to be mentally content with his very old wisdom and knowledge (for there is a distinction between the two). He is satisfied with the truths that remain constant and which have been transmitted over century upon century. Even if these are seen with a new interpretation, he hardly recognizes the need for even this concession to historical development and the evolving culture.

His music remains like a pool where ebb and flow are stilled, where the evolution of musical forms is less pronounced, and where the gravitational pull is always towards the past. But many artists in the North might regard this as inertia.

With the coming of Independence there has been a recovery of balance by Indians; there is a rational but also emotional urge towards a rediscovery of themselves as Indians, without regional emphasis, in the cultural sphere if not in the political arena. For the first time for a very long period, and on a scale never achieved before, a deliberate interchange between Hindustani and Carnatic musicians is taking place. It is still only in its infancy and there is considerable dragging of feet, but All India Radio and the various federal cultural agencies have made a conscious effort to break through this cultural blockage, as well as individual musicians such as Ravi Shankar who have introduced Carnatic raags into their Northern repertoire. Ironically though, more creative interchange may come between musicians from East and West than between those of these two regions.

Four thousand years of history milling around them have not changed the South Indians to any considerable degree. They are indeed for this reason the steadying factor in the tidal swings that have occurred in Indian development. This very conservation which has bequeathed to them such an integrity is also their halter, jerking them back from any radical experimentation. North Indians in this respect regard them with a mixture of envy for their inviolability, but despair for their obduracy in defence of such cultural chastity – the holy writ of traditional principles upon which all their arts of sculpture, music and dancing are held to be founded.

Although the fundamental grammar of the two systems is similar and the main raags are the same, to the musicians of each system the corresponding musical result is meaningless. The Carnatic raga is rigid to a North Indian. The formalism seems to hold it in thrall. In the North various gharanas handle one and the same raga very differently, but again and again I was informed by my South Indian friends that I would hear the same raga performed in different areas of the South without deviation except for certain human elements of musicianship. I am not competent to corroborate whether this is true or not but Dr Narayana Menon, as a South Indian who has lived long years in the North, can speak with some impunity on the difference in attitude between the two systems.

He has written: 'The South and the North agree on the fundamentals although the nomenclature both of ragas and talas differs. The difference is mainly that of style. Instrumental music is more developed in the North. The North has also brought into the main current a temporal element which has had healthy effect. In the South even today the leading composers are preoccupied with the writing of mystical religious songs. They faithfully copy the standards set by the great Thyāgarāja, in form as well as content.'

One other thing has to be said about the South which has an inhibiting effect upon the creative musician there. Again it is both a vice and an astonishing virtue. This is the intellectual knowledge of the audiences. In Madras I attended a concert which was wholly different in atmosphere from those in New Delhi. One felt the intensity of concentration, the humming of the melody, the nodding of the head as though each and all were plugged in mentally to the same electrical circuit. In fact they were. It has been truly said that the patrons of Carnatic music have been the people, not the princes, and it is the common people who express their distaste if they do not get what they expect in the old tradition.

THE TWENTIETH CENTURY

There is overall, however, a very acute problem for the creative artist in India at the present time. Whereas the painter, writer, dramatist, composer and sculptor in our hemisphere has regarded change, fresh examination of the rationale behind the mechanics, and rebellion against established principles as the *sine qua non* of his having been born a sensitive explorer and portrayer of the human condition, his Indian *confrère*, and more especially the true Hindu, feels ill at ease at such a suggestion. Acceptance, not rebellion, has been the artistic and social norm which controls the Indian character.

Our historical sense demands of us a movement forwards in finite time; their metaphysical sense demands the investigation of truth in the infinite sense. Because of this, none of the great streams of artistic tradition has been allowed to break its banks; the flood-waters would be as catastrophic as those of the mighty Brahmaputra if these treacherous rivers of experiment were allowed to swirl through the long stretch of artistic growth. So today, those who are restlessly creative and wish to channel a less turbulent but nevertheless, changing, passage are caught mid-stream. Even in the pictorial arts where tradition is least strong, only a very small minority of artists have escaped into the open plains where their individual integrity is the only signpost into the future. Whereas no-one decries musical composers such as the American, Henry Cowell, who incorporated melodic phrases from Indian ragas into his Thirteenth Symphony, Julian Bream, who created raga from the medieval air Greensleeves, or Yehudi Menuhin, who recently sat down cross-legged to play on his violin a raga with Western overtones to it, the Indian musician who transgresses the rules and steps into unknown territory with the free flight of the artistic spirit, is regarded by his fellow countrymen with real distrust and misunderstanding. The traditions have been denied – and that is enough for their audiences to deflate their efforts. Augustus Willard, writing even at the end of the eighteenth century and commenting upon those musicians who were taking liberties with the limited numbers of authentic melodies allowed by Indian purists of that age, said that 'what the more reputed of the moderns have since done is, that they have adapted them to their own purpose, and formed others (ragas) by the combination of two or more of them. Thus far they are licensed, but they dare not proceed a step further. Whatever merit an entire modern composition might possess, should it have no resemblance to the established melody of the country it would be looked upon as spurious. It is implicitly believed that it is impossible to add to the number of these one single melody of equal merit. So tenacious are the Indians of their ancient practices.'

Even knowledgeable and modern Indians who may well accept social and economic change as a necessary corollary of their nation's coming to terms with the twentieth century, still refuse to accept the same for their music, despite the fact that artists and sculptors have broken out of their inhibiting framework. Perhaps music is such an intimate and sentimental involvement that it arouses passions which the pictorial arts do not. One of North India's best traditional sarod players, Hafiz Ali Khan, a man of the old school who can trace his ancestry back to Tansen, has been known to assert that 'change is profanity'. To him the only true music is the ancient dagar style of dhrupad–music made for peace. It will be interesting to watch how his talented son, Amjad Ali, shapes in the future as a sarod player, encouraged as he is by his father to try the khyal style which is difficult for the sarod as it has no frets (unlike the sitar which can, therefore, 'follow' the human voice more easily). Dalip Chandra Vedi has expressed similar scepticism: 'The notes should be almost meditative in their repose and dignity. All those little taans (trills) used with such facility in khyals and thumris conjure up an entirely different mood. They are a most unfortunate innovation.'

Yet these have been an accepted part of Hindustani music for the past generation! Tansen himself could introduce a new juxtaposition of notes with an E♭ and both varieties of B and so create a new raga, Miyan-ki-Malhar, from an original raga, Malhar. In fairness it has to be acknowledged that even in our own countries music has been the slowest of all the art forms to change, and audiences are still very conservative in their acceptance of the new music.

The experimental musician in India is damned from the beginning and loses his friends, or makes mistakes which he is too sensitive to admit in the face of such pervasive suspicion. Or, worst of all, he will be accused of succumbing to Western influence. This is a very fragile area to probe after 250 years of European rule. Naturally Indians wish to establish their own pride of culture again, but this psychological need restricts the creative artist at the very moment when the whole world of communications is opening up global areas to the searching spirit of his fellow artists abroad.

Experiments are, however, taking place in Indian musical forms –but very tentatively. Ravi Shankar, Pannalal Gosh when he was alive, Ali Akbar Khan and Vilayat Khan to some extent, and many of the film musicians, as well as older dancer/musicians such as Uday Shankar and Rukmini Devi Arundale at Adiyar in Madras, and some of the AIR musicians, are attempting orchestration, the notation of scores, and the incorporation of new themes into the raga system. Even a generation ago, Omkar Nath Thakar was showing the way; he played Western music and was as conversant with it as with his own.

The most courageous effort has been the composition of a concerto for sitar by Ravi Shankar, which was given its premier performance with the London Symphony Orchestra under the direction of Andre Previn in January, 1971. It will be discussed in more detail in a later chapter.

I have to admit that earlier rather uninspired experimentations in harmony undertaken by the AIR orchestra left me with the sense that the music had been emasculated. This does not mean to say that it should never have taken place however. Artists have to be taken on trust, for the restless ferment will come to India sooner or later. She can no longer isolate herself from the movement of culture on a world-wide scale. Radio, the jet-plane and easy physical interchange of people have changed all this. There can be no going back. Yehudi Menuhin has taken his stand. Indian musicians have suddenly achieved fame from Helsinki to Rome, through Paris and London to New York and San Francisco, and so on into innumerable college campuses. George Harrison has been to Bombay to study for a few months under Ravi Shankar's tutelage; Palghat Mani Iyer and Bismillah have visited the Edinburgh Festival; Balasaraswati, the great dancer, has sung her padams in the august halls of London's Victoria and Albert Museum and taught Indian dance on American college campuses; Julian Bream and Ali Akbar have collaborated in Calcutta; Ravi Shankar has been called to London by Jonathan Miller to compose highly original music for the BBC television production of *Alice in Wonderland*–which succeeded despite all the doubting Thomases' expectations of failure. Schools of Indian music are springing up in Western cities; every other week some new Indian influence is noted, either in Western fashion or in Gandhian influence on the political philosophy of non-violent protest or in art-gallery exhibitions of Tantric art or in the discovery of the new cult of gentleness. But above all, the long-playing record has made possible concentrated listening to Indian music and study of its system, and therefore, possibly, ultimate cross-fertilization between different styles and detailed notation of individual renderings of ragas. This latter painstaking undertaking is already being done with the same degree of devotion as any Indian shishya would display for his guru by a young English music student and composer, John Barham, whose transcriptions of Ali Akbar's Sindh Bhairavi and Ameer Khan's Marwa I have used for illustration of certain techniques in this book. This kind of integrity among the young cannot be decried. The one sad characteristic about Indians on the whole is that they too easily criticize–

especially their own nationals who show any courage of originality. India has set herself about her own social revolution no matter how halting its progress. This means that the culture also can no longer remain static. Artistic integrity can be their only guide and this Indians surely have in the greatest measure of all – if they care to cultivate the roots of their civilization. Their musicians then should have freedom to experiment and be given a breathing-space in which to make mistakes. It may well take years to achieve an equilibrium, but it is important for the enrichment of the whole world's artistic accomplishments that they have this freedom. Indian music is so vibrant and expressive of individual search that it certainly does not have to fear the process of change.

There is some point in tracing the historical development of Indian classical music, if only to quarrel with the purists of today who frequently quote texts of Sanskrit treatise of the seventh or twelfth century to debar or damn experimentation in the twentieth. Reading between the lines, an outsider can soon sense that creative minds have been at work on the Indian raga over centuries and effected subtle changes despite the rules. India's greatest master musician – Tansen – was one such. He is often quoted as the sustainer of orthodoxy. But D. P. Mukherji, with his unerring sense for falsity of Indian orthodox argument, demolishes such an attitude as he does the inherent snobbery which says that all things ancient, *ipso facto*, are good.

He points out how throughout Muslim rule, at least 600 years of history, classical music and regional folk-music were continually changing: 'The opposition of orthodox scholars was overcome by equating the new courtly styles with ancient ones. Darbari became coterminous with classical. If two or three melodic types were blended, older terms for them were just diphthonged, or new names with Sanskrit flavour were affixed, or the name of the Muslim composer was used as an adjective to the original Hindu substantive; numerous were the novelties which were blessed by being mentioned in Sanskrit texts composed in the Muslim period. Today if a virtuoso commits a mistake in the demonstration of one such, he is cursed with bell, book and candle by his Hindu and Muslim listeners who just do not suspect its parvenu character.'

It is a disillusioning process for someone such as myself who believes in Indian tolerance to discover at the intellectual level a growing intolerance against her own creative people. It is too easy for the spectator to decry; only those involved in the agonizing search and reappraisal can really know how best to bring about the evolution of new forms in the raag without losing an overall integrity. Intolerance is a retrograde step in India.

One man who creates controversy is Ravi Shankar. He has been criticized by some Indians for jazzing up his music to suit Western audiences. This may have happened in the initial impact during the fifties, but now that he is free to do completely experimental music his actual classical playing has reached a new maturity. Anyone who has listened to his renditions during his 1967 tour and from then onwards, will realize that the lengthy dhrupad style of playing major ragas such as Darbari Khanada, Marwa, Bageshri, and recently the Carnatic Parameshwar, is making no concession at all to Western audiences. They now have to accept Indian music on its own terms. He too has had to abide by the long discipline and retains respect for the good in the tradition, even as he attempts to change it and bring in new influences.

'Even if notation comes', he once explained to me when he was conductor of the Air Vadya Vrinda orchestra in 1954, 'we must never lose the relationship we have between guru and pupil. The guru is the teacher whom you devote yourself to. It is like using up body and soul. I shaved off my hair, wore a dhoti, worked so hard I can remember now those difficult times.' While he talked in the studio South Indian flute players shook their tight-knotted Brahmin buns of hair while a North Indian tabla player with a sarangi and veena traced the melodic theme of a composite medley of ragas. They were attempting a rudimentary kind of Western harmony where certain thematic movements overlapped.

'I was lucky in my guru,' he went on. His guru was the great Ustad Allauddin Khan, who is now said to be more than one hundred years old. 'You have no idea of the purity of his life, utterly devoted to music. He lived music. I was indeed lucky,' Ravi said, fingering his gnarled and scabbed joints where the strings had bitten into the flesh from the power of his playing.

'During the latter Moghul rule there was a different attitude to the music. A teacher would beat you up, shout at you, treat you as a master to a servant. The princes encouraged music but a court musician was nothing more than a performing bear, like the juggler or a clown. There was a bad atmosphere. But a Hindu has to discipline himself. The shastras demand it. Even if we slip we always feel the pull back again. The guru is a truly devoted man and as a Muslim also insists on discipline. It is inside him, in his heart, in his soul, and you have to give everything up to be a good musician. It has meaning inside.'

The pure artist must be free, free to absorb all influence and to mirror the whole world of universal man where affinities are greater than divisions.

On this matter the final words go to that seemingly orthodox South Indian, the gentle Jayaram Iyer. One night he was listening to records of Gregorian chant in our house in New Delhi. He was enthusing about the affinities he felt natural between our two musical systems, even including Louis Armstrong and Dave Brubeck as well as the early church music and Gustav Holst. We had been listening to a recording of the Planets by this composer.

'This is much like our Todi Raga,' he remarked of the Gregorian chant. 'It is exquisite and solemn and quickens the mind, is full of pathos. You feel no feeling in the end,' he slowly enunciated.

'All is at rest. You know, there is a special group of musicians near Tiruchurapalli in the South, at the temple of Srirangam, who are veena players. They have been given a lot of land by the temple and they just play, nothing else. It is music that does not excite or sadden but it is music that composes the mind. It is like this chanting. It is not like Holst. That disturbs me, especially Mars. But this is music that is close to God. You do not have to think or feel. You are set at rest. This is being near the Lord, isn't it?'

In Sanskrit there is a word for this sense of tranquillity-abhyudyaprdm, अ॰ युदय प्रदमू-music leading to salvation. This is the only important thing one can ever ask of a musician and orthodox treatment, whether in composition or playing, has nothing whatsoever to do with the inner process of creation, laboriously but exhilaratingly undertaken by each musician, artist or writer as he faces that dreadful chasm-the uncreated moment before he communicates across that area between executant and the expectant audience awaiting that communication.

Chapter Four

THE GRAMMAR OF THE RAAG
Passion and Precision in the Craftsmanship

'Indian music has continued unperturbed through thirty centuries or more, with the even pulse of a river and with the unbroken evolution of a sequoitry.'
YEHUDI MENUHIN

It is dangerous indeed when attempting to explain Indian music to seek for likenesses to our own system, based as ours is upon the fundamental rule of harmony. The analogies never quite fit. I do however feel most strongly that some attempt has to be made in order to make sense in general and simple terms, so that the long-held feelings of strangeness, the idea of an exotic oriental music totally alien to our senses, can be dispelled once and for all. There are, on examination, more meeting points than have previously been allowed.

Therefore, any analogies that I have tried to draw must be taken in the spirit in which they are made, rather than as strictly accurate definitions of the mechanics of the music.

My prime concern within the scope of this book is to interpret the spirit that impels Indians to express their beliefs in certain forms of artistic endeavour rather than in others. It is not a musicological manual. I make no apologies for this – I am a listener, not a practising musician. This has not detracted from the sheer joy of the music. Indeed, my fears grow that the due processes of scholastic analysing which are being undertaken by some Westerners as the music becomes more familiar, might result in drawing away the ras, leaving only the shell of technique.

There are admittedly difficulties if one has never been to India, nor felt India in bone, thought and fibre. But over-elaborate explanation may defeat its own purposes. We have again and again to forget our own terminology even in the very act of using it. It is vital to recall the processes by which Indian musicians learn their precision of craftsmanship through painstaking years of close-knit family training, so carrying on the hereditary traditions that existed in a similar manner in the concentrated talent of the family Bach.

Indian musicians do not verbalize their theory. They play the notes and learn the melodic ornamentations in complex phrases until these become their *alter ego*. Ustad Hafiz Ali Khan has dismissed scornfully the idea of considering oneself a musician after a few years in music school: 'There can be no degrees for learning—and no time limits,' he says. 'One may achieve something in between 12 and 20 years. Once I was asked to teach a few students for 3 or 4 months. The attitude implied in that was wrong. What could they possibly acquire in that short period ? It is a great slight to the art of music. I refuse to undertake such instruction. Three years is the least for a fundamental grounding. After that it is an endless course. All one's life one learns. There must be intense relationship between teacher and disciple—but the spirit of dedication is now gone.'

His own son, Amjad Ali, at present making a name for himself as a sarod player (contemporarily with Ashish Khan, Ali Akbar's son), seems now to feel the same urge to return to these traditional relationships. He has experienced the excitement of the West, of enthusiastic audiences in America and Canada, but the pull towards sanity in the old ways remains. He has been quoted on his recent American tour: 'When I was playing, oh, I was lost in music and I was in tune with the audience and they with me and I didn't care where I was. The young people there; they want to break all the bonds, all inhibitions; they don't even want to wear clothes; they don't want to observe the conventions of any relationship, even with their parents; they are against the establishment; they don't want any barrier, even in music, and Indian music answers their needs because it is free and improvisatory and meditative.

'But sometimes, alone in my room, I would wonder: Why am I here ? What am I doing in America ? Why am I not in India where I belong ?

'I remembered the accounts my father gave of the old days when if you belonged to the Gwalior gharana and you stayed in Gwalior, anybody who wanted to hear you had to come to Gwalior to do so . . . Why shouldn't somebody who wants to learn come to me, learn the ways of devotion to the teacher, imbibe the atmosphere

here, instead of my going there carrying my music out with me ?'

An Indian musician often, however, finds it extremely hard to explain to a foreigner about his music; he himself takes so much for granted. He may, in fact, be inarticulate about intellectual principles laid down by the pandits of centuries gone by, but he does possess the acute accuracy of ear that the aural guild tradition of the guru/shishya system demands. He instinctively imbibes the family knowledge and the idiosyncratic singing or playing of his own gharana. He knows almost from intuition how to distinguish ragas from each other by the most subtle shades of differentiation, but to express this in theoretical and scientifically accurate terms is beyond his capabilities. It is only those who have ventured forth into our Western world that can catch an insight into our predicament, the predicament of finding even a small foothold.

The great need is for Indian scholars who are versed in Western music but who can also sift through the Sanskrit, Tamil and Telegu treatises and be sufficiently conversant with the English language as well to be able to interpret the one to the other without swamping the language with the deadening touch of academic jargon.

Some scholarship in India is now being undertaken on very early manuscripts with the keen eye of analysis rather than with the previous, devotionally slanted attitude of sanctity. Even then there is often failure of communication between regions in India, some regions being a great many times the size of the United Kingdom and speaking more different languages than all the countries of Europe combined. There are many nationalities which have co-alesced into the unity of India, and their own interpretation of the music and traditions differs also. In the North too there was a period of 'burning the books' during the iconoclastic Muslim invasions of the thirteenth and fourteenth centuries. What was handed on by word of mouth may well have been corrupted or contain new invention away from the purist line of descent which South Indians claim for Carnatic music. One Indian will often be refuting another Indian for this very reason and a raga might well have a shift in emphasis among its specific notes that another gharana from another region will not have given it. This tends to confuse the outsider – as Mr Fox-Strangways well knew when he set about writing his *Music of Hindoostan*, for he himself followed with verve those individuals who told him what they held as their own individual truth.

THE GRAMMAR OF THE RAAG

An amalgam of all these individual truths is the sum of the truth in India. No single person can embrace such a comprehensive view for it would mean the devoted single-mindedness of a lifetime to track down each musician. He would have to walk in pada yatra throughout the length and breadth of India, taking down in miniscule notation all the variations on a single theme. That would indeed necessitate many reincarnations to accomplish the task thoroughly! It is salutary to remind oneself that in the hugeness of India there are almost as many truths as there are individual Indians. I myself have been told one set of facts by Indians from one region, only to have these same facts confounded by Indians from another region with different language and upbringing.

This book came to be written because of these confusing personal experiences. The analogies I have turned to and the imagery I use are born of these passionate encounters and the need I always feel to break down the barriers, so that those who come entirely without warning to the music do not flounder in some of the pitfalls that I stumbled into myself. Even living as I did with the music all around me I had to hack away at the rockface by persistent inquiry. Befogged as I was, many Indian friends simply assumed that as a Westerner I could not possibly wish to know. Initially, and fortunately in my innocence, I just let the music ripple through my blood because of an instinctive sense of belonging to India. Perhaps if I had approached it the other way around, I might have been alienated for life; I have known Westerners of some musical inclination who could never bring themselves to sit through an Indian concert, so overcome were they by their preconceived ideas, reinforced by too intimate a knowledge of their own musical system which ultimately stood in the way of their letting go and allowing emotion to play a large part in their spontaneous response to it. I know that Ravi Shankar himself is concerned at this inhibitive attitude of some Western classical musicians who approach Indian music with too many of their own value-systems, without trying to assess Indian principles without this inbuilt intellectual bias. The Asian has always had to make reciprocal mental adjustments in coming to know and be conversant with our culture, for the simple historical reason of colonial rule. It is now time to repay the compliment. However, ignorance of all musical systems may indeed be bliss–which may also be a comfort to all those who come to Indian music concerts somewhat tentatively and aware of their own

THE GRAMMAR OF THE RAAG

ignorance of music in theoretical terms and its definitions. In a certain sense the music is so concentrated emotionally that it speaks directly to the heart. If one co-operates emotionally and consciously denies that half of the mind its tendency to compare what it is hearing with our own music, then half the battle is won. But there is no doubt that involvement does mean going further than this. Appreciation cannot rest forever with just the emotional impact and the empathy it arouses. Having come through to the other side I have begun to discover so many other excitements and challenges as the principles of the music have begun to open up; the enjoyment has become that much more enhanced, heightened by the balance of intellect and emotion which is the necessary requirement of any permanent artistic appreciation.

WESTERN *v.* INDIAN MUSIC

Our system is based on the architecture of harmonic depth and chordal strength rather than on the single-mindedness of purpose in one melodic line. It is also based on the tempered scale which contains a set combination of tones and semitones in either a major or minor diatonic scale. Few accidentals (flattened or sharpened notes) are used in comparison with the numbers employed within certain defined rules in an Indian raga, either repetitively—as being expected in a certain melodic scale—or characteristically—in the singing of a certain musician or the style used by his gharana.

In Western music, two or more melodies may be going on at the same time, so creating counterpoint. This is not to say that the same is not happening in Indian music, even if in an elementary form; it actually does, but it is more by accident than design.

Two or more notes may be sounded simultaneously in our music; this chordal harmony is the thick base against which everything is to be heard, especially in symphonic music. On the other hand, when our music is performed solo, or even in small groups such as is chamber music, it can sound extraordinarily 'thin' to an Indian. There appear to be great gaps in the structure. Sometimes even I have felt that a piano solo has no body to it, if I have been listening for any length of time to Indian ragas. The clipped and precise tones of the piano are the exact opposite of the resonances of any solo instrument in India. That is not to denigrate it. The sensation is only temporary and perfectly natural because Indian music is

123

made up from other strata compressed together, like geological formations of rock layers which become the ground-base of the surface soil where the single melodic line is implanted. This line is what one has to cling on to and hold in the ear, recognizing certain emphasized notes which are contrasted and held in relation to each other, to be returned to again and again.

Finally, although our own system possesses rhythm as a constituent element, it in no sense functions in such a complex and vitally integral way as the drum-beats and rhythms of the Hindustani and Carnatic systems. These can stand on their own as a specific strata within the structure of the raga. A piece of music is for us generally divided up into short lengths or bars, which on the whole are equal and of regular stress, most frequently using two, three or four beats to the bar. In Indian music the most commonly used beats number at least 20 different kinds, symmetric and asymmetric, but there are said to be in existence well over 108 main and distinct talas or beats, and perhaps as many as 300 or more variations upon these! The main talas each fit into a regular overall laya or rhythm which comes around in great cycles within the performance of the piece of music. These can be subdivided into all kinds of corresponding symmetric or asymmetric divisions so that rhythm in Indian terms is neither a mechanical nor a rigid process. It fluctuates, sometimes unobtrusively giving support to the soloist, sometimes asserting its prowess in dominating the melodic line.

While the ear is straining after the flights of drummers' fancy the instrumentalist may be carrying on a rhythmic 'conversation' with the percussion player at the melodic level, and all the time at the deepest level of the formation is the continuous fingering of the drone, deliberately selecting the tonic of the melody in play and its dominating note. This is stated over and over again like the refrain in folk-melodies of our own earlier musical development, but also in a steady continuum which is more akin to the bagpipe's drone.

The listener gradually becomes aware of this emphasis, recurring with absolute and unchanging regularity. All the spaces are, so to speak, filled in. Subtle rivalries between percussion and melody (carried by either vocal or instrumental performer) carve out the levels of depth that chordal harmonies do for our ears. In fact, a form of harmony is implied. The perpetual sounds of the drone often overlap and conflict with augmented or diminished notes which may have been natural in ascent, but shifted to 'accidental' in descent. This clash between drone and melodic line sets up dissonances which are carried in the ear, or are held on the sympathetic strings of an instrument like the sarod or sitar while other phrases are being carried forwards. So in no sense is there the shallowness that the absence of our kind of harmony would presuppose.

Constantly in searching for the right description for this evocative music I have turned to a picture image. Music being the most abstract and mental of the arts, it is the most elusive and defies the concrete term. It is often easier to 'see' music. Theory is often very difficult to assimilate for those who do not play an instrument themselves. I am well aware that many people have the enjoyment of music killed for them by reading about it in erudite terms, but unfortunately, like any living language, the grammar has to be spelled out for the real enrichment to come. Then the grammar can be forgotten and the poetry and high prose can take over.

INTERVALS AND SRUTIS

SRUTI (22) or SHRUTI	Sa	Ri or reh b	Ri b	Ri ♮	Ri #	Ga b	Ga b	Ga ♮	Ga #	Ma #	Ma #	Ma ♮	Ma +	Pa	Dha b	Dha b	D ♮	D #	Ni b	Ni #	Ni b	Ni ♮	Ni #	Sa	Ri b
SVARA (7)	Sa	Ri or Reh				Ga				Ma				Pa	Dha				Ni					Sa	
DIATONIC Sol/Fah scale	Doh	Ray				Me				Fah				Soh	Lah				Te					Doh	
CHROMATIC 12-tone scale	C	Db	D	Eb	E					F	F♯	G			Ab	A			Bb	B				C	

This is an arbitrary and pictorial image of the Indian chromatic scale of 22 intervals within the octave of 7 pure, substantive tones, the svaras. It is by no means the musical truth. This scale is never sung in consecutive order. Its importance lies only in the way an individual musician uses the satellite srutis as major or minor tones (in our sense) to approach a svara note, either by curling towards it or slurring away from it, or again by using the many sympathetic strings and resonances (of the gourds) on their stringed instruments to overlay the serial line of full tones with a host of connected quartertones or semitones – depending on how sharp or flat they are compared with our less acutely differentiated scale-system. I have attempted this visual scale with the help of the English musicologist

125

and composer, Mr Crossley-Holland, and Pandit Ravi Shankar. Nevertheless it is still an approximation; nor does it hold good for Carnatic music which, to all intents and purposes, uses only 12 tones in different pitches.

Why then have I bothered to create an inaccuracy? The simple reason is that, after my own baptism of fire where explanations were in abstract terms and where hours of listening carried me yet further into the realms of the non-visual, I longed to 'see' the music. I think it is almost impossible for any musician, be he Asian or Western, to understand one iota of the difficulties for those of us who are really spectators at the musical feast. Even those amateur music-goers who can carry a tune in their head and whistle it, are lucky compared with those who have to read a score and see it visually before they can understand the relationship of notes and place them in their proper tonal gradations.

It was not until I came to sit down, years after hearing that first magical encounter with Bismillah Khan, that I suddenly realized what Indian music was about. Previously it had been an intuitive and emotional experience, but murky for all that. Now I wish that someone had shown me such a diagram, despite its faults, so that I could see in Western terms just where to make a start. Without such a guide there is a great amorphous mass of knowledge and no telling where to begin. The Indian musician has, over the centuries, come to accept as the ground-base of his artistic discipline this finely graded system of unequal intervals, and no matter where he chooses to place his keynote, sa (our doh), on our fixed keyboard, the ratio of intervals will move up or down in accordance with sa like a slide-rule or a musical transposer diagram.

To make matters more complicated for outsiders, there are actually nearly as many versions of where these microtones cluster as there are Western experts trying to decipher and notate the ever-elusive quality of these tones. One of the real difficulties, as Mr Clements laboured so hard in his book[1] to point out, is that references to modern srutis have no connection with those names mentioned in earlier treatises. Their vibration values, and their places among what we would call the chromatic notes of the Western scale, have changed over the centuries. Now today we may be fortunate as bystanders for it appears that gradually a good many Indian musicians are coming to sing or play a 12-tone scale using

[1] *Lectures on Indian Music*, E. Clements.

the finer shades of tone the more sparingly. This may be a deterioration for Indian music and some Indian musicians ascribe its recent occurrence as rising from the use of the harmonium, which is very unsuitable for Indian music.

The scientifically measurable accuracy of the srutis can be questioned. The stretch of interval, no matter how small, and the accumulation of intervals, can vary by diminution or augmentation according to the unique training of the individual vocalist or player. His knowledge is not theoretical, as I have so often pointed out. The srutis and their exactitudes have been quarrelled over and redefined in texts since Bharata, twenty-two centuries ago. Measuring the length of intervals by logarithmic cents or by oscillographs can, however, turn music into an algebraic formula which only experts can appreciate. It is devastating to the musical appreciation of the ordinary listener and is not the purpose of this book anyway.

Much of the confusion to the layman lies in the definition of the beginning of the scale. In this respect some ancient theoreticians and Bhatkhande count the srutis from different points in the chromatic scale, and Alan Danielou gives 24 srutis in his exposition of North Indian music. In the South, various Tamil treatises distribute these intervals differently again. Does it in fact begin, as Mr Fox-Strangways questions, with the sa interval leading to the full substantive note which is the Indian ri[1] (D) of 600 vibrations, or are the shrutis counted from the Indian shadaja note sa (C) of the universally accepted 540 vibrations? All this is nowadays a rarified mathematical splitting of hairs for the concert-goer. Who in fact, if we shift our ground, appreciated Stravinsky or Bartok any the less for not knowing the measurable intervals between substantive notes? It may be of interest to the musicologist or to some practising composers of the new atonal music, but to the music-lover who listens for the aesthetic pleasure it has to be put into its proper perspective.

The music must be seen in its comprehensive whole. A painting can be analysed closely, seeing every single dab of oil-paint laid on thickly and encrusted with the palette knife, but it gives one no sense of the great dimensions of the canvas seen as one steps back, away from the divisions and intervals between crests of paint, as in, say, a Jackson Pollock or a Van Gogh.

Only when seen entire, as layers and planes of composition interrelated, can the full message, the sensations, the subconscious

---

[1] From now on this note will be referred to as reh.

depictions or the abstract design–depending on the artist in question–come through. At a distance the spirit and the composition are of supreme importance. So it is in a raga.

Mr Fox-Strangways has kept his head clear on this matter when he points out that the srutis are theoretical, being sung only as 'increments' of other larger intervals. He uses the word 'heterotonic satellites' to give the impression of their existence dependent on the svaras. 'Stress has been laid on there being 22 of them,' he has explained because of misapprehension about the nature of sruti. 'The scale has come to be regarded as an octave with 21 places upon the way. We have seen that this is wrong artistically, because melodies rarely use 2 of these, and never 3 in succession. But it is wrong scientifically also. For the sruti did not arise as a division, equal or unequal, of the semitone. *It has no independent existence* [my italics]. It is only a difference between two intervals considerably larger than itself. A sruti is not the smallest audible sound but the accurately audible sound–that which is "heard" in accurate relationship *to some other*.'

In fact, as Indian musicians are quick to point out, the notes of an Indian scale do not remain static or fixed. They undergo many variations in pitch according to the vocalist, and the degree of augmentation or diminishing depends on the number of srutis incorporated into the svara as the raga scale demands. Flatness and sharpness are thus regulated by this process of what is expected by tradition.

Dr Bake has pointed out also that sruti are important in practice in defining the character of parallel modes with similar intervals: '. . . a sruti smaller or larger in the one mode than in the other creates a different mood or atmosphere.'

In fact, many a warning is given from Sanskrit and Hindi treatises by Pandit Bhatkhande at the beginning of each new section on a different raga. He quotes an old treatise, *Chandri Kayam*, on the subtleties of Jai Jawanti Raga.

'Dwinishada,	dwigandhara,	reyanshā samvadi	panchama
(Both ni's	both ga's	reh is just a slight touch	pancham is samvadi)
Sauratyangat		evāisha nishi	jai jawanti'
(From the touch of Saurat		in the beginning	is Jai Jawanti

Raga [i.e. it involves a touch   of   the   night   Raga)
of Saurat Raga; implied is   [nishi]
the hint: *therefore be careful*]

For this reason srutis, no matter how infinitesimal, can make a great difference between ragas employing the primary scale or thaat, such as Kanada, Bageshri and Kafi. If taken in Western terms these are of the A mode: CDE♭ F, G, A♭B♭C.[1] Mathematically subdivided, the intervals, when measured in vibrations (known to musicologists in technical language as musical cents) from sa to sa, differ in only small degrees between one major note and the next. Nevertheless, in the division between notes when using our scale of C D E♭ F G A♭ B♭ C, the range between D and E♭, and E♭ and F can be as much as 25 cents. This means that on the more sensitive stringed instruments of India, the degree of flatness of E♭ can be made less in one raga than in a related raga using the same D and E♭. The division between the flattened sruti and the next in D♮ is smaller in mathematical cents. In fact, as my Indian friends delight in explaining to me, in some of these closely related ragas the only interval between two major notes which does remain constant is that between ma (4th) and pa (5th)!

It is said in Sanskrit texts that sa and pa are 'shant'—that is, calm or immobile, without wavering to either side—like a sea which is static after the sway of the waves have rippled over it in the rest of the notes, reh, ga, dha and ni. These are known as movable or kānt. Ma is the only ambiguous note in that it can never be flattened, but is said to be ugr, sharpened or piquant.

It behoves us, therefore, to train our ears more assiduously from the lazy way we listen to sounds at the moment. There are many examples of this differentiation which one finds as one's knowledge of the functioning of srutis grows with familiarity with the music. It has taken me about eight years to recognize some of these fractional differences and then only because certain Indians have deliberately sung predominant phrases to me. The reh[s] for instance of Raga Kafi (D♮ if sa is middle C) or Raga Desh (reh, ma, ga, pa ni sa[t] reh ga sa[s], ni dha ma[t] pa ga reh) is different from the reh[t] (D♯ literally in Indian terminology, but D♮ on our keyboard) of

---

[1] The symbols ♭, ♮ and ♯ are used to indicate flat, natural or sharp notes in Western terms. In Indian terms, [k] (komal), [s] (shuddh) and [t] (tivra) indicate the flat, natural or sharp state.

Kalyan or Asaveri. According to Indian theory this latter sruti has more minute vibrations than the reh[s] (D). It is, in fact, only tivra (sharp) in relation to the preceding sruti of middle D, but it is actually D♮ in relation to the next sruti along the line, the sruti that makes the note become E♭.

Architecture can perhaps best explain the layout of this system of lines and partials in terms of layers and spaces, planes and proportions, because it is the most straightforward and solid of the arts. Such relationships in spatial measurement are the essence of good music, no matter how abstract that music is.

MUSIC FORM IN BRIEF

Srutis and Svaras

Indian music can therefore be said to rest on these 22 foundation-stones, the srutis upon which 7 great blocks have been placed. These are the notes of the octave corresponding to our keyboard scale of C–the 7 svaras. Together these two layers add up to the 12-tone scale now being used by our own experimenting musicians.

To continue the metaphor, the cementing together of these foundations is done by the ever-present drone. It gives homogeneity and firmness to the structure by the very recurrence of the same sounds throughout the lengthy playing of a raga. In this way it detaches those sounds from the particular melody and, so to speak, holds them out prominently for the ear to note clearly and continually. In fact it also serves to emphasize those full tones of the raga which coincide with the drone notes.

Another layer has to be placed on these blocks and foundation-stones. These are the architectural pillars and outer buttresses of the tala, the percussive element which gives a sense of space and definition to the long line of bricks which is the elongated and single melodic line tracing its way through every raga. This percussive tala strenthens the whole edifice of tones.

So this is the essential architecture; but like a building it would be stark without decoration, windows to provide a view, painting, and other suitable ornament to add variety. Classical dhrupad music is in fact stark–architecturally plain and massive–but the greater part of Indian classical music has sought to please the ear with every kind of artifice and delight.

Long improvisations, when a musician is composing instan-

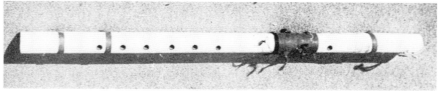

15 Bansari

16 Venu

17 Pannalal Gosh at the Flute

18 Violin, with T. K. Jayaram Iyer

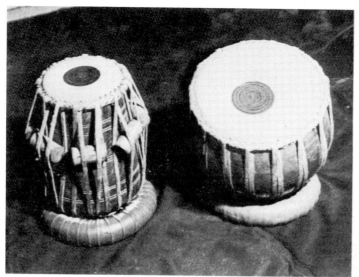

19 Tabla

20 Pakhāwaj

21 Dholak

22 Palghat Mani Iyer at the Mrdngam

23 Mrdngam and Pakhāwaj

24 Chenda

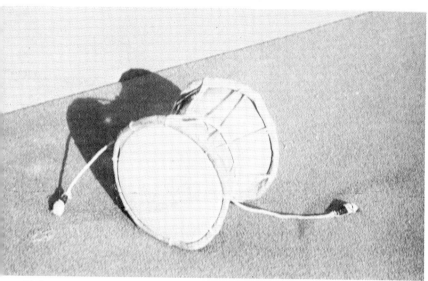

25 Dumru

26 Kanjira

27 Dhol

28 Ghatam

taneously on a prescribed grouping of notes, are the windows to the raga, for each raga can be played entirely differently by individual musicians. They can also be played entirely differently by the *same* musician at different times. Each musician is the window to the soul of the melody. What he opens up with his own insight and skill may be very different from the aspect created by the next musician.

Essential Decoration

The surface decorations can be many, depending on the architect– the solo instrumentalist or vocalist–and the accompanying drum player. There are certain well defined and established harmonious designs: the gamakas (pronounced 'gummuk'; = grace notes); the tanas or taans (melodic figures which fill in the melody in fast runs or sweeps); the alamkara (ornamental variations which appear to form into 'graphs', regular in pattern except for perhaps one change in order of notes up or down); and the matras (infinite varieties of permutations in the beat of the tala).

At this point I must once again stress the need to remember that there is a difference in meaning sometimes, when using the same terminology for Western and Eastern systems. Decoration is not an extraneous part of Indian music. It is fundamental to it. No melody is sung along a thin melodic line like a medieval air or a ballad. Everywhere the grace notes are playing around the tones and shading in the sensations to the sounds. Just as all the multitudinous gods and goddesses who twine and unite in embrace around every conceivable free area of wall *constitute* the Indian temple rather than just decorate it superficially, so the graces of Indian music are an integral part of the raag. They make the raag. In this way they differ from our own *appogiatura* of which the dictionary definition is: 'an ornament consisting of a short note inserted a whole tone or half a tone higher or lower than a note forming part of a chord *without being an essential part of a melody*'.

Grace is absolutely essential to the Indian system. The way musicians approach the svaras which make up the vertebrae of the raga, by slurring upward to a certain note or by breathing a gentle hint of many overtones before they come to rest in the dead centre of a full tone, is what makes Indian music so unique and breathes life into the raag which without gamakas would be slender indeed in content.

These actual architectural proportions, the lintels, fluted columns and their capitals of different scroll design, the shape of the roof and the colour of the brick, are really to be thought of in terms of Corbusier architecture. Nothing is surface ornament; decoration is melted into the stone; and whatever is added is necessary as part of the organic design. There are no neoclassical arabesques which could be stripped from French architecture of the eighteenth century or from the later Italian copyists of the Greek originals, leaving the simple structure to speak for itself in denuded apologia. You cannot strip Corbusier designs. Whatever is ornamental has a *raison d'être* and is inextricably part of the architecture.

Raga Form

The proportions are noticed when you stand back and see the music as a whole. The introduction to a raga may be long or short, the middle section also, with a certain overall rhythm making itself felt gradually, and then the third area comes into view, finished at great speed or worked on with infinite variety and complicated tooling. These three sections are the alaap (or alapa), jor and jhalla, all making up the raga alapana.

Then finally there is the fixed composition which is precomposed, the gat (pronounced 'gut'), the final recapitulation of all that has gone before, its design accentuated by a predominance of tala. This is the coda which brings space and shade to the whole raga, like sunlight and cloud effects on architecture.

STARTING AT THE FOUNDATIONS

According to Indian theorists 'musical sounds are first perceived as relative pitches and intervals and when they have lasted as such for some time then alone are they able to communicate to the mind any idea or expression'.

This is noticeable on instruments such as the sitar, sarod and the veena, especially the veena when played by an artist such as Abdul Aziz Khan of Patiala, whose recordings can still be bought, or by South Indians of the stature of Balachander or that young master making a name for himself in the South, Chittibabu. Notes in lower octaves float as swollen resonances around the gourds, pregnant with emotional overtones. Full tones and partials float in space like overblown balloons, slowly turning where no wind blows. The same is true of the famous Khansahib Abdul Karim Khan whose sudden vocal swerves into higher pitches still carry with them the remembrance of the last few tones in a lower pitch. Sometimes his voice with its astonishing range can transfer itself into the soprano pitch so that it is difficult for a foreigner to distinguish whether it is a man or a woman singing.

Mictrotones can be forgotten as the melodic line gathers momentum in shafts of fluid arrow-sound. The fractional divisions fuse into wholeness. This creates a paradox that is not an uncommon characteristic of Indian life. Opposites are always working towards unity and synthesis so that the listener is never made consciously aware of any compartmentalism, or miniscule fragmented divisions. Rather he is given the feel of a flowing unity. This is an essentially Indian attitude of mind, a compulsion born out of Indian philosophy and the use of Sanskrit language. Nearly every aspect of life has been broken up into its atomic particles – lovemaking, taste, emotions, dance postures and hand gestures, eating, habits, yogic āsanas, what should be eaten and with whom, etc. – and yet after the fragmentation a process of merging into one entity takes place. Wholeness is all.

In this perpetually evolving, steady state, Indians are interested in analysis not as a scientific end in itself but as a means to a greater wisdom about how to live life in the hopes of gaining liberation from it. So it is that the divisions of sound into these thin slivers of microtones do not in the least cause a jerky, staccato or cellular music. Notes are axial, with the graces revolving around them. They come into focus as if under a zoom lens which picks out details, highlights them, then lets them fuzz at the edges as the focus changes. Notes are in fact flattened and rammed together into groups, rather than picked out individually as in the crystal sparkle and clarity of a Bach concert. Astonishingly enough, in the vocal chords of master-singers like Bade Ghulam Ali, or the two Pakistani brothers Nazakat and Salamat Ali, they glitter like the minute, globular facets of a chandelier. It is a *tour de force* when the vocalist moves into the main section of the gat and the tempo increases. Each atomic particle is there with no fuzziness at the edges for the singer – yet to the listener only the whole effect can really be appreciated. In no way can this be compared with Bach or with a soprano singing the long cadenzas of a Verdi opera.

The musician comes to rest, after some intended tension while one awaits the resolution in the ear, on the centre of the note. This can be heard from the immediate outset when a vocalist starts to 'describe' the ascending scale. Perhaps four or five notes will be passed over and breathed upon before the tonic is reached. It is a familiar pattern to be repeated subtly throughout the whole performance, like this but in much more elaborate detail:

or even more simply:

Indian notes are never separated 'from the evolving process'. Of all instruments it is the veena which most exemplifies this 'evolving' process and its techniques in Indian classical music. This most ancient instrument is described in full in the Glossary, but we must note here the especial niche that the veena holds in musical lore and the evocation it brings to an Indian mind of an enrichment far beyond this worldly level.

For one thing, it is India's oldest instrument, tracing its lineage back to a far distant primitive veena of 4000 years ago, mentioned in the Vedic texts, and, according to some scholars, itself evolving from an earlier Egyptian lute called the vena.

In Hindu legends the veena is always played by Saraswati, Goddess of Arts, Music and Learning. To be able to play the veena is to be able to play any instrument, so delicate are its nuances. Built as it is with 7 strings stretched on 2 high bridges over 22–24 frets fixed in wax and therefore slightly movable, it responds to the slightest variations in finger pressure. Sometimes it is played with a glass egg sliding along the strings which gives a zither-like effect of illusive notes. The South Indian saraswati veena which is played with the right-hand fingers wearing plectrums, is extremely sensitive to the subtleties of the 2 resonating chambers attached to the long, carved, wooden bridge.

No wonder then that that famous law-maker of pre-Christian times, Yagnavalkya, declared: '. . . he who knows the art of veena playing and struti shastra (law-books) can attain God easily'.

In recent years though, the best example of this technique of gathering up a multitude of fragmentary sounds into a smooth, gliding quality of grace, is to be found in the unique instrument which Pannalal Gosh perfected before his untimely death a few years ago. His three-foot-long, bamboo flute can still be heard, fortunately, on LP recordings. The melodies stand out more clearly than on the 'twanging' stringed instruments, but the quality of the notes is still unmistakably Indian. To listen to his playing is an essential lesson in absorbing the flowing quality which srutis bring to the music.

We Westerners concentrate on the dead-centre of the note, as anyone listening to Joan Sutherland or Elizabeth Schwarzkopf can recognize from the start, but in India it is a 'sonorous fluid ascension from the fundamental (ancestor) to the overtones (successors) and leading to successive octaves as from one generation to another'. This is how Mr Goswami sees the process.

The scale of twenty-two srutis is never sung chromatically, and the intervals are not important one to another but only as *groups* of intervals, 'the precise vibration value of which depends on their *position in a progression, not on their relation to a tonic*'.

Srutis are never seen in juxtaposition to each other but as in a figure of speech where there are many commas interspersing the words. This is why it is best, once the sruti has been theoretically recognized, to forget about its existence. Mr Jairazbhoy, one-time lecturer in Indian Music at the School of Oriental Studies in London and now Professor of Music in Canada, has questioned the premise put forwards by the French scholar of Indian music, Alan Danielou, that the sruti can be measured specifically and with separate identity.

In a paper presented at London University he has stated: 'One of the fundamental concepts in Danielou's works appears to be the belief that a raga achieves its coherence through a balance of expressions inherent in the specific intervals of that raga. There appears to be no tolerance in his attitude – no allowance for the human element. According to him each individual sings or plays certain exact intervals in any particular raga. The intervals in any particular raga, he maintains, are constant all over India, irrespective of the tradition or school of the musician. He postulates an equally perfect audience, endowed with abnormal sensitivity for distinguishing the finest shades of intonation and experiencing a particular and invariable emotion from each of these. For instance, the musician and the audience must be able to differentiate clearly between an interval of 884 cents and another of 906 cents (a difference of 22 cents, or less than half a quartertone) and to find in each of these a distinct expression – the former, soft and calm; the latter, restless and playful.'

This is territory for scholars. The scientific analysis of srutis and the way they are used by differing musicians is now made possible by the technical sensitivity of oscillograms as Mr Jairazbhoy has shown in an interesting paper.[1] For those who are professional musicians this is obviously a subject of keen controversy, and it would appear that Indian musicians and both Asian and Western musicologists need to come together in conference to define srutis if their existence is to be established as an exact science. I have had such conflicting things said to me about their existence, their potentialities and usage that in this particular context of scholarship it would seem to be a question of semantics that does not concern the ordinary listener nor affect his bewilderment and enjoyment at the first encounter.

Professor Mukherji has quoted the mystic musician, Inayat Khan, as having given a demonstration in the old hall of the Calcutta University Institute during which he produced distinctly all the twenty-two srutis, and even more, with his masterly voice. Yet Mr Jairazbhoy quotes Bada Ghulam Ali as saying that srutis occur only in slides and shakes, and are not held as steady notes because 'to all intents and purposes we sing a twelve-tone scale'. He should know, since he sang them all the time and blended them into a marvellously expanding sound, as expansive as his own Falstaffian girth. Perhaps it is as Mr Popley succinctly suggests in his book on Indian music: singing all twenty-two srutis in succession is the art of the acoustic – but is not music.

'What is important', T. K. Jayaram Iyer my South Indian mentor once explained to me, 'is *how* we sing the note or play it. There are no sliced divisions. Indian music is like water.'

Indeed I often find myself visualizing water: the unbroken swell, the long curl of a wave, its crash, wash forwards, and run back-

[1] 'Intonation in present day North Indian classical music', *Bulletin of the School of Oriental and African Studies, University of London*, Vol. XXVI, Part 1, 1963.

wards; the swirl of a pool and the inward pull towards the centre from the banks; the rippling, bubbling stream falling over the sloping land, shimmering down in a long glissando. A vision of Allauddin Khan, the greatest of contemporary gurus, playing in willow-green shade over a so limpid pool returns again and again to haunt me, when I recall in a nostalgic flash that evening under the scalloped arches of the Red Fort in 1954 when he lifted us all into another dimension with his gifted playing of the sarod. And this when he was reaching his nineties. But of srutis, I can remember nothing!

Srutis could exist after all in Western music if one cared to split hairs, to mix the metaphors! Greensleeves has been played in such a manner by Julian Bream on his guitar. Ali Akbar Khan has returned the compliment and played the same medieval air on the sarod during a performance of Bhairavi when he made a necklace of ragas (Malika) and presented Greensleeves somewhat in the manner of a coda. There is no end to the experiments which could be undertaken and which would marry the two approaches from West and East. Any strongly repetitive melody could be taken in our own music and a particularized grouping of notes could be extracted and worked upon. Then each of these notes could be isolated and subjected to all manner of slurring sounds which joined it to the note that followed or glided gently over intervening notes to the next but one up the melodic line, giving just a hint of the other tones in between. Then the melody could be pieced together again, group by group and restored to its complete flow. Folk-melodies are especially susceptible.

The ballad of Barbara Allen is one I always wish to see metamorphosed this way. Its scale is the fundamental one of Indian music–Bilawal or C major–and it also embraces the octave within the first three bars. The middle lines of each verse carry a 'shape' in the melody which is essentially Indian: a pull away from the tonic in top C (sa) down through B (ni) to G (pa); a movement on either side of the tonic into the 2nd and 7th notes of the scale and back to the tonic; a lovely glissando down from the tonic C through B to G; and then an elaboration around the 5th dominant note (here it is G, pa in the Indian scale).

There is already an implied grace in the line 'Made every youth cry well aday', from the 5th to 6th note (pa to dha), and in the wobble on the first syllable of 'Allen'.

Such slurs and turns and slithers from one note to another occur among a good many negro singers (Mahalia Jackson for instance). I do believe that enforced listening to pop music during years of teenage children has made me come to see how attuned this generation is to joined and tied sounds. Echo-chambers have accomplished what drones have been doing for years. Our hearing is now not averse to dissonances and fuzzed edges, such as these:

This kind of grace and turned notes is not uncommon to our music but it will, I know, seem heretical to equate such popular kinds of music with classical Indian. I have felt however for a long time that a healthy irreverence is no bad thing in India. As it is, there is too much sanctity about the music, which often dehydrates it. The full rich joy of the melodies, however, knows no bounds. It is impossible not to sway to some Indian ragas, to let the body live in the way provoked by musicians such as Ali Akbar when he is playing in a raga with an imperative lyrical sway or the Ali brothers when they are singing a thrumri in Sindh Kafi Raga. The atmosphere is electric with eroticism. The pulse beats in one's blood along with the drum; one really feels the 'dying fall' of a superb slide down the notes–Bade Ghulam Ali could elevate this into a real, physical ache in the heart.

In this sense classical music and popular music are the same. Of course, the latter may provoke a more momentary lifting of the spirit whereas the sound of Bach or Bageshri Raag remains in the memory a long time afterwards and is a permanent experience in the realm of the spirit. However, Hoagy Carmichael, Josh White, Sonny Terry and Brownie McGhee (these latter two imitate vocal sounds on their instruments just as in reverse Indian vocalists, such as Keserbhai, imitate instrumental sounds with their voices) can, with a sudden swerve of tempo and a coming-together on the beat, create the same emotional thrill that body and mind inevitably feel in both classical and pop music at moments of complete identification between performer and listener. Our two worlds are not so far apart as we have been led to think. I wish someone had said to me in the beginning of my discovery of this world where the emotional impact is so strong and yet not to be denigrated, 'Just give yourself to it and after a time you will find that the effect upon you is much the same as when you are responding to what you like best in your own music.'

If you happen to like Bach and the early forms of jazz, you are well on the way to stepping over that imaginary divide which rests more in the mind and with old-fashioned prejudice than in the reality of the music.

We are, after all, hearing srutis all the time, although we do not know it for a fact. In Bach and Handel there are many moments when, just as in Indian music, the ear longs to be drawn to a resolution of the preceding sounds, as in a cadence towards the tonic (especially the upper doh) for instance. Bach does not follow through from the leading note to the resolution but slurs over the tonic and makes the listener wait in suspense. This is not a common occurrence but it does happen; in Indian music it is happening all the time. However, here it is more clearly differentiated in the ear than in Bach and Handel where full notes are joined together in chordal harmonies which leave their own reverberations. This function is performed in the cellular spaces between melodic notes of the Indian structure by the fragmentation of sruti.

There is obviously a difficulty for the Westerner who may be trying not only to translate the language of Indian music and its terms, but also to fit the inflexibility of our own fixed octave within the elasticity of Indian tones. These live and have their being in relation to each other in a kind of serial order, not in relation to a fixed keyboard where A♮ and A♭ and B♮ are known quantities and recognizably measured notes.

As an experiment I have spent painstaking hours trying to isolate on the piano keyboard the tones of Raga Miya Kaa Malhar as played on the sitar by Vilayat Khan accompanied by Imrat Khan (his younger brother) on the sumptuous voice of the surbahar. It is quite impossible with our tempered scale to capture the fleeting, elusive movements between tones and semitones. The layers of sound imposed one upon the other by the wallowing echoes of the gourd, the drone and the shimmer of sitar strings, are as slippery to capture as globules of mercury sliding around on ice.

The actual phrases peculiar to Miya Kaa Malhar are: reh, ma reh sa; ma reh; pa; ni^k (7th flat)–dha, ni^s (7th natural) sa upper. The start on reh sets the emotions of the raga. A second phraseology is the following: sa ni^k pa, ma pa; ga^k, ma ga^s ma, reh, sa. The vadi or dominating note is sa.

The movement or rather slide from D > D♭C D♭ > D, repeated both an octave and two octaves lower by the surbahar, the flowing, swaying tones from D > E and the lightest of falls from F♯ to F, remain tantalizingly in the ear but defy the precision we demand. To tell the truth, theirs is so fine a definition that it defies analysis. The interpretation has to come from within the active imagination of the singer or the instrumentalist, depending on the creative spark of the moment. The swirl upwards to a top A is like the merest breath of wind lifting an autumn leaf–effortlessly, effortlessly! No notation can ever quite encompass the 'feel' of this, a point which Indian musicians make great effort to emphasize. Another interesting and graphic illustration of the problems inherent in this elusive component of Indian music is the Yehudi Menuhin/Ravi Shankar recording (West Meets East–EMI ALP 2294) of Raga Goonkali. In Raga Goonkali there is an especial slur (a lingering waver around the reh note–in this recording reh is D♮) which has an inescapably evocative impact on a knowledgeable Indian listener; one has to inherit this 'feel' of a note unconsciously from birth, along with that inexplicable emotional content that Indians imbibe from their way of life and religious and social disciplines. Western musicians, despite all their technical skill and genius in musicianship, have real difficulty with imbuing a note with this 'inside' feeling.

There is no adequate way of explaining graphically these subtleties of pressure, either on a string or in the larynx of the human voice, that make two ragas–using the *same* notes–very markedly different from each other. But there is no doubt of the tender melancholy with which the note reh can be invested when an Indian vocalist sings it and approaches it in the descent and wavers either side of it. Goonkali is a morning raga; the Indian scale if the keynote is middle C is this:

Its special phrase or pakad is this:

The 3rd and 7th notes are always omitted. The 2nd and 6th are flattened. It is in fact a pentatonic, five-note scale and the particular phrase to be quoted is this lingering drop from the 2nd to the 1st note—a combination of reh, reh^k (flat reh), dha, and a concentration around dha, dha^k, ma^t (sharp ma) and reh^s (natural reh). In the Menuhin/Shankar recording the tonic sa is C♯. Our C♯ scale runs thus:

but in Indian terms the 3rd and 7th are omitted in Raga Goonkali, and the 2nd and 6th notes are flattened, so the Goonkali scale with sa on C♯ runs like this:

A recording of this raga which brings out the full flavour of th's particular fall from reh to sa is that sung by Bade Ghulam Ali (HMV/EALP 1258). His keynote is D♮. The Western D♮ scale is this:

But again in Goonkali the 2nd and 6th notes have to be flattened and the 3rd and 7th notes omitted, so using D♮ as sa the raga scale this time stands in the ascending order thus:

There is a very marked phraseology of falling notes in the descent. The lingering way Bade Ghulam Ali caresses the ma, reh, sa at the end of a long elaboration is characteristic of Goonkali.

There is also a close connection between the dha > pa (= B♭ > A) and a slur upwards again from A > B♭. This vocalist spends a lot of time 'wobbling' between these notes and upper sa. It is a soaring kind of singing. The relationship between the upper D > B♭ A is the same as in the lower half of the tetrachord between G > B♭ D♮. Here again one could say there is an implied harmony. One's memory carries the first pattern while the mind is engaged on the singing of the other.

What appears so complex at the outset settles into place quite clearly. Bade Ghulam Ali can even later in the recording be heard to sing the descent of the scale entire:

and even to reach upper A and G where the same phraseology repeats itself from upper G > E♭ D♮.

Only when our own composers have experimented more unself-consciously with serial music will we perhaps reach a fuller understanding of the acute precision of definition in Indian classical music within the quartertones and the shifting emphasis they give as they build up during play around certain substantive notes. It is the pakad of Goonkali which clearly reflects this 'making of a raga', the combination of reh, reh[k] and dha[s] and the playing around dha, dha[k], ma[t] and reh[s], illustrated here:

dha   ma reh

Tonic - Sa - C♯

I have mentioned the difficulty of translating straight into our musical context even the Indian terms used for their notes. For instance, when an Indian musician names notes as ma[s] and ma[t], he does *not* mean the literal translation as it would be into Western notation, i.e. F♮ (lying between F♯ and E♭) and F♯. He is in fact singing *two* F♮ that are slightly different in shades of tones *in relation* to their adjoining notes to which they may be connected as grace, or in a procession of graph-like cadences.

There is inevitable distortion in translating this kind of technique into our notation. Many a time if one reads the Devanagri script one comes across a ma^k (F♭) or a dha^t (A♯) which can in no way be transferred into our terms of E of B♭ respectively, for these are what F♭ and A♯ become in Western notation. For one thing, the tonic may not be our C♮ and these notes may be elsewhere on our keyboard. They only have fixity in relation to their own sa. This kind of acuteness of play, a tautening of the tension wires in the mind, is the marrow of Indian music.

Svaras (Sol-fa Notes)

In the traditional treatises it was discovered that various pitches aroused different emotions and that these could be specifically analysed. But the musicologists did not leave it at that, as a scientifically acoustical division. They related the intervals to the psyche, grouped into five sections—keen, tender, large, compassionate, moderate—running the whole gamut of human emotions from the bass sa, where the mood is sad, tender, loving, calm, up to the upper octave.

These passed through the microtones around reh, which evoke delight and passion according to the Hindu theorists, to ga with its strong, brooding emotions of hardness and determination. Ma is supposed to bring to mind the 'feel' of peace, moonlight and sensuality; ma^t (F♯ if sa is middle C), intense grief; pa, sunlight and joy; dha, deep sorrow. Ni mirrored the sense of awe and trembling agitation, and after the violence the svaras again led up to the plateau of tranquillity and simplicity, expressed in upper sa.

Svara (sva = self; rajri = to shine) means something that is complete in itself, shining within.

The designations of the sol-fa notes in Indian music and in Devanagri script are as follows:

C	D	E	F	G	A	B	C
doh	ray	me	fah	soh	lah	tee	doh
सा	री or रे	गा	मा	पा	धा	नी	सां
sa	ri or reh^1	ga	ma	pa	dha	ni	sa

---

[1] Reh is now more used in singing sol-fa passages. It takes its name from another spelling of the 2nd note of the scale, i.e. rehkab.

Occasionally in some Hindi books on musical theory, the full chromatic scale is given instead of saying that a note, dha for instance, is komal (flat) or tivra (sharp).

C	D♭	D	E♭	E	F	F♯	G	A♭	A	B♭	B	C
sa	rah	ree	ga	gee	ma	mi	pa	dha	dhi	na	ni	sa

The majority of these syllables end in the half-open 'a' as in the pronunciation of the first syllable in the word *Pun*-jaab. Some musicians do however sing the sargam or sol-fa notes with a heavier emphasis on this vowel–gaa, maa, paa, as in Pun-j*aab*.

This particular detail of phonetics is important to Indian vocalization as the flow of syllabic sound is based on the principle of ease: the ease with which it is possible to emit this sound of 'ah' and the facility with which it can be dwelt upon as a pure sound, to be savoured by the musician as an abstract art form, just as the sculptor may carve abstract shapes into stone or metal for the pure joy of bringing out its intrinsic quality or molecular characteristics, rather than for creating a representational piece of work.

This movement in the throat has been described by Mr Goswani as necessitating 'the play of the deepest part of the vocal cavities down to those of the lower cavities'. This is an idea not unfamiliar to the practice of yoga where each cavity of the body is absolutely relevant to the others. Of course, we may say this is a self-evident truth, but the Hindu never takes this for granted, and in yoga deep breathing is the first thing to be consciously concentrated upon. With the lungs fully extended, right down into the diaphragm, in a way that makes our own unconscious breathing seem very shallow indeed, the yogi logically surmises that right breathing is the first prerequisite to right thinking. This theory appears graphically and explicitly in the chakras (wheels) of Tautric Art.

Shadja or Shuddha Note

This is the pure, substantive note; the sol-fa note sa can be established at any pitch. For convenience one fixes it at middle C and from it are created the basic scales in use in present-day India. All scales are modifications of the basic shuddha C major scale: C D E F G A B C with no sharps or flats.

For this we have to thank the one man who in the early part of this century set about simplifying Hindustani music, throwing out all the irrelevancies and barnacle-like additions which centuries of development had accreted since Tansen's major overhaul of the system. Pandit Bhatkhande is often referred to as the father of modern Indian classical music. He systematized the ten scales most predominantly used in the Hindustani music of North India, and their derivatives. They are now known by the names in the following table, and all ragas derived from them carry their own special names or compound names of the prime scale designation, e.g. Puriya Kalyan.

One word of warning: it is misleading to see them notated in Western fashion, in the sense that no account is made of the special ordering of notes in phrases as the raga develops upon the skeletal melodic line, or of the way certain notes are handled (for example, lingered over or 'pulled out' for pathos) or are placed prominently to the fore in the exposition of the raga. Nor do these scales illustrate even the special grace notes which may swing either side of some prime notes like the wobble around A♭ or E♭ in Raga Darbari Kanada. And to confuse the issue more, some notes change their pitch slightly in different ragas, e.g. ga^k (E♭ if sa is middle C) in Kafi compared with ga^k in Todi.

The derivative scales are not listed here; these are known as mixed modes and are made up of more than the 7 prime notes, often having accidentals (used in the Western sense) or modified notes in the descending scale. These are called aurav- sharav- sampooram, 5-, 6- or 7-note serial lines.

Finally it must be emphasized again, so that there is no misunderstanding when seeing the scales transcribed as follows from a fixed middle C, that each singer or instrumentalist can choose the keynote or tonic sa according to his own convenience, even though during a great Sangeet Sammelan he may be singing a variety of ragas for hours into the night. A change of sa to a different key in the Western sense of a fixed scale would displace the tuning of all instruments, including the drums. They too are tuned to the sa chosen, and to the ma and pa, according to the systematic pattern of the raag – Malkauns, for instance, omits pa – in relation to this chosen sa. This applies also to the tampura or drone used. If two musicians perform together, each can use his own drummers who have tuned to the sa being used by each vocalist. Therefore the Indian sa, fixed in relation to other notes in its scale, can be used as a slide-rule on our own tempered keyboard; transposition of our own scale must then follow from wherever the Indian sa rests.

The Ten Basic Scales or Thaats

Hindustani	Carnatic	S R G M P D N

Bilawal
seven notes all pure
Derivatives: Bihag, Durga.

Shankarabharanam

Vadi
or emphasised note

Khambaj or
Kamaj
1 vikrit or changed note: ni[k]
Derivatives: Tilang, Jhinjoti, Jaya Javanti.

Kamboj or
Harikhaambhodi

Kalyan
1 vikrit note ma[t]
Derivatives: Kedāra, Shyam.

Mechakalyani

Marwa
2 vikrit notes: reh[k], ma[t]. Marwa Raag derived from this deliberately omits the tonic sa as much as possible, and the 5th, pa.
Derivatives: Hindol, Puriya.

Gamanashram or
Gamanapriya

Bhairava[1] or
Bhairon
2 vikrit notes: reh[k], dha[k]. It is not to be confused with the other Hindustani thaat Bhairavi.
Derivatives: Saurashti, Jogiya, Lalita, Rāmkali.

Mayamalavagaula or
Malavgaurak

Kafi
2 vikrit notes: ga[k], ni[k]. It is extracted from Raag Sri but not the whole of it.
Derivatives: Piloo, Saranga, Bhimpalasi.

Kharhapriya

Asāveri or
Sindhi bhairavi
3 vikrit notes: ga[k], dha[k], ni[k].
Derivatives: Jaunpuri, Desh.

Todi or
Nata bhairavi

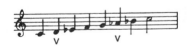

Sri (Shri)
Purvi (Puravi)
3 vikrit notes: reh[k], ma[t], dah[k].
Derivatives: Mālāvī, Gauri, Puriyadhanasri.

Kaam vardhani
(passion/increasing)

[1] Bhairava is the fundamental scale from which Carnatic musicians learn all their alamkaras (configurations). Purandarasa composed from this scale.

Bhairavi   *Hanumantodi*
. vikrit notes: reh^k, ga^k, dha^k, ni^k.
Derivatives: Mālkauns, Bhupali.

Todi   *Vrali* or *Pantuvarali*
. vikrit notes: reh^k, ga^k, ma^t, dha^k.
Derivatives: Multani, Gurjari.

In this last group microtonal variations are frequently used. Reh is often called ati-komal in this thaat, meaning a half-diminished tone or quartertone lower than a normal flattened note. Dha and ma will be less than fully sharpened or flattened semitones also.

Thaats

A thaat is the lowest common denominator in ordering Indian music into a system. Sanskrit texts mention the word 'ranjaktaa', meaning that a thaat does not necessarily engage the attentions in the same way as a raag, which is coloured with very definite characteristics. In fact a thaat is nondescript.

In the more capacious and comprehensive Carnatic system, Ravi Shankar has written in his book *My Music, My Life*: 'This system was finally classified in the seventeenth century by Pandit Venkata-mukhi in his *Chaturdaudi Prakashika*. According to the present Hindustani system of the North, there are 10 primary scales called thats. Unlike the South with its uninterrupted, continuous musical tradition, the North has no one system of classification of the scales or primary ragas. At the turn of this century (that is, 250 years after Venkatamukhi) an attempt was made by V. N. Bhatkhande to recodify the system ... into 10 thats. ... I myself, however, as well as a number of other musicians, do not feel that these 10 scales adequately accommodate a great variety of ragas, for there are many ragas that use notes not contained in these 10 thats. We therefore think it is more reasonable and scientific to follow the old (72-scale) melakarta system of the South because it can sustain almost any raga, no matter how unusual its ascending and descending structures.'

From these primary scales as many as 10, 20 or 30 ragas inherit their characteristic shape. In the Carnatic system the texts speak of 'mela swarsamnha syaad ragavyamjanshaktimaan', mela being a particular combination from which the raga is created with the force of its expression. In all, about 50 or 60 ragas have well defined, clear-cut forms. But of course there are 100s of hybrids sometimes with more than the seven notes, or as combinations of two ragas. These are not mathematical rearrangements by permutation of the notes of the parent scale, but are different in degree by the notes singled out for emphasis, or by the way the same notes are put together in a different order or motif to be repeated many times, or by the way certain oscillations or grace are affixed to a shuddha note, Raga Darbari Kanada, for instance, mentioned later in the main section on raga.

Many of these derivatives are associated with certain seasons, or composers such as Tansen. These are prefixed with his title Mian kaa or Mian kee, depending on whether they are male raga or female ragini.

None of this enlargement by process of permutation on the prime scales should seem strange to us. Looking at our own music in severely mathematical terms we have over the generations used every conceivable permutative process also. The wonder is that the permutations seem to be so infinite and that new melodies appear from modern composers in all their pristine freshness.

Indian music is therefore governed by this principle of a succession of single notes in an ascent and a descent. This principle may seem unbelievably 'thin' when set against the vigour of chordal harmony. This is a misconception. The soloist is not (in effect) playing a single line. His own instrument with all its sympathetic strings, the background resonance of the drone, the criss-crossing currents of the percussion, often a unison with the soloist, the playing of alternating phrases, and possibly other accompanying instruments adding rival elaborations almost like counterpoint against the melodic line–these together create a composite mosaic of tone colour.

This is particularly noticeable when a vocalist is accompanied by the stringed sarangi, a delightful and versatile bowed instrument with 3 main strings and 1 of brass–and sometimes as many as 18 sympathetic strings. The sarangi can be heard cavorting in and out of the melodic line echoing a passage which the singer has just executed, or zig-zagging across the singer's melodic line, weaving motifs in and out of it.

The ear becomes after a while accustomed to this other harmony, and in fact literally forgets the drone. But were the drone to be left out then the ear again would signal that something was wrong.

Dr Narayana Menon, with his intimate knowledge of Western traditions, has understood this most explicitly: '. . . it has become almost impossible for the Westerner to conceive of melody without the implications, tacit or explicit, of a harmonic system. In Western music, a melodic line is really the top or surface line of a carefully constructed harmonic structure. This is the building-up of melody, the harmonic implications of substantive and passing notes, and the relationship of these play an important part. Also, Western melody has a tendency to develop around notes which are harmonically related to the tonic. Indian melody is made up of notes which are related *purely by their continuity* . . . It is not the number of notes we use that is important. The important thing is how small an interval is of direct use and interest to us.'

RAAG OR RAGA

This question of interval brings us from the skeletal components to the main body of the raga, the word derived from ranja (= to please) and ghan (= doing). It has been said of raga in an attempt to describe it with precise definition that it is 'an arrangement of intervals in a definite order (not necessarily a consecutive order) upon which a melody is founded'.

Breaking down the word into its component Devanagri characters it can symbolically stand for the following: र = roop- रुप = pattern, a specific pattern of movement of sound based on certain modes (time, note and rhythm); the long A vowel denoted by the upright stroke । = अ = अधार (aadhar) = basis or foundation; and ग = गति (gati) = movement.

In Bhatkhande's treatise *Hindustani Sangeet Paddhati* (system) this definition of raga is given:

योयं	धनिविशेषस्तु	स्वरवर्णं	विभूषित:
Yoyam	dhunivishaishstu	svaravarun	vibhushiteh
That what	in that way becomes	a (note) specific	kind of sound

रंजको	जनचित्तानां	स राग:	काथतोबुधै:
ranjkō	janchittānam	se raag	kathitō budhayeh
the flavour which	people-heart-	that is raag	say the wise
makes attractive	that (which amuse)	(the wise people call that raag)	

149

It is certainly not a scale; these scales of ascent and descent peculiar to each raga are but the springboard for the imagination and creative power of the musician from which he can leap into the higher reaches where transcendental feeling takes over and where mood and the inner flavour – as mentioned previously – transform the struck note into an expressive sound, a catalyst for all manner of emotional and spiritual connotations. In fact, in actual play the most complicated patterns within a raga are formed in a stage of highest ecstacy – at the stage when the relish is most savoured by performer and audience alike, so much so that the listener can be lost physically yet feel like dancing as a man transformed, devoid of intellectual sense but moved by the harmonies of emotional energy.

There is in fact a structure, a mathematical one consisting of a selection of 5 notes (aurav), 6 (sharav) or 7 notes (sampooram) with an interrelationship between a chief note (vadi or amsa) and its samvadi (harmonically associated note); there are lower and higher limits to the melody; and there are certain characteristic turns of phrase, always running against an ever-present contrast with the drone.

In all ragas there is a dominating note (not our so-termed 'dominant' note, the 5th from the tonic) and a subdominant, which is often four intervals away from this assertive svara. The musician will give these much attention and treat them to this pivoting and axial tension, like a muscle pulling at the bone structure of the main body.

'The musician', writes Mr Goswami, 'often does not reveal the full implication of the vadi note; he simply gives a hint of it repeatedly but deliberately postpones it by using delaying notes. This postponement of the dominant suitable to the raga at the critical moment creates a sense of a tension in the listener who desires it to be removed. This is a very clever trick of the Indian masters corresponding to the *appogiatura* of the Western musical system. If the raga happens to be a cheerful one the tension is, eventually, removed successfully . . . If the raga is of a sad or dull disposition the tension is not removed at all and instead a dissonant note is used to make the effect more specific.'

In order to do just this Indian musicians use 'only those notes as leading ones which either precede or follow the primes by a semi-tone'. The performer is never acting on whim, although free to improvise almost eighty per cent of the time if he is an accomplished Ustad or Pandit. Improvisation has not, however, the same connotations as those with which we invest the word in relation to jazz. The vocalist or instrumentalist is working within strictly defined rules, never written and only set down in 'scaffolded' notation in the various treatises. These basic patterns of notes from which the edifice is built are learned from the age of three or four when a beginner first sits down on the duree alongside father, uncle or teacher and imbibes by ear the uniquely personal interpretation of the svaras and their microtonal idiosyncracies which his family or gharana have used from time immemorial.

The following is one example given by Pandit Bhatkhande for Miyan kee Malhar: reh ma reh sa; ma reh, pa; ni^k dha, ni^s, sa. In descent it follows this way: upper sa, ni^k, pa, ma pa, ga^k, ma reh sa (sa being middle C):

The special grouping are these:

Sa or ma are the vadi notes.

This is the scale given in its basic foundations for Yaman Kalyan, one of the most sensuous of ragas:

with many variations on this special ordering of notes:

Another raga, Jai Jawanti, is given this scaffolding: sa reh reh, reh ga^k reh sa; lower ni^k dha pa, reh, ga ma pa, ni sa (upper). This is the main phrase which is returned to again and again. The special phrase in which reh is the vadi note (and sometimes ga^k) is this:

Often long phrases end with: ga^k, reh ga^s, ma ga, reh ga^k reh sa, ga ma reh ga^k reh sa.

It is also cautioned that Jai Jawanti must be given a touch of ga^k, otherwise it can be mistaken for Raga Sonath. This gives an indication of the fineness of differentiation between ragas. The slightest touch of the wrong note may shift one raga into another and damn the exponent as less than a master, Hence, the function of India's *memoria technica*. A gifted musician should be able to move with logic from one group of notes constituting the main raag to another group representing a different raag with coherence and consonance of sound. However, even the greatest, such as the vocalist Girija Devi, can be called to task by an Indian music critic who can write: 'She is far from being a grammarian, that is her strong point in fact, but the way she was treating dha in Bhopali was definitely suggestive of Raga Deshkar.' Such orders and groupings of notes and their consequent 'shapes' have been branded into the mind of the musician by the white heat of concentrated listening and disciplined musicianship in the technique–sometimes ten to fifteen years in the making. This is called riyaz in the North.

From then on as the musician matures within, the technique shifts to a deeper metaphysical level where the mathematical permutations are forgotten. It is then a question of exploration in depth.

Each selection of tones and their relationship, and the way they are played expressively, is redolent with emotion. Each raga carries in its 'arrangement of intervals' this evocative mood and the listener is drawn, almost inevitably, to centre his own emotions there, developing, analysing, exploring, until the whole experience is exalted in the metamorphosis that occurs in any great art form. The individual is taken out of himself and refreshed by a vision from other realms.

Repetition of certain orders of notes, subtle catch-phrases or pakad begin to occur as the raga proceeds in intricacy. Half the fun for the newcomer is the recognition of these phrases, or of the way a certain note is used, such as the wobble or shake upon dha (A♭ if sa is middle C) in Darbari Kanada and the repetitive dha-ni-reh (Ab-B-D) which is typical also of this raga). A discerning ear and constant listening to a few well-known ragas will help in this recognition.

In fact, these arrangements of intervals do not become a raga with a specific name until they fulfil certain conditions in organization of their scales. One of these conditions is the special ordering of notes so that they are organically related like molecular structures which, because of their own intrinsic and unique shapes among molecular groupings, although belonging to the same kinship, are different in outward delination. Two ragas may in fact consist of the same five notes but it is the way those notes exist one with the other, the way they are ordered when the musician returns to the tonic sa or the dominating note as he completes an elaboration, the register they occupy most of the time, and the emotional feeling which the musician extracts from them by varying the mechanics through pressure on the notes, that are the genetic constituents marking out different personalities of raga.

For instance, Raag Bhopali and Raag Dehkar have exactly the same arohi ascending scale:

sa   reh   ga   pa   dah   sa

In Bhopali the lower part of the tetrachord is emphasized whereas in Deshkar it is the upper part. In Bhopali the play is around the shuddh note ga; in Deshkar, dha has to be emphasized.

The phrases in Bhopali run like this in the preliminary exposition, the sthayi:

```
ga  reh  sa,  reh  ga,  ga  reh  sa
ga  reh  ga  reh  sa  dha  pa¹
dha  sa,  reh  sa  ga    ·    ·
dha  pa  ga,  pa  ga,  reh  ga,  ga  reh  sa
```

and expand further outward and from the centre in the antara:

```
ga  pa  dha  sa,  sa  reh,  sa  dha  dha
pa  ga,  reh  ga,  ga  reh  sa  dha  pa  ga
```

¹ A dot under the svara denotes lower octave; a dot over denotes the upper octave.

reh ga, ga reh, ga reh sa
dha pa ga, sa dha pa ga,
dha pa ga reh, ga, reh sa.

Pa > ga is a typical way of approaching ga.

In Raag Deshkar with exactly the same arohi scale, dha is the prominent svara in the sthayi:

dha, dha pa, ga pa, dha, pa, ga reh sa,
sa reh ga pa, dha dha pa, dha pa sa
dha, pa reh reh sa, dha pa dha dha
sa, sa dha pa, dha pa ga reh sa,
dha dha pa, dha dha dha pa.

The antara expansion this time starts from pa:

pa ga, pa dha, sa, reh sa,
sa reh ga reh sa, reh sa dha pa
dha, dha reh sa, dha dha pa, ga pa dha sa
dha pa, ga pa dha pa, ga reh sa dha, dha (slurred into)
pa, ga reh ga reh dha.

Professor Mukherji has written the following in trying to explain the fine shades of difference to Westerners: 'It is the way in which the note is used, rather than the note itself, which is important in the execution of our music. Taking a broad view, raga is a whole structure and the sense of its wholeness demands at least a pattern of notes.

'Thus it is that our musicians demonstrate:

(a) a dominating note, a vadi, equivalent to the king in his court
(b) a subdominant samvadi which has been compared to the chief minister, the relation between the two being 1:5 (this is consonant with or in harmonic relationship with the vadi–and according to Indian theory should be nine to thirteen srutis from the vadi).
(c) an ally (anuvadi).
(d) an enemy note which is not to be mentioned (such as the tonic note in Raga Marwa which it is customary not to touch in the singing even when the force of the melody makes the ear long to hear it, the pa in Bageshri Raga, the reh and pa left out altogether in Hindola. These are known as varjit swara.)'

He continues: 'These principles are not, however, sacrosanct because dominance, meaning thereby a longer dwelling and treatment in the place of rest, or the reposeful point to which notes of the raga gravitate, may not be one note but may as well be two according to the exigencies of movement and decorations or the temper of the artist.'

It is this very factor, the determination of mood, which makes the raga form unique to music. The notes of the raga define the mood, determine the time of the day it should be performed (although of course this rigid doctrine is no longer abided by in modern concerts) and can also be related to the seasons of the year.

Apart from the actual scientifically measurable componant parts of the raga which can give it certain musical qualities to mark it out from the next raga, there is of course the far more illusive touch which each individual musician brings to the melody, so enhancing the spirit of the raga that its inherent personality becomes inescapable. Kafi is one such raga, sensually emotional and evocative of a highly romantic mood. Played by Nazakat and Salamat Ali, the effect can be as heady as a high moon and good wine!

It has to be repeated *ad nauseam* that an Indian musician is both performer and composer because he is free in the spontaneity of the moment of performance to create as the spirit moves him. What he has carved out within his own spirit through his own training and by dint of his character, personal agonies and rewarding moments of happiness, is bound to be reflected in the emotional and intellectual content with which he invests the raga. I shall return to this point later when comparing how several musicians can interpret one specific raga in a variety of ways although the principles which govern that raga are identical.

The artist's capacity for expressing the inner spirit of the raga – the fragile, intangible core or suksham svaron (delicate departments of notes in Sanskrit) – is aided by a number of technical devices. If analyzed in more detail these embellishments and figurations could be shown in geometrical terms. They are not created in a haphazard fashion. From the set notes of the raga a succession of melodic figures builds up, repeated with slight variations with each restatement. These are the varnas or movements. In the most simplified forms they start off like this cut-to-the-bone progression: sa, reh, ga–reh, ga, reh–ga, ma, ga–ma, pa, ma, etc., or sa, ga, reh–ga, pa, ma–pa, ni, dha.

These melodic figures can expand or contract by different usage of ornamentation in alamkaras: the decorative sweeps of svaras backwards and forwards or stepping upwards and downwards in flexible 'shapes'; or the swift-running 'taans' or oscillating arabesques (for want of any more accurate phrase to describe them); or the abundance of swinging fractional grace.

A most useful book to read on this score is Mr Fox-Strangway's book which has at last been reprinted after a generation of being almost unobtainable. *The Music of Hindoostan* gives abundant examples of Indian principles in the only way that makes an immediate impact–that of Western notation. Perhaps by present-day analysis he may not be entirely accurate, but he was doing a pioneering job in the 1920s; this in itself is a miracle considering the difficulties he must have laboured under in tracking down the accuracy of renderings of various ragas, and in getting musicians to explain verbally (which they are notoriously clumsy at doing) the principles from which they are working.

What is even more useful in this book are the frequent analogies drawn with our own music and the cross-references to similar processes at work, be they in a Beethoven symphony or a simple Scottish air. This similarity to Scottish folk-ballads is immediately noticeable. Celtic music is similar because so many folk-airs confine themselves to five notes of a scale–they are pentatonic like many Indian ragas. Many also include the augmented 4th–ma^t–but it is not this mechanical affinity alone which brings Ireland or Scotland to mind. There are deeper ethnic affinities than this; certainly, much of the Irish and Indian outlook is in harmony. There are even further socio-religious links, such as the caste system, very similar to the Hindu stratification of society, which existed in pre-Christian Ireland; and there are now theories being mooted of Indo–Aryan links and Celtic migrations into the heartland of Eurasia.

A Celtic theme phrase which is illustrated by Mr Fox-Strangways for a khyal, makes more clear than any words the actual physical processes at work in the Raga Mālkauns, a derivative of the Bhairavi scale, one of the major ragas of Hindustani music. It is a late-evening raga depicting heroism, using the notes sa, ga^k, ma, dha^k, ni^k (C, E♭, F, A♭ and B♭ if sa is middle C). Mr Fox-Strangways points out how the use of the B♭ as leading note is very akin to its use in Scottish laments, as are the formations of these notes. Ma

(F) is the amsa or predominant note to which the melodic figures glide or return:

This theme phrase is returned to over and over again:

Intervening are all manner of combinations of the basic notes but particular to this raga are the glides upwards to the top F, like a river tern swooping in a graceful climb:

Then there are the inverted descents by thirds to the theme:

Here the middle F echoes the higher register where the F was attained in the run upwards:

These figures of ascent and descent are typically North Indian as is this kind of regular alamkara of movement into a higher octave. Note how the note pa (G) is left out entirely in this raga. There is always the danger in such a clinical analysis of a raga, of stripping it bare of its real quality. No Indian ever thinks of these elements or isolates them consciously in the process of savouring a raga in play. Its integral whole is composed of so many elements: the lengthy passages of ascending steps, the curling motions and zig-zags, the slurs, trills and glides down into lower octaves to repeat the process all over again but with a slightly different permutation of notes, the deliberate overstepping of a svara and the recoil.

All these indescribably minute fractions of sound bring lustre to the whole playing of a raga, so much so that in fact there is no escape from its intrinsic emotional personality. Luminosity is basically the right English word for the effect of 'shining within' that the root words 'rajri' (to shine) and 'sva' (self) bring to the concept of svaras, the cornerstones of the whole edifice of raga-building.

Ravi Shankar himself uses the French word 'vivant' to describe the quality given to the notes, investing them with French connotations far beyond the literal translation, 'living'. This is precisely what the Sanskrit word 'praña' breathes into each life-breath of the note sung by the human voice. Praña quite literally and bio-chemically gives the human voice note a luminosity, so making it vivant.

The clarity of emotion held in these luminous notes explains why there is still such a pull of the compass towards the theory enunciated so many long centuries ago which says that certain notes and their combinations give rise to varying devotional or emotional moods – or bhava – and their culminating relish – rasa.

NAVA RASA OR NAAVRUSS

Music distils emotion and captures all the fleeting nuances which I have categorized earlier. In the first musical treatise this theory of nava rasa or nine sentiments was analysed in as much detail as the srutis and graces were. In fact, part of the mythology of the musical history of India is the belief that a twenty-two-stringed veena was put together so that the early masters could determine the emotive value of each of the twenty-two srutis and identify its relationship with sa.

Groups of these srutis were gathered together under nine headings working up from the 2nd note of the octave, reh (D♮, sa being middle C).

In Sanskrit the corresponding flavours arising from the play around these prime notes are as follows:

Sanskrit	Bhaav or Bhava	Raas or Rasa
utsah	bravery, effort, determination	veera
krodh	anger	raudra
bhaya	fright, alarm	bhayanaka
ascharya	marvelling	adbhuta

vismaya	amazement	adbhuta
rati	love	sringara
hasya	mirth	hasya
jugapsa	censure, disgust	vibhatsa
shohk	compassion, grief	karuna
sham	meditative peace where there is an absence of passion	shaant

There is a further rasa in Hindu philosophical thought: the tenth, which is not so commonly known and it is not applicable to music. This is vaatsayala, embodying the tender unerotic love relationship between parent and child.

Such a relationship is easily transformed in metaphysical terms into the symbolic relationship of man with the heavenly Father or Mother. Love is religiously sublimated. This is common to all religions. Depending on whether a society is patriarchal or matriarchal, God is mirrored as the Father or the Mother.

In India, where matriarchal societies have flourished, certainly along the southern Malabar coast and in some hill societies of the North, there has always been the equal balance between male and female forces so that the godhead has been personalized in Shiva/Shakti imagery, or as Iswara/Maya, Krishna/Radha, Rama/Sita or Vishnu/Meenakshi. From these unions have come the worship of their children, the 'Son of Man' principle of the Christian religion. Ganesh the Elephant God, son of Shiva and Parvati (i.e. Shakti) is one manifestation of this and his devotees lavish upon him a warm, understanding affection as a parental devotion. The same quality of loving worship is poured upon the baby Krishna at the time of Janam Ashtami, his birthday. Then he is not the avatar of Krishna, the god of the gopis, the reincarnation devoted to sensual love, but the recipient from his human worshippers of an effusive concern which is totally asexual, vaatsayala.

One may not agree (when testing such a theory by playing the notes) that such definitive categorization can be possible, but there can be no doubt that major ragas do fit this pattern once one comes to identify certain figurations that are continually emphasized and which drop like persistent raindrops into the mind, playing upon so many nerve-ends until the mood is inevitably created and sustained there. And there is certainly no doubt, when one listens in the very real and vibrant atmosphere of an Indian audience, that the response is warmly reciprocated from the discerning listener who awaits with expectancy those evocative phrases and refrains. To savour the music without this evocation would be like tasting a wine which appears enjoyable when seen in the glass but is sadly flat in reality.

In the philosophical treatise of Hinduism where the arts are concerned, rasa is believed to have three constituents:

(a) sthayi bhava: a permanence in the steady-state where emotions remain in a latent form;
(b) vibhava: that state which arouses the appropriate emotions;
(c) anubhava: the experience which comes from physical expression and which gives rise to these emotions.

One intriguing flight of the imagination has been allowed himself by Mr Swarup in his writing on the theory of Indian music. As an illustration of this principle of nava rasa he has analysed Hamlet's famous soliloquy and 'put it to music'. First of all he dissects the psychology of Hamlet's thinking with 'its utter disgust of the world and the great disappointments at the troubles of outrageous fortune'.

The sentiments expressed by Hamlet 'are grief, anger, disgust and determination, giving rise to karuna, vibhatsa, raudra and veera rasa. Appreciation and love are altogether absent, so sringara and adbhuta are excluded.' He concludes that the notes to be played upon with emphasis would, roughly speaking, be C, E, F, A♭ and B♭ and 'the tune Malakosha (in modern spelling Mālkauns) would approach this very nearly as it has no reh (D) or pa (G) and has its force on sa, ga^k and ma. It has of course no mi (F♯).' Our old friend Mālkauns with all the soulful melancholy of a Scottish lament inherent in its scale has been harnessed to the evergreen equation of Hamlet!

However, it is obviously ridiculous to believe that one note in isolation can express a specified sentiment in such potent, distilled form, sa and reh standing in for heroism and wonder, for instance. It is the use of a certain note, its duration and expression and the ornaments of its graces that can influence the mind e.g. F♯ for Kalyan Raga has an undoubted 'yearning' quality about it. Of course examples of this art could be taken from Western music as any film-composer realizes. Background music in a certain pitch, playing upon certain notes, consistently heightens the mood in theatrical and cinematic productions, and in fact enlarges the expectancy of an audience almost unconsciously.

The truth about nava rasa is not literal therefore. This is consistent with aspects of truth in India; it is to be taken more in the spirit of what lies behind this theory than in the actual fact. Much depends anyway on how the musician feels emotionally. The hypersensitivity of the true artist is conveyed as by an electrical filament into the playing of the raga. For instance, I have myself heard Ali Akbar play Sindhi Bhairavi with two separate and distinct emotional interpretations.

This is a morning raga of great beauty, creating images of pathos, peace and restfulness in its minor key, using four 'black' notes in ascent if sa is middle C: the 2nd, 3rd, 6th and 7th. The melancholy of the notes flavours the mind long after the playing is finished, a certain muted anguish like a woebegone love song. Perhaps this is because of the important characteristic of this raga which is a wavering around the pa or 5th note; one might call this the ethos of Sindhi Bhairavi.

This is the ascending scale as transcribed by Ali Akbar Khan:

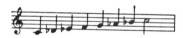

and the descent which gives it this especial flavour:

Again and again according to our way of thinking accidentals appear in his playing, shifting the dha^k (A♭) to A♮ and then back again; sometimes modifying the reh^k (D♭) to D♮, and diminishing even the pa (G) to what we would term an F♯. The irregularity, if such it may be called, of this sequence—A♭, F♯ F♮ E♭ D♭ E♮—is like the shuttle of a loom sliding either side of the main strand. Abdul Karim Khan, whose early recordings have now been transferred to LP, brings out the saddened quality of this raga most clearly in his singing, dwelling as he does upon the minor 6th and 7th notes and then coming to rest upon the 5th note, pa or G.

But once, in London, Ali Akbar Khan played this raga and

admitted to me afterwards that he felt very much at odds with the world. He used it this time as a launching-platform from which to reach out to other associated ragas, so creating a necklace of ragas, known as a ragamala (or raagmaal), threading one into the other with an interspersing of the melodic line of Sindhi Bhairavi. He did not care to do this on the appropriate note which would normally be the catch with which to unlatch the door to the next consonant melody, but chose angular notes of dissonance for the veering away at a tangent. In so doing (and I may say with extraordinary virtuosity and the final paradoxical harmony of the integrated artist working in depth), he chose all manner of ragas in minor keys, with the result that the feeling of anger was passionately displayed.

He struck the appropriate dissonances with heavy accentuation, thus arousing all manner of complementary senses: disturbance, unease, yet at the same time vibrant expectancy. Even his accompanying tambura player, Prodyot Sen, was shaking his head, amazed at the quality and sheer brilliance of his play that night. Sindhi Bhairavi will never be quite the same again after this singular performance. So it is with Indians who remember well loved ragas associated with certain moods or incidents, and recall them with intimations in a Wordsworthian sense of readiness, awaiting the exposition as a musician prepares to create a raga anew.

There are other ragas that stand out clearly also and demand a certain way of playing because of the predominance of a well defined mood arising out of the svaras in use and their relationship with each other.

Using the association of veera rasa with the dominant note reh, there is the classical severity of Abhogi Raga with its stately procession of tones. The use of ma in Malavi Raga brings out its sweet lyricism. I heard it played in Paris by Ravi Shankar at a great UNESCO concert; suddenly I was astonished to find myself humming September in the Rain across the melody, so closely are popular and classical intertwined.

This is in no sense a derogatory reflection on Indian classical music; there are many occasions when it is easier for a Westerner to recall a melody from a great musical of the Rogers and Hammerstein genus or a Gershwin tune, simply because their single-line melodies are so marked and embossed in comparison to the complex chordal harmonies of symphonic music or the diffuse music of a chamber quartet. Even *The Times'* music correspondent at a concert of Indian music discerned phrases in the descending shape of Sindhi Bhairavi 'strongly reminiscent of Gershwin's It Ain't Necessarily So' and, in the second section, reminders of Merseyside beat-tunes.

To liken the one with the other is inevitable for the Westerner: melody and rhythm are so pronounced in Indian classical music that jazz and our lighter musical themes are bound to spring to mind; themes from *Porgy and Bess* and *West Side Story* and Scottish ballads are easily whistled. One doesn't need an orchestra to evoke such music, but it is difficult to hold Bach in the mind without the aid of instruments. Simply because popular music is still regarded as second best by our own classicists, it does not mean that Indian music which occasionally arouses memories of these kinship melodies has to be relegated to such a secondary position. Such aesthetic compartmentalizing is not only a misnomer, but a false premise as well. Classical and light music are of equal relevance to the human condition, and the work by the Pink Floyd, The Who, Deep Purple and Led Zepperlin, and George Harrison and John Lennon, have as much merit, by any standards of judgement, as works by other musicians.

There are ragas which stand out particularly in my mind because of associations of ideas, but which therefore mean little to the next listener. I remember Bhatiyar, a morning raga of great dignity and solemnity playing on the major tone of its tonic, sa, as being inextricably linked with the tranquility of that opening sequence in the famous Aparojit trilogy of films made by the prize-winning Bengali producer, Satyajit Ray, where the sweep of doves in curving flight fall over the glinting waters of the Ganges. I cannot help but recall my own personal memories of the early heat of the sun in Benares as it fell upon the dawn crowds while we all sat upon the worn steps of the Das Aswamedha Ghat. As I reflected on the majestic sweep of the sacred river at Benares, all of India seemed to chant, 'Ram kaa naam . . . Ram kaa naam' in worship of God, while fat priests lazed under their gigantic plantain umbrellas. Here is a mood, never to escape the opening passages of Bhatiyar Raga.

There is Chandra Kauns fluctuating around the 7th note, ni, with its pensive minor mode; and Todi, the king of ragas according to some Indians, with its scale of four 'black' notes: reh^k, ga^k, ma^t, dha^k (D♭, E♭, F♯ and A♭ if transposed into our C major scale) recalling similarities with a five-note pentatonic scale and, for me, always conjuring up the stately muted grace and mellowness of Brahms' well known Clarinet Quintet in E minor.

D   N   S   R   G   R   G   M   D   N   S   N   D   M   D   M   G   R   G   R   S

If one cares to listen to the Ali Akbar recording of this raga one can feel the sombreness brought out in the wavering passages from the reh^k to the ma^t and the total absence of the 5th note, pa, in both ascent and descent. The two-tone separation between the dha^k and the 2nd pure substantive ma in descent, only adds, by its dissonance, to the doleful effect of this raga, as does the juxtaposition of ga^k, reh^k and sa.

One raga that personally grows in import and subtleties over the years is Marwa Raga. It concentrates its force on five notes and deliberately omits the 5th note, Pa, and its 1st note or tonic, sa, except for the passing effect of touching it when it is least expected, so heightening the tension in a quite indefinable and tantalizing way. Its scale begins with the tonic sa, reh^k ga, ma^t and dha, passing over the upper sa to upper reh^k and omitting the tonic in descent.

To me it is a Beethoven of ragas. Played by Ravi Shankar at his most austere it was set in an impressive devotional mood in a memorable concert at the Wigmore Hall in London years ago, and the concentration of all his power upon the passages from the 2nd note (flattened) to the neighbouring ga onwards through ma to the 6th note dha (always omitting the 5th) underlined the emotional seriousness and poignancy of the music. This was the spiritual ras at its most powerful.

Sung by such an individualistic master as Ameer Khan it is transformed into a raga of great tenderness, even sensuality, as he uses his lingering voice almost in a whisper in the lower register, moving slowly over the alaap, expounding and enlarging as a meditative thinker on the opening sthayi or level exposition of a few notes.

Ameer Khan's interpretation of Raga Marwa, transcribed by John Barham and Leela Charles.

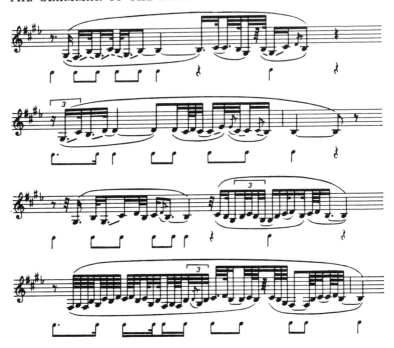

It is interesting to watch how he gives his own unique rendering of this raga. He sings in the key of D♮ so that the whole scale needs to be transposed in Western terms, the tonic sa moving up a tone from C to D. In our keyboard it would be transposed thus:

D♮,	E,	F♯,	G,	A,	B,	C♯,	D♮.
doh,	ray,	me,	fah,	soh,	lah,	tee,	doh.
sa,	reh,	ga,	ma,	pa,	dha,	ni,	sa.

But in the Indian scale for this raga the note reh is komal (flattened) and ma is tivra (sharpened). Pa is totally omitted. Even sa is un-emphasized. So Marwa scale as sung by Ameer Khan runs as follows on the Western keyboard:

D♮ E♭ F♯ G♯ B C♯ D♮
Sa Reh Ga Ma Dha Ni Sa

He especially lingers on the dominating note reh (E♭), coming to rest on it at the end of most phrases, or on its samvadi note dha (B), and uses the tonic note only lightly as a leading note to the vadi or dominant reh.

Once the tonic has been established, only then does he remind the listener of its presence *en passant*, or he touches it in mid-phrases where it presents a curiously dissonant sound. This ability of the Indian vocalist consciously to omit a specified note if tradition has laid down that this rule is to be obeyed within a certain raga, is teasing to the subconscious urge within one's own listening to slide towards this very same note, it often being a necessary complement to the next note within tonal laws. Considerable tension can be created this way, which is an intrinsic component for arousing the emotional 'pull' of a raga. In the following passage Ameer Khan is effectively playing on four 'black' notes and on the B♮ or samvadi dha which he deliberately emphasizes by pausing on it. Note the almost total absence of sa and D♮, and the pakad: dha ma ga reh (B♮ G♯ F♯ E♭).

Ameer Khan's gravel voice is a curious mixture of the Negro

depth of timbre with a top layer of the soft soil of operatic richness; the whisper of the meditative passages is pure poetry in the lower register, flowing 'over the ear like the breath of the sweet south

> That breathes upon a bank of violets
> Stealing and giving odour'.

An English musician once used the word 'ravished' when he talked of the effect Indian music had on him. Marwa Raga can be said to do just this through the voice of this unusual master-vocalist.

These are further characteristic phraseologies, as notated by Debabrata Chaudhuri, the young sitar player who in 1967 emerged into the Western world as yet one more successful such artist:

Raga Marwa:

Sa = C as tonic.
    Reh is komal; ma is major 4th slightly sharpened.
    Pa is totally omitted.

A dash is used as a pause between short phrases; in Indian notation the dot below indicates the lower register, above – the upper register; a line under a note means komal, a stroke above, tivra.

etc.

Note the lingering pause before the final tonic, the repetitive phrase of ma^t, ga, reh^k, and the reaching for the upper reh in the sixth line. This is also noticeable on Ameer Khan's recording.

Pandit Bhatkhande gives these phrases as the sthayi or level phrasing in the first introductory exposition:

ni reh^k ga ma^t ni dha–ma^t ga reh^k ga ma^t ga reh^k sa–
ni reh^k ni dha   ma dha sa–   ni reh ga ma   ga reh^k sa–
 · ·   · ·   ·

and in the antara, the enlargement into the upper register of a raga:

ma^t dha ma^t ga ma^t dha sa–   ni reh^k ga ma^t ga reh^k ra–
reh^k ni dha ni   dha ma^t dha ma^t ga reh^k ga ma^t ga reh^k sa–

In the taans or quick notes of these phrases Bhatkhande gives the following (sa = middle C, vadi is reh^k, samvadi is dha):

taan slide

Marwa has been recorded on a French disc by Ramnarayan, the sarangi player, (the brother of the late Chatur Lal, the tabla player), as though it were a Gaelic folk-song telling of a lovers' parting as it slurs repeatedly over the reh, dha, ni to the sa. One could wish for a longer exposition as it is somewhat abruptly terminated. The keynote is transposed, sa being F♯, so that the scale in our keyboard interpretation would run:

F♯	A♭	B♭	B	C♯	E♭	F	F♯
sa	reh	ga	ma	pa	dha	ni	sa
doh	ray	me	fah	soh	lah	tee	doh

But in Marwa Raga reh is komal, therefore A♭ becomes G; m ais tivra so B becomes C; and pa (C♯) is omitted altogether. Marwa scale in this transposition therefore runs: F♯ G B♭ C E♭ F♮ G, and the descent line: G F♮ E♭ C B♭ G F♮ E♭, slurring back to F♯ (sa): reh ni dha ma, ga, reh ni, dha.

There is constant play in the contrasting dissonances of the E♭ to C and the lightly touched note sa (F♯) as Ramnarayan passes from reh to dha in the fall from G, through F♯ to F (ni) and E♭ (dha). There is a lovely cadence from upper E♭ (dha) through B♭ (ga) to G (reh). Most of the phrases come to rest on the vadi note dha, which is E♭. The poignant relationship of these particular orders and usage of the notes conjures up all the sadness of Irish ballads telling about death at sea, the mystery of the deep ocean, the racing of the scudding spray–this added to the call from the lonely voice singing mournfully in the sarangi strings.

Darbari Raga, one of the serious ragas most popular with Indian audiences, so well known and awaited with such awareness in their concerts, is taken in slow tempo with few flourishes except for the characteristic shake on A♭ (dhaᵏ) and the E♭ (gaᵏ).

It is known as the Prince of Ragas, depicting as it does the mood of dignity and grandeur of the great courts or durbars held by the Moghul emperors.

These are the figurations given by Pandit Bhatkhande:

(a) ni sa, reh ga^k, reh sa,
    ma pa, dha^k, ni^k s̈a
(b) in descending phrases:
    s̈a, dha^k, ni^k, pa ma pa, ga^k, ma reh, sa

with a repetitive pakad that marks Darbari out, the vadi being reh, samvadi pa:

The time for playing is midnight. (To indicate how Indians respond to this raga I quote a recent critique of a musical concert in Delhi in the summer of 1970: 'Darbari played on the sarod by Sharan Rani was a connoisseur's delight. This is the kind of raga where the training and the understanding of the artist are both put to the supreme test. The moment the first "reh dha" was touched the performance was on all fours. The ga and dha in this raga are achieved correctly with the help of microtones and gentle oscillations delicately but clearly touched upon.')

In complete contrast to such a heavyweight raga is Lajwanti, composed by Ustad Ali Akbar Khan for his daughter of the same name. It is full of mellifluous sound, lilting and sweet and nostalgic all at the same time, with its characteristic shakes on dha (6th note) and ga (3rd).

Raga Lajwanti

These then are some of the basic patterns of ragas which have been pruned to the bone. The spirit cannot be defined. Much depends on the musician's skill in conjuring up the intrinsic nature of the raga. A well known Indian writer on the subject of arts and aesthetics, O. C. Gangoly, in his book *Ragas and Raginis*, makes this point: '. . . no amount of mechanical reproduction of its symphonic structure can put life into the melody . . . and unless it is alive in the song or instrument it does not fulfil its purpose. A raga or ragini is something more than its physical form–its symphonic structure–its "body". It has a "soul" which comes to dwell and inhabit in the "body". In the language of Indian poetics, this "soul"–this principle–is known as the rasa, or flavour, sentiment, impassioned feeling and . . . a successful performer (sādhăk) must be familiar with the image form as well as the sound form.'

If the burden for the musician is so much, how much also must be the sympathetic understanding from the audience, being *au fait* with the image-building. This constitutes especial difficulties of rapport with Western audiences unfamiliar with either the technique or the spirit of such music. We have to become like the devout old woman who suddenly and spontaneously sings to God in a pew of that vast cathedral of St Peter's in Rome when there is no service being conducted and when people are milling around her. She is much nearer to intuitive oneness with the Indian people and the richness of their enjoyment of life than we who sit rather stiffly as audiences, inhibited by our conventions of concert-going and our self-control. If only we could climb out of these psychological strait-jackets, despite our fears of making fools of ourselves, it would all be so much easier! And certainly one would be freer to discover what Indians experience as they share the exploration of the music along with the performing musician. I have asked Ravi Shankar whether he does not find it dampening to his spirit to play to Western audiences when they do not know how to respond. He admitted that it did sometimes affect his playing and that he relied on his fellow musicians on stage to reinforce the ambience of the occasion. He was not at his best, so this is why he prefers student audiences, who give of their emotions more enthusiastically.

I have dealt later on with the effect audiences do have on their great masters but it is also relevant here as we discuss what a raga can do to the emotions of the listener by the repeated concentration on certain salient points of the melody. Professor Mukherji has taken account of what must strike a good many foreigners when they first recline through the lengthening hours of an Indian concert: the abstract figures which Indian musicians, most especially singers, carve into the air with their arms and hands, more often than not with their eyes closed.

'Apart from the physical need,' he writes, 'there is another meaning of such movements, and listeners would do well to follow them. The Indian musician is in a sense a conductor with hands as a baton. The true reason is that Indian music is contemplative even in its execution. So at least two contemplators, the musician and the listener, must meet. The third is the accompanist. Contemplation may be of various types, religious, philosophical and aesthetic. But all types tend to conform to the angelic types of each raga. The attainment of the dhyan-murti–the angelic–the divine or the archetypal form, which can be sensed only by contemplation, is the supreme endeavour of every artist. Musicians believe that if the proper notes of the raga are struck, the presiding spirit, devata, stands out in the fullness of being. Numerous stories are told about how rains came, flowers blossomed, and the goddess appeared in human form before the ustad, the master. Beautiful stanzas depict the image–dhyan-murti–in detail. The Indian musician, if he is worth anything, is constantly trying to bring up the image and unfold it before the vision of the sympathetic listener. It is a double process–invocation and evocation. The listener too should not be ignorant of the contour and substance of the image. By shutting the eyes and moving the hands, invocation, evocation and exchange are facilitated. But modern listeners often fail the contemplative musician.'

I have quoted both these writers at length because they exemplify the essentially Indian frame of mind where imaginative response and emotional inspiration are trained into the one channel of spiritual enlargement. There is a moral in it for us, in that we shall have to become much more learned in their philosophical background and their culture if we are ever to be worthy audiences for their best musicians when they visit our hemisphere. They have for a long time been conversant with our civilization and its culture; they give our classical musicians, dramatists and artists years of study even early on in their education. It is only equitable that this imbalance should now be righted.

THE COMPONENT PARTS OF A RAGA

Alaap or Alapana

The raga as played in most Sangeet Sammelans and private concerts is made up of two sections. The first consists of an *alaap* pronounced as written. This is the introduction or prelude which is in slow free time at the beginning; it is thoughtful and expository. It is essentially 'linear' music, the effect being from one melodic line without the deepening effect of an overall rhythm. The important notes are dwelt upon, the motifs are established and returned to for emphasis. The exposition of the alaap plays around the first four notes of the scale in use (i.e. the first part of the tetrachord in which the vadi or predominant note is usually located), which is usually in the middle octave and just below middle C.

This reiteration of the vadi note sets it in the ear of the listener and performer, and helps to contrast it against the tonic note recurring very frequently on the drone strings. If it so happens that the vadi note appears in the upper part of the scale (from pa to upper sa) then the subsidiary dominating note, usually two or three tones away from the vadi, is placed to the forefront of the sthayi section. Movement is very much restricted. In many ways the alaap is the most acceptable part in Hindustani music (although not necessarily in Carnatic), once the intrigue and excitement gleaned from the virtuosity of percussion-playing has abated for the newcomer. When played on such sensitive instruments as the sitar and the sarod this section is vibrant with melody and after several performances can become familiar enough even to the Western layman to enable one to hum an accompaniment to it.

The tempo of the alaap gradually increases in rhythm – this is the *jor* – and then passes into a rapid and complex graph of sound when the theme and phrases that have to be established in the main body of the raga at a later stage, are placed again and again before the listener. This is the *jhalla*.

The alāpana of a Carnatic raga is not so important, nor does it divide itself into sections like this.

Gat

The gat is the final fixed instrumental composition after the alaap, comprising a number of different but related sections which are given special thematic treatment in the shuddh notes so clearly stated before. Short phrases, for instance, are repeated rapidly with emphasis on the sum or emphatic start to a rhythmic cycle. Certain ratios of notes–6 notes followed by 4, followed by 6–are used in patterns after each other, repeated for several 'bars'. These movements are called tisram, mishram (7 notes followed by 4) and chatasram (8 notes alternating with 4). Melody notes are rapidly interspersed in the jhalla with 1, 2 or 3 notes struck on the drone strings, and there are short repetitive phrases played over 3 times culminating on the sum. These are known as tihais.

At this point when the gat commences so does the all-important tala or beat, introduced now as a well defined pulse to the music to replace the rhythm or laya which one senses as a ground swell, rather than as individual waves, in the alaap. The actual tala chosen is up to the main artist, and never the drum player, unless of course he is playing solo. About 12 main talas are in common use nowadays. As for the ragas, an artist of middle-ranging calibre will have mastered about 75 to 100 ragas and will perhaps be able to expound about 35–40 to fuller depth, without any sheet notation at all.

RAGAS AND RAGINIS

As each raga has such strong emotive values, the mental picture of a raga was conjured up during centuries of evolution, and these qualities took on masculine and feminine personality. Their emotional content was therefore categorized and depicted in paintings which appeared in the Moghul period, 'visualized music' as Percy Brown, great lover of India art and one-time principal of Calcutta's College of Art, has called it.

Ragas were thought of as masculine and depicted male qualities of wonder, courage and anger. Raginis expressed feminine qualities of love, laughter and sorrow. These were conceived of as feminine by Indian theorists because of 'their subordination to the tonal structure of the raga'. Neuters expressed fear, disgust and peace.

The most explicit interpretations of these charming miniature paintings has been given in O. C. Gangoly's *Ragas and Raginis* where he dissects with his analytical perception the 'multiplicity of moods' down to the finest detail: '. . . the pangs of separation alone have been classified into a dozen types distinguishable by age, season, locale and the earlier emotional predicament. Crossed in love, expectancy, half-crossed, double-crossed, angry, self-abasing, aggressive – each mood is marked by its own features, colour, background, and the musician singing a song or playing a raga is expected not to depart from, but to conform to them to the best of his ability.'

Interestingly enough, in contemporary underground experiments with Western music, colour relationships with certain tones has come to the fore again. This is clearly catching up with Indian thinking, for astrology long ago tabulated the correspondence between colours, musical notes and flower scents. These were related to the zodiacal influences of the planets and the personal temperament of human beings.

Rimbaud, Newton and Goethe have all expressed theories on the association of colour and vibration. Newton regarded the spectrum as an octave. Goethe gave colours to the timbre of musical instruments and Rimbaud tried to create a language of colour: white E, red I, blue O and green U.

Only recently a letter from a Mr Gerald Denley of Coventry was published in the Sunday *Observer* in Britain; in this he referred to the Indian Raga Bhairavi which found its way into Europe through Andalusian music: 'The predominating colour of the Bhairavi is orange, and its effect on flamenco music is to make it glow with warmth, for this music invigorates the entire nervous system. It is not by chance that orange and red are the predominating colours of the gypsies. If "colour is not in the rose but in ourselves" then sound vibrations of varying lengths may affect us as much as colours do, with very similar results!'

It now only needs scientific research into the structure of sound and colour to discover if there is correspondence between the two sensory perceptions and, if there is, to interrelate them in psychosomatic terms. The earliest Hindu thinkers of over 4000 years ago might then be proved correct.

DRONE

To give the drone any particular importance will seem strange to Indians but when listening to any Indian music the first comment often made by the newcomer is about the drone. The repeated and continuous sound, the general reverberations, make a mesmeric effect upon anyone unfamiliar with this ubiquitous element of

Indian music. Sometimes it is even difficult to concentrate on the playing of the raga because of the continual process of being 'drawn back' to the tonic or the fundamental note which is thrust into one's consciousness by the drone.

It contributes the hypnotic effect of which Yehudi Menuhin so often speaks. The drone is somewhat akin to the permanent drone of the bagpipes (although not so sombre nor strident) and runs as a horizontal thread through all the clusters of intricately beaded sound, giving both unity and a curious liberation.

The first reaction to this sense of liberation in the mind is suspense, a waiting for the resolution upon either the tonic or the emphasized note of the raga.

It is as though the magnetic pull was of overpowering force, demanding this resolution, this coming-together from all the varying spirals and swerving eddies of sound which the figurations and melodic movements have stirred up. Out of the apparent confusion all the interlinking lines fall gracefully into one unending line, like the resolution of a cat's cradle.

It is on one of these two notes, vadi or samvadi, that the emphatic beat of the sum starts up a new cycle of rhythm, both instruments, melodic and percussive, should meet as a general principle, although this is not a hard and fast rule. It is at this crucial point that the drone should stress the tonic.

Indian musicians have told me that it is very difficult for the Western mind to appreciate the full impact of this culmination in drone technique – this 'drone-feed' so to speak from tampura player to solo vocalist especially or to instrumentalist when in full flight of imagination. It is as though a hypodermic needle had sent them on a trip and they were projected forwards on a thrust of adrenalin. Such is the actual physical thrill of the experience to master-musicians who are each going their separate ways on cycles of improvization when by instinct and the force of grammar they come together on the sum with a kind of spontaneous combustion causing a sudden firing of all the artists.

Intellect and emotion are totally identified at these rare moments of supreme identification. When listening to Indian music at the beginning of one's experience it is a help to single out the notes played on the strings of the tampura, the most frequently used drone instrument. This does aid the mind to follow what the soloist is doing, and to pick out which notes he is choosing to rest upon for emphasis while building up the structure of the melodic theme. At first one does tend to lose track, being so absorbed by the general rush of tones and vibratory overtones. Then like the swoop of the hawk, the ear pulls the mind back with a sudden jerk to the notes being carried on the four strings of the tampura.

There is no absolute rule on tuning the pitch of the drone. This depends on the main artist and his selection of a basic pitch, or level of sa which remains the same whatever raga scale is used. A whole concert may be played thus; with the one basic pitch even two musicians singing together will have to tune to the same keynote. This in itself undermines serious experiment in counterpoint and the criss-crossing tonal structures inherent in the overlapping of different strata in Western musical compositions. Uniformity of pitch poses problems of dynamics for Indian musicians who wish to experiment in conjunction unassailable. Ravi Shankar with his searching spirit and exacting professional standards has now made the first honest attempt with his 1971 Concerto for Sitar. This blends certain Western principles of pitch and the volume of a full-scale Western symphony orchestra with the constancy of tuning of his own sitar, (c♯ = tonic) and its delicacy of sound. With ingenuity he has constructed certain methods of hooking the main strings of the sitar so that at the end of one movement the pitch can be shifted slightly without the full-scale intricacies of retuning such a finely attuned instrument as the sitar. He was able to move the tonic from D in Raga Khamaj to B in Sindhi Bhairavi to E in Raga Adana and back to D in Manj Khamaj. This is no mean feat, even if the ragas were chosen for their affinities. These are their melody lines: underlined notes accord with Indian diminished tones, not Western.

Khamaj (tonic = D; stress on ga and pa):

Ni Sa Ga Ma Pa Dha Ni Sa   Sa Ni Dha P   M P D M   G M P G M R S

Sindhi Bhairavi (tonic = B):

S R N S G M P G M D N Ṡ   Ṡ N Ḋ N D P M G R G R S

Adānā (tonic = E):

<u>N</u> S R M P <u>N</u> M P Ṡ   D <u>N</u> P M P <u>G</u> M R S

Mans Khamaj (tonic = D; stress on ma and dha):

S G M P G P M G M P D <u>N</u> D N Ṡ

<u>N</u> D P M G P M   G M R S <u>N</u> S <u>N</u> D

In a sense this experiment is a beginning. There is still a compromise in that the orchestra is still used in unison, but when one thinks of the formidable obstacles that Ravi Shankar has already overcome in bringing a complete Western orchestra to the task of following Indian melodic structure and rhythm, one is grateful that he has the knowledge of both systems which enables him to dare where others fear to tread. Imitative passages between orchestra and solo sitar may sound strange, to Western ears, but the entire experiment has opened up further stages of exploration, now that this musician has mastered the knowledge of Western orchestral functioning. One's private hopes remain that suggestions of counterpoint, contrast and harmony may be the next step although Ravi Shankar strongly believes that these elements, once established, might destroy the essence, the bhaav (previously discussed) of the raag.

With an annoying and ironical obstinacy I was even aware of the missing background of drone. Perhaps someday an orchestra is going to have to engineer such a feedback if Indian music is to sound authentic in partnership with Western instruments.

In the true Indian experience, hearing a raga for the first time is like standing in a great marshalling yard where trains and their coaches are shunted back and forth, taken out on the track as befits the ordered mind of the comptroller, and then returned to their sidings while another set of different length and style are brought out for use; the shuttling is going on all the time. Or it feels like travelling on some fairground wheel of gigantic size, always returning to base no matter how long the intervening lapse of time. And when one does return there, one can hear, coincident with the underlying recall of the drone, the emphasis of the drum upon the tonic or the dominant 4th or 5th note. All the phrasings of the melodic line and the drum line coincide on the sum. The signal is instantaneously given for another 'letting out of the line' before reeling in the listener again towards another resolution.

I often see the drone in terms of painting and tapestry; it is the backcloth on which the artist weaves his pictures of sound with all the embroidered ornamentations that are possible without its becoming florid and baroque.

I am constantly reminded of Botticelli's famous painting of Primavera, the Allegory of Spring, arranged in a frieze-like pattern of unusual linear quality. Each group of figures is curiously self-contained, unrelated to any other: Venus in the middle stands alone, a painting within a painting; the three Graces move solely within their own orbit also; Mercury at the far left remains static, playing no part in the general scene, yet provides the stopping-point in the movement. The same quantities and characteristics are there in a raga. The drone gives wholeness. The tala breaks the linear shape into recognizable quantities. The movement and restatements upon a theme, the pakad (special grouping of notes like a refrain), are there, self-contained and standing in their own right.

The interest is heightened by the duplication of shade and tone upon what is already there in the background. The merging gives luminosity and depth of plane; and the contrast of colours (when the embroidery of graces are jagged and unblended purposefully in dissonances) alerts the mind to the tension which is in all disequilibrium.

Because Indian music is modal it is based on the same complex and magnetic relationship as painting. The interrelationship of the svaras or full tones and their fragmentary graces with the 'permanent invariable' note – the tonic – and their own introspective relationship one with another (svara and sruti), both undergo the same detailed build-up between planes of activity as a Cézanne oil-painting.

As the music becomes more familiar the ear tends to forget the drone. It is there, and that is enough. But without the tampura or the sarangi or the in-built drone strings on a resonating stringed instrument, the vocalist especially would be lost. He relies on the constancy of the drone to enable him to use the dissonances and accidentals not common to a specific raga in order to decorate its limited notes. There is a very real purpose in the drone's maintaining a steady level, in order to sustain the comparison with the pivotal note, the amsa, which may appear high (and the tone spirited) or low (and the tone reflective). Against this background continuity a vocalist can compare what he is singing at any given moment. Such vocalists can be seen in performances cupping their hands to one ear to aid them in doing just this. In this way they pick up the consonances generated by the harmony of the drone; it acts as an anchor from which they can launch forth into further voyages of exploration – the passages of improvization.

Mr Goswami says in his book on Indian music that 'the passage from one note to another is *not made abruptly but as smoothly as possible*'. This is very different from our own music. It is the general practice of the artist to return to sa (doh) and the dominant while singing, 'so as to compare his voice with the fundamental'. Hence the fascination for the beginner in following the drone and comparing it with the melodic line of the raga when it becomes unmistakably clear.

And so the raga is complete. The joy of new discovery is always there. Each time one comes to it after a long absence, there is a freshness of new interpretation. The summing-up I can leave to Jayaram Iyer. In his patient and understanding way he was always willing to explain in terms understandable to even the slowest-witted alien how his own music functioned. He had himself composed a theme based on the very old South Indian raga, Mukhari, the scale of which runs: sa, re^k, reh, ma, pa, dha^k, dha, sa. I caught a hint even in those early days in New Delhi before I ever journeyed South to my spiritual home, of the lingering pathos swaying in the soft South Indian flutes.

He confirmed my thoughts. 'This is a sad raga. There is no oscillation as you see. Oscillation you do not like. I know how foreigners feel. You know, our ragas are like people. Each has its own personality. If you meet a man you remember his face. He has a personality in a room with many other men. So our ragas are like this. Some of our purists, the old orthodox musicians, would say that one raga has one emotion. Only one. It would be wonder, love or martial anger. But I do not believe this, even though I am a South Indian; you know that they say we are the same as we were 5000 years ago!

'I have been doing work on this and I find that there are many emotions in a raga. Emotions can be created in several ways. The musical note itself–a major–expresses happiness, love. And what you would call a minor key or flattened note expresses sadness and despair. Then the pitch of that note can influence our minds.'

He sang C in all the octaves.

'One octave higher from doh and it is more interesting and commanding. The sol-fa middle C is a dull note. It is like a man who is dull. You do not want to meet him for a long time. He has not much to say. But another person you can bring out.'

He sang C an octave even higher, with a ringing quality, elongating it and drawing it out.

'That has the quality of a speaking note. It can express love and joy. An octave higher and it screeches. Things have gone wrong. There is unhappiness.'

Then he jumped down to lower C.

'Here is night. It is mysterious, there are ghosts; in the darkness there is sense of foreboding. Many moods are expressed in the pitch of the note, you see. Then there is tempo and rhythm. A long slow tempo is like a man talking evenly and equably. He speaks smoothly. Too smoothly. He may put you to sleep! There is no jarring. But that can shake you up.'

He sang staccato.

'We are now dispirited, upset. Or the tempo can be fast and even. And always in our music there is tension. Notes are pulling this way and that, never quite coinciding with the dominant. The main ragas have so much in them to elaborate that you can go on expounding them for half an hour, an hour, even more.'

This is so. My husband and I sat many a time under the stars listening to concerts that sang and played their way long past the midnight hours, and more often until the dawn was well established. There was one occasion when that greatest of vocalists, Bade Ghulam Ali, sat for two hours developing the grandeur of the Raga Todi (pronounced with a palate 'r'–'Tori'). The hour of three in the morning came and still the audience was lying there on the cool lawns, some in armchairs, some sprawled in the shadows on carpets, some occasionally moving out of the crowd for a coffee from a nearby paan seller or to stretch their legs–this is permissible in the informality of India and in a concert where there is no fixed interval and where a musician is free to expound or contract according to his own inspiration of the moment and to when he feels he has given the raga all of his talent and skill.

Time is irrelevant.

Yehudi Menuhin has said that Indians have had more time to meditate than any other nation and that they have put it to good use. 'Most of life's experiences, thoughts, actions and divinations have their exact time and place, and music is no exception.'

I felt, certainly among these audiences bound as they were by indefinable ties of accepted traditions – a steady framework of un-questioned belief – and by the frail filaments of sound that coalesced into a tenacity of force and influence to which even I was susceptible though a complete outsider, that their music was indeed the yantra Dr Menon once called it.

This was more than music in the purely secular sense of com-mercial entertainment. Devotion had settled on the night air laden with the weight of the perfume from the raat-ki-rani blossom, and I experienced perhaps a touch of that comprehensive oneness that seems to suffuse the very air of India at times of potency such as this.

Chapter Five

MEMORIA TECHNICA

'*A stately pleasure dome decree . . .*
. . . a miracle of rare device.'
'Kubla Khan'
SAMUEL TAYLOR COLERIDGE

In the contemporary arts much of our preoccupation at the creative level of imagination now lies in the intangible world of matter as well as in the realm of spirit and mind. The disintegration of the outward forms of matter under the probing influence of science has led us on into the seemingly ineffable nature of existence and reality. Inevitably our concepts of space and form are changing as our comprehension is influenced by the new perspective which nuclear physics and biochemistry unfold in our curved flight into outer space, and by our perception of cells, molecular forms, crystallography and our knowledge of atoms, protons and the elusive neutrino particle.

Art is not a cloistered occupation. Every scientific concept is bound eventually to percolate through and to effect the artist's view of life. The Indian musician is as much concerned with this inner kernel of reality and its expression and statement in the flow of sound as the artist is in his struggle to give expression to what is so fugitive in representational art. The final, despairing statement of this search is, to me, a canvas by Mark Rothko in the United States. It is painted white–and left at that! There is no other way for this artist–it would appear–to show the ultimate moment when nuclear acid spurts into life and regeneration takes place in the ebb and flow which is the condition not only of man's existence but of the whole of the created universe.

Particles are always flaring into being in the vacuum of space and cosmic gases. Energy is constantly being made tangible.

In actual concrete terms the Indian musician captures this illusive process, but in absolutely the opposite way from Rothko's denial of form. The very concreteness of certain techniques which are put to work in Indian music achieve the same effect–para-doxically–by the melting away of so many specific outer forms which fuse into an inner abstract reality. The intense concentration of mind on the fractional details that constitute the expandable framework of the raag, forces one's own mind to explode beyond these finite limits, the rigid detailed grammer, into the abstract. Just in the same way the yogi, turning his eyes towards one specific pinpoint of light also blots it out paradoxically in the actual point of concentration, so moving beyond into a liberated area of experience where discipline releases the spirit rather than confines it.

Yehudin Menuhin clearly felt this when he wrote so intuitively about the experience: '. . . to appreciate Indian music one has to adopt a completely different sense of values . . . one must orientate oneself and, at least for the period concerned, forget there is a time-clock ticking away, and merely sink into a kind of subjective, almost hypnotic, trance. In that condition the repetitive features of Indian music, both rhythmic and melodic, acquire an extraordinary fascination and charm . . . despite the domination of this hypnotic mood, a characteristic of Indian music is that far from deadening the intellect, it actively liberates the mind.

'It is characteristic of the East to search itself, and for the individual to concentrate for hours, days and weeks upon one single object, be that a sound or a thought. In fact, the meditation of India is done in an attempt to cleanse the mind of trivial, transitory or inessential thought, leaving only a kind of exalted essence, a kind of superexistence, in which neither time nor space nor any of our material notions enter.'

It is told in India of the great saint Ramakrishna, who lived at the turn of this century, that on one of his tours he passed through Brindaban, the temple city east of Mathura, near Delhi. There he had a great desire to listen to a stringed instrument, the veena. For this purpose he journeyed to Benares and sought out the Pandit Mahesh Chandra Sarkar, an acknowledged master of the veena.

As Sarkar began to play Ramakrishna felt himself going into samadhi, a state of physical unconsciousness when the mind is withdrawn from outward sense of the body; literally one could call it 'being out of one's mind'. In fact it is just the opposite. It is a state of such concentrated awareness, far more intense than everyday consciousness, an activating meditation of the most inwardly creating kind.

This is what superexistence means to even the most untutored Indian mind.

How then is the structure of this stately pleasure dome built up, and in the process the attainment of liberation reached for the architect and viewer alike? In Indian music the melody is, after all, on its own; it has no support from the foundation-stones of harmony nor is buttressed by the layers of phrasing which counterpoint supplies. The architectonics have to be supplied therefore by all the minute and systematized techniques carried in the memory—the decorations and magical devices of grace and motifs and figurations, those short musical phrases which assume a distinctive character in the raga by virtue of their repetition and by the traditional approach to the notes of the chosen scale.

GAMAKA ALAMKARA OR GAMAAK ALAMKAAR

Gamaka and alamkara, taan and meend, tala and sensual caressing of the full tones with resonating voice and string—these constitute the architectonics. The echoes and the vibrations carry over, note to note, filling in all the spaces and bringing to the ear a sense of depth long after the musician has passed on to yet another passage being built up from the skeletal and basic scaffolding.

It has been said by experts on the two systems of music that ornamentation is essential to the Indian musician whereas it is incidental to the Western; but that the vibrations, the long slurs and trills, the tremolos, are only different in degree and style, not in kind. Indian instruments are, moreover, played with enormous wrist movements to emphasize these embellishments which are their flesh and blood. Grace notes are produced by a slight touch to the adjoining note, or by subtly passing over it using it as a prefix to the next note or as a suffix to the one just played.

It comes with a shock to listen to Western exposition of song in immediate contrast with an Indian vocalist of, say, Bade Ghulam Ali's calibre. Take Joan Sutherland for instance singing an aria from Bellini's *La Sonambula*. Her falling glissandos, the oscillation, slurring and grace notes are all there—but in a totally different quantity in the singing of her counterparts, Hirabai Barodekar or Keserbhai or Begum Akhtar. Her soprano voice cuts the notes one from another with diamond sharpness. There is no blurring into fuzziness at the edges. Even the glide is different, with not a single fusion of notes, and when she sings accelerando the notes still stand out, crystal clear, with none of the taanbazi of Indian vocalists. Taans are a peculiar characteristic of Indian grace notes, a rapid shimmering of successive notes in quick rhythm, creating a pattern of coherent sound. They give a spectacular display of dexterity in the cascade of notes, but not one note stands clearly apart from the next.

VARNA ALAMKARA

The *Sangeet Ratnakara* states that an ornamental vocalization which is known as an alamkara is a combination of several melodic phrases which make up altogether an overall movement or varna. These form into a geometric symmetry, a shape or a graph, using both shuddha (or full substantive) notes, or vikrit (modified) notes, according to the prescribed notes of the raga being played.

These shapes – the only word I can think of which is fitting because certain ragas with predominant movements do certainly take shape in the mind (an old recording of Ravi Shankar and Ali Akbar playing a dhun or light and romantic air from Palas-Kafi Raga illustrates the use of an unmistakable phraseology easily recognizable because of its likeness in shape to a melodic phrase from *Porgy and Bess*) – these shapes grow in different ways depending on the mood of the performer at the immediate moment in time, or on the characteristics of a certain raga. Jerky shapes, for instance, denote disquiet and are very different from the serene, smooth-flowing ligato phrases expressive of meditation found in, say, early-morning ragas, this being the time of prayer in India. Or they can be idiosyncratic to a certain performer, as some of Ali Akbar's performances become when he takes his characteristic plunge into the lower register from the middle level of the sthayi.

A flute player or vocalist on the other hand may be especially dexterous with fast-moving oscillation on fractionally separated tones, as are Bismillah Khan, Pannalal Gosh, Nazakat and Salamat Ali; or he may prefer long runs of ascending and descending notes, as Subbulakshmi does on occasion or Ravi Shankar when playing the fast gat. Such runs are not unlike runs in certain arias when a soprano wishes to display the technique behind the voice production, rather than its melodiousness and timbre; these emerge in the

slower, lingering passages. Such singers in India are of the orthodox variety; vocalists like Bade Ghulam Ali, Semmangudi Srinavasa Iyer and Subbulakshmi have no need to show off their mastery
of technique (which they could do if they so desired) but sing with
sentiment and rich, warm tones, their voices fluted and miracu-
lously floating in the air like the purest bird-song.

There are four different kinds of varna alamkaras, derived as
they are from four different varnas or types of melodic movement
known as sthayi, antara, sanchari, and abhog.

VARNA MELODIC MOVEMENTS

Sthayi or Asthayi

A melody which holds the same note repetitively and moves around
it fractionally, or which moves up and down the special scale of the
raga in these shaped phrases of two or three connected notes
moving in progression (1 2 3, 2 3 2, 3 4 3, etc.) above and below the
keynote, returning again to the starting note at the same level where
it began, coming to rest upon the keynote, is termed sthayi or
asthayi. This is the first section of a raga. This term is still used and
is of importance in 'getting to know a raga' and being able to recognize it, because what happens in the beginning is the statement of
what is to follow throughout the raga. It will be heard, echoed,
repeated with minute variations (and half the fun is to be ready for
these surprises when they happen—or, for the novice, to be able
even to recognize them!), moved an octave up and down, or taken
up and spoken in the drum language of the second section, the
antara.

Antara

The whole section of the sthayi swings around a prominent note in
a very limited way so as to place it well and truly in the listener's
ear. The second movement or succession of notes to be organized
organically is based on the ascending scale. This movement takes
the melodic line up in gradations from one note to the next and
flings out figurative streamers, scoops or slurs around those notes.
But even then it is not to be mistaken as a *logical* ascent, taken note
by note upwards.

A similar treatment of the descending scale is known as the

avarohi. This is the most accentuated of the two scales, containing in ninety-five per cent of the cases the modified notes.

Sanchari

This third movement and its 'examination' by the instrumentalist or the vocalist takes the raga forwards and like the first movement is of no fixed length. The duration of this exposition is entirely up to the soloist, his inspiration, mood and inventiveness. Some gifted vocalists could spend half an hour in extempore exploration whereas a lesser musician might touch only a few of the permutations possible.

This mixture of the previous two movements opens up many avenues for the competent musician to explore. If we arbitrarily take our own B♭ scale just as an exercise in this, a particular way of grouping the notes – even using the B♮ as an accidental – might take place around the B♭, A and B; or there might be a slide down to the G, F, E♭, as in Raga Bahar:

1 4 5 3♭ 4 7♭ 6 7♮ 8 8 7♭ 6 7♮ 5 4 5 3♭ 4 2 1 7♭ 6 7♭ 2 1

Here is the wobble around the 6th note, the 7th and the 4th, and again in the phrase: 5, 4, 5, 3, 4. A movement around the F, G and E into E♭ may develop, and the wavering around B♭ and A may move down into the lower register. This is a much simplified illustration of what a musician does to create a movement forwards, taking upward and downward sweeps and intermingling them. It is second nature to him, and even if he is asked to play a scale in Western notation it is immediate to the ear that the notes do not descend chromatically and in consecutive order as a moving escalation downwards, but rather in groupings of notes which slightly reverse the downward flow in order to play around the notes which are constantly to be accentuated as being important to a particular raag. Since those early days of Matanga this principle has become highly elaborate and embellished with every conceivable kind of microtonal device, grouping and tied notes echoing and underscoring the prime notes of the scale from the sympathetic strings of the instrument or from the vibrations (or garglings as it first seems before familiarity with the use of the voice dispels this idea) of the singer's vocal chords.

In the decorative phraseology, sthayi is straightforward vocalizing on a level, easing back in repetitive patterns to the same starting note or to its octave or tonic, etc.:

S S R R S S R R G G R R G G M M G G M M P P M M

Arochi are the ascending ornaments, working around one note then moving up and starting again on a different and higher one:

S G R G M G P M P D P N D N S N

Avarohi are just the opposite from the above, working down in reverse order, but in a different pattern:

S N D N D P D P M P M G
etc.

Sanchari are the mixing up of all the three previous forms into really elaborate interweavings and permutations of a complex multitude which often sound like a whirlpool of sound:

etc.

Again, this is a very arbitrary transference to our piano notation. It is a distorted simplification but it illustrates visually an approximation of the principle behind the *memoria technica* which every musician carries in his brain from years of hard labour memorizing by ear. It is only put here to indicate again a visual image of what is happening in a far more sustained and splintered way as the notes are joined in quick light runs.

Abhog

Abhog is the final coda, a reiteration of all these elements and their mixing up, but complex though the dense patterns may become, the principles are always there in an essential simplicity. Now it can be seen why an Indian concert can be so elastic. There is no end to the mathematical formulas. All manner of structural devices can be build upon the melodic line of chosen notes in the scale. Great skyscrapers could be founded on two or three notes alone if a musician wished to loose all sense of proportion and go berserk with structural permutations. But he never does because of that ubiquitous sense of discipline which devotional training gives him, and the powerful Indian desire for balance between the two forces of symmetry and asymmetry, the intellectual demands (in the mathematical design) and the claims of emotional release (through rasa).

Inwards and upwards go the geometric designs. There can be a simple graceful shape, curving like the dome of a mosque and repeated without much change in structure, or an involuted, spiralling construction like a curving staircase, or perhaps a long stepped-up flight of stairs. The length and the period sustained are up to the individual performer. He may linger in the sthayi, the first straightforward statement, with sensuous joy as Ali Akbar and Amjad Ali do after a long-sustained striking of the tonic or dominating notes. Then there may be a swift alighting on the notes of the raga scale and a long pull on the string, elongating the notes so that they are suspended and curling in the echo-chamber of the instrument.

The following notation by John Barham of Ali Akbar's recording of Sindh Bhairavi provides by far the most exact translation into Western terms by any young Western musician working in the dual field where Indian and Western music begin to merge quite naturally. His piano rendering of Raga Marwa, to be recorded along with Ashish Khan's composition in quartet form, is something to look forward to as an exciting and integrated development of the two great streams of music. This particular passage begins at 1 minute 11 seconds from the beginning of the recorded performance, HMV ALP C2, alaap and gamaks in Kharaj.

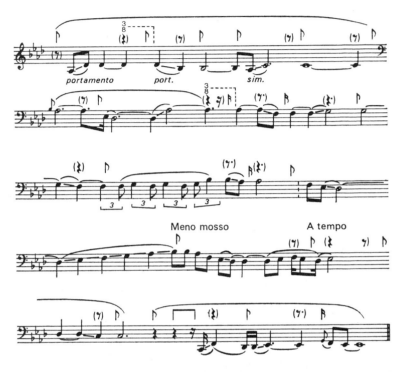

The musician can disjoint the graph and make it wobble and 'gargle' and then swoop to a long flowing passage in contrast.

This may appear to be a painstaking degree of artifice, too elaborately formalized. It is certainly not when played. The subtleties can never be described verbally nor the qualities of voice of people like Subbulakshmi, Bade Ghulam Ali and Ameer Khan, whose voices touch the taans, these long, zig-zagging figurations, like whispers of perfume lingering in the atmosphere. In fact, very few Indian concerts leave one emotionally untouched. The edifice may be mathematically based in principle, but the heart is never estranged from the mind. There can never be a cerebral intellectuality for Indians because they consider balance essential in the human spirit. They quite rightly recognize this as false to the human condition. Fortunately they have in all their philosophy escaped the tendency to divorce heart and mind, emotion and intellect. And to accompany the melodic line there is the constant demanding challenge of the drum language answering the dialogue created by the instrumentalist or vocalist. Even such young musicians as the talented Ashish Khan (son of Ali Akbar) and Zakir Husein (whose father Alla Rakha can well be proud of him) show an amazing quality of joy in their exchanged glances from embattled but friendly rivalry, and sheer physical stamina in their duet of melody and percussion.

The fierce discipline, dinned and drilled into the subconsciousness of Indian musicians since childhood sees to this. In this way a musician will show the stamp of his master, just as someone remarked to me once when Annapurna was playing the surbahar alongside her husband, Ravi Shankar. 'How like her father she plays,' was my neighbour's comment because of her ability to play sliding meends, the glissandos which were a marked speciality of her father Ustad Allauddin Khan, the great sarod master.

The astonishing thing is that these ornamentations are carried in the head. They are not notated as in Bach, nor arrived at impromptu as by Duke Ellington or Stan Getz on the alto saxophone, but are foreseen and manoeuvred by a 'seeing eye' in a photographic memory.

To the purist or the theoretician it seems that, by the strength of this aural tradition, certain ragas should be sung with only certain figurations and permutations of these melodic figures and only certain graces playing around the emphasized notes.

This tradition is particularly strong in its influence in South India, where the connoisseurs are past counting, and is referred to as sampradaya – the tradition of music handed down from one guru or vidwan to a pupil within a musical family and therefore carried on with a collective wisdom from generation to generation. Nowhere is this so rigid as in the South. In Hindustani music many musicians go beyond the established bounds of the raga by singing some ragas without their rightful gamakas or even their rightful order of notes, or by giving these notes entirely different emphasis and length from that expected by the teacher. In one way it could be said that Muslim influence, the freedom of the individual to express himself outside the Hindu canons of taste and established custom, has made Hindustani music more open to natural mutation. Such musicians who do attempt the unorthodox are in good company, for it is said that while singing Raga Yaman, Khusru, the eminent vocalist of the twelfth century, used two notes ma^s and ma^t (F♮ and F♯ if sa is middle C) when only the one note ma^s (F♮) is allowed to this raga. In so doing he created spontaneously the new derivative raga Yaman Kalyan which now uses both ma^s and ma^t. Thus, apocryphally, are ragas born!

For this and many other reasons notation will be constrictive for Indian music because, although a raga might be written down, the performing artist must feel free to launch forth whenever the spirit moves him from a given notated note into an entirely new shaping of an ornamental phrase or melodic figure.

G. N. Balasubramanyam, referred to as 'G.N.' in the South where he was well known as a vocalist and composer, has written of his own music in the Karnatakam that 'in basic structure and pattern it has remained essentially the same through centuries of tradition, whereas the Hindustani system is more elastic and flexible and comparatively free from inhibitions and restrictions. For instance, in the North there are several gharanas each one handling one and the same raga differently. In the South everywhere raga is rendered alike. Again in the Hindustani system several ragas have arisen from a single root with noticeable differences. For instance the phrase: ga, ma, reh, sa in Kanada Raga has given birth to Darbari Kanada, Kafi Kanada, Atana Kanada, Nayaki Kanada . . . The most noteworthy feature of Karnatak music is the gamakashuddha (the use of grace note) . . . which may be said in our system to be more emphatic.'

The use of gamaka or grace is such a complex study in this music that, as G.N. has said, 'our scholars have proved the futility of notating our ragas and even kirtanams (South Indian popular religious songs) in their real and full spirit. For instance, the note ga in Raga Sahana acquires three distinct values in terms of sthaana (place or position), gamaka (grace) and sruti in different contexts. This cannot be studied from a textbook, but can be learnt only by listening to a traditional and sampradaya rendering.'

GRACE

There are said to be many forms of grace in Indian texts, passing like shadows from one note to another. In the actual playing of the music this theory is misleading. Grace notes are used in the same way as in Western music, only more exaggeratedly so and more often. These gamakas fall conspicuously around the full, prime notes like summer bees buzzing round the nectar of a flower. A flurry, a throb or a ripple are distinguishable in general terms, but except for the highly trained perception of professional musicians such portamentos cannot possibly be deciphered in any real detail by the layman.

Their transitional nature, so integral to this music, has been ingeniously suggested to be derived from the beginnings of Rigvedic Sanskrit. This language, the root of many of India's fourteen main languages, slurs the sound of consonants next to each other; vowels are often compounded in the middle of words. They are also carried over in liaison from the end of one word to the beginning of the next. When chanted in saman music this naturally created similar slurrings and slides.

Movement is always swaying sideways and coming into the prime notes as if from a tangent – but made into a composite whole by the abundant use of those grace notes or shrutis. Whenever, for instance, a raga commences, the musician never strikes the tonic first. He slides from side to side of it and then comes to rest in its centre, as is shown in the previous notation of Sindh Bhairavi by John Barsham.

In the following examples, figure A is an ordinary grace most common to the music. It is a melting-away from the main note to a higher or lower pitch. It used to be called the humpitam and appears not in the melody itself but attached to certain defined notes of the melody of the raag. Figure B is the andolitam, swaying motion or swing that happens either side of a prime. This is sometimes difficult for our ears to appreciate fully. In general, the Western ear tends to hear a movement around the substantive note before reaching it (as in jazz), rather than hear the opposite – the full note and a move away from it. Figure C is a long meend or very lightly executed glide or linam (perfectly displayed by Bade Ghulam Ali who scarcely appears to touch the notes in his singing; his voice falls with the curling grace of an autumnal leaf in the still air). Figure D is the throb, the zam zamma much beloved by vocalists. The mordent sign above it means that the note should be struck twice in rapid succession with a tone a minute degree above or below as the sign indicates. This one lowers fractionally.

The meend when executed by a performer arouses gasps of

appreciation from a well attuned Indian audience. It can touch all the intermediary sounds running the whole gamut of a scale, as one can hear in recordings by Bismillah Khan with his shehnai. It gives one the visual sense of running down an escalator, and when used by two such musicians as Ravi Shankar and Ali Akbar playing on these rare but spellbinding occasions together, then it surpasses any other liquid sound I have ever heard. For delight it could be repeated more often than it is, but rarity heightens its value. Self-gratification is never succumbed to and so the audience is never quite satiated – which is as it should be.

On stringed instruments it is easy to build up these fractional pitches in the grace because of the thin, flexible strings of the sitar and the many sympathetic strings of this, the sarod, the veena and the sarangi. Their snapping and breaking in concerts from the very force of playing is not unknown, which gives some indication of their fineness.

Full tones need thick strings at a high tension. But Dr Goswami has explained how 'quartertones make it easy for Indians to use thin and long wires at a low tension, which enables the player to deflect the string without disturbing the peg. The stopping of a finger of the left hand makes the note, which the right hand then plucks, and while it is vibrating the left hand deflects it, which sharpens the note.'

Because of the very nature of Indian grace it is difficult to pin it down without a very elaborate notation. Mr Fox-Strangways realized this in his many attempts to set down Indian songs. A grace, he discovered, seldom consisted of the diatonic notes of the raga, and the whole matter of improvisation forced him to notate 'heads without tails' because 'the time is variable and entirely at the will of the singer which is influenced by the context in which they (the notes) occur'. The duration of gamakas, although defined for some ragas (as reh is in Bihag Raga) or in relation to some notes, is variable according to the idiosyncrasies of each musician.

IMPROVISATION

It does not take much imagination to envisage the possibilities open to a musician with all these tools of his craft at hand. I have only touched on a few of the techniques for ornamentation in order to avoid confusion for the layman who is not a conversant theoretical musician. But like the stone-mason working on a piece of sculpture, the Indian can use all manner of these small devices to perfect his form. What he chooses is for him to decide quite spontaneously, but within this known framework. When one talks of impromptu improvisation in Indian music it is somewhat of a misnomer. Ali Akbar Khan has said that improvisation is 'five years hard learning of technique'. But once these techniques are mastered with consummate skill and fluency, then all these means of decoration can be used impromptu and as the spirit moves.

Over the centuries our own music became so set in its traditional forms and pegged down by the guy-ropes of notation that we forgot until the most contemporary musicians came along that extempore passages were allowed in our early plain-chant, and that even in Mozart's and Handel's day the baroque singers were free to improvise in the cadenzas – again within the set framework.

Here again the guild system works its positive benefits in that the particular styles of singing and their complicated graces and ornamentations and permutative processes are imbibed along with all other subconscious childhood impressions.

In concerts in India one can see sometimes a cluster of vocalists behind the main singer. They are pupils singing 'behind' him, literally and figuratively. The great majority of musicians in musical families grow up in this secondary role of accompanist, slowly learning the intricacies of these embellishments almost as second nature. They become as natural to them as the use of their feet in walking effortlessly without thought for the mechanical processes of muscle and tendon and nerve vibration with the brain.

CRITIQUE OF INDIAN MUSIC

Seen whole, a few quotations from Indian critics will suffice to show what in India is considered important in a concert, and how musicians are appreciated.

Shrimati Girja Devi, a well known singer of Benares, 'displays precision and aesthetic balance in the rendering of khyal', this being the popular style of lighter, classical singing, preferred nowadays to the austere dhrupad.

Gopal Misra, a famous sarangi player also from Benares, which is a great centre of musical learning, brings 'astonishing adroitness and dexterity as accompanist, and his solo recitals are notable for their clarity, diversity and use of grace'.

The Daggar Brothers, noted classical singers, 'have developed a massive mode of utterance which is eminently suited to dhrupad. The imaginative quality of their singing finds eloquent expression in the graciously rendered expositions of their style.'

Shakur Khan and Ghulam Sabir, both sarangi players, reveal 'nimble and alert intelligence and remarkable skill and address in following the singer's flitting patterns of rhythm and melody with commendable accuracy'. This is certainly a feat to note because there is no warning of what phraseology and elaborate embellishments are to come from the master-musician and such accompanists can be heard echoing and answering every melodic figure with incredible *élan* as well as speed.

Shrimati Moghu Bai 'lavishes loving care on portraying a raga till its form stands out in conspicuous relief; another notable feature of her singing is the consummate skill she displays in synthesizing the variegated melodic and rhythmic patterns into an artistic scheme that is highly satisfying to the mind'.

Bada Ghulam Ali's thumris, even more romantic and popular than khyal-singing, are 'rich in erotic values and profusely embellished with colourful intonations, leaving a sweet aroma in the listener's heart'.

Bhaskar Rao Bakhle 'fully understands the prakriti (nature) of each raag, and all elaborations were strictly in harmony with it. He treated each raag in a particular way. In a raag like Darbari he would give importance to slow elaboration and in a raag like Adānā (often called proud with a strange phrase: pa, dha, ni, dha) of the same scale his treatment would have been totally different, with stress on intricate bol-taans and swift and brisk taans.'

RHYTHM AND BEAT

Tala or Taal

When all is said and done and when the concert is complete, the most riveting experience for any Westerner will have been the rhythmic content–the tala. This makes an immediate understandable appeal because of the dramatic nature of the feats of memory which combine the technical aspects of drumming with the art of harmonizing with the musical composition of raag melody.

Tala (= palm of the hand) is a complex organization of rhythms or differing beats (unlike the constant beat of our music) in multiple groupings or thekas which are again subdivided by the individual components of the beat, the fractional matras. All these elements add up to an astonishing range and virtuosity of playing, which culminates in the final coda of the raga, the fixed composition called the gat in which the gradually increasing rhythmic momentum matches the accelerating, climactic statement of the melodic line.

A master-tabalchi (a North Indian drummer of consummate skill) carries a computer in his head: the technical memory of fractional cross-references in the percussion, and a veritable storehouse of derived techniques gleaned at the foot of a great teacher. I have seen Western audiences transfixed by the mathematical attainments of such tabalchis as Ustad Alla Rakha (and, pleasingly, his young son Zakir, who displays the same acute prowess as his father in playing difficult and little-known talas with crispness and clarity), Jan Thirkwa and Shanta Prasad. The rhythms used are so complicated and asymmetrical and yet so wholly blended into harmonious partnership with the overall laya, the rhythmic swell of the melodic playing, that the ultimate in aesthetic satisfaction is reached; it is far beyond the possibilities of even the best jazz drummers, such as Louis Belsen, or those pop group musicians as accomplished as Ginger Baker, now independent, of The Cream.

There is a well known aphorism which is always being quoted in India to the effect that if shruti is the mother of Indian music then laya is the father.

Laya

Laya is the tempo of the music of which tala plays the detailed part. Laya again brings to mind certain imagery of the painting craft. An oil-painting from far off gives a pleasing and well defined composition seen, on closer inspection, to be made up of layer upon layer of detailed, individual strokes and clumps put on with the scalpel. This is the relationship of the individual brush-stroke to the complete canvas. Laya leaves its imprint on the raga; it is most distinctly felt in the alaap where no tala intrudes on the melodic line with its insistent beats. It is the syncopation and the sway, the pull which draws even upon our own bodies when we first hear it.

Tala, therefore, is the division of the distinctive groupings of beats that constitute the long phrases of the laya.

Matras

Matras are the smaller individual beats, each matra being determined in length by the pace of the overall rhythm. If the tempo is slow, for instance, then the matra would be of crotchet duration and would be marked with a single, upright stroke thus: ⏐ . In druta laya (fast tempo) a matra could be the length of a quaver or semiquaver, marked thus in notation: ⊔ or ⊔⊔⊔ . These are the counted divisions within the tala and in their turn add once more to the fractional sounds of Indian music. They will be the ground-base to the linear melody.

Tala is absolutely intrinsic to the classical tradition, being at one and the same time a disciplined intellectual exercise as demanding as a Bach fugue and an appeal to the excitability of the audience's emotion. In the sophistication of the art, in the complexity of crisscrossing rhythm and in the wide range of time measure, it has no parallel and can be said to be the most distinctive feature that marks out Indian music as so different from any other. To hear Palghat Mani Iyer, the most famous South Indian mridangam player of today, is to see all our own drummers at the toddler's stage. Percussion has never played such a necessary part in our own classical music, but *without* it Indian classical music would lose its vertebrae. It holds the body of melodic movement together. It shapes the raga at one level; in a sense it gives the raga breath.

Of all the elements of Indian music it is the most readily acceptable to our ears and almost unconsciously we respond with admiration. The heavily accentuated beat of the sum is quickly understood and unmistakably picked out with a beat of the hand or a flick of the finger, such as is going on all round an Indian audience. The emphasis is accentual, not quantitative as it is in our own regular time structure of measurement, where short bars are divided into a number of equal, *slightly stressed* beats not graduated in intensity, like the kettle-drums in a Beethoven symphony. Intensity of sound is not important to the classical musician in India. Accent is in the form of time stress. One has to remember that in the whole of 2000 years of historical development when no 'books' were written and all learning was passed on by Sanskrit slokas, stanzas learned by heart, stress in the form of time measure, became an exact art. There is no 'scanning' of verse in the Latin sense where metre is all-important in the formation of word syllables of the right length. Words are incidental to Indian rhythmic pattern – rather, words have to fit into musical time beats rather than the other way round. Anyone who has had the privilege of attending a play in Sanskrit (as I once had the good fortune to do so in New Delhi when Alkazi presented his Bombay Theatre Group in the famous drama *Shakuntalla*) will be struck by the force of time measure in the magnificent weight of the Sanskrit verse.

This emphasis on matras and beat persists even in the other languages of India. The verses of any song, a thumri for instance like the following one, can be put to any time measure by using repetitions of the words in phrases and syllables of these self-same words juggled into the talas to fit the metres. This thumri is in a vernacular, a mixture of Punjabi, Sindhi and Urdu, with very special emotional connotations that cannot truly be expressed in English – an Indian sense of yearning in which the torture of infatuated love for the beloved is a heady and burning quality equalled only by the Indian sun!

Tati ro ro main vaat nihāraan
   sāmvăl mōr muhāraan.
Mann mann mantaan pir munaawaan.
   Mullah kōl tareer (taveez) likhaawăn.
Sad Sad (chhadd chadd) josh phalaa paawaan
   Main kardee haan (hoon) yattan hazārōn
   sāmval mōr muhāraan.
Chōr Farīd 'na yaar da daamăn
   Jendi keeta judr kaar kaamăn.
Dōhaan jahaanaa da saada daamăn
   Unōn ki veh main diltōn basāraan.'
Sāmval mōr muhāraan.

My unfortunate self, frustrated with longing for you, I walk along
   the path you have taken.
   Dear one, turn back towards me.[1]
I promise, oh I promise, to do all that God wishes of me if He hears
   my prayers now.[2]

[1] 'Mor muhāraan' refers to the turning of a horse by the reins.
[2] . . . and so fulfil my heart's longing.

I go to the mullah to write a holy word[1] to grant my dearest wish.
I will renounce my egotistical self and place the long scarf (phalaa)
   around my neck as a sign of humility as I bow to God.
I make thousands of these attempts.
Dear one, turn back towards me.
Oh Fareed[2] says: 'Do not leave the dupaata (daamǎn or scarf) of the
   friend
With whom you have become infatuated,[3]
Who is my saviour in both worlds.[4]
How can I possibly forget the friend who has possessed my heart?
Dear one, oh turn back towards me.

This thumri has been recorded on 45 disc (HMV 7 EPE 1356) and is
called Nakkivaat in Raga Sindh Kafi, sung by Nazakat and Salamat
Ali in a tala called Kahrvaa, of 8 regular beats:

$$\left|\begin{array}{l} | \\ x \end{array}---\right|\begin{array}{l} | \\ o \end{array}---\left|\begin{array}{l} | \\ x \end{array}---\right|\begin{array}{l} | \\ o \end{array}---\bigg| = 4 \times 2$$

twice over, with the first mantra accented, the second an unaccented
beat not hit by the palm of the hand but by a wave of the hand. It
could as a song have been sung as equally well to a more difficult
tala, such as jhaptal of 10 beats divided unequally: 2–3–2–3. In
Indian music tala has become so vital perhaps because of the very
abstract nature of svaras and melody forms; something was
needed to give a skeletal framework upon which to hang the melody
line.
   This process of condensing words to fit the individual matras is
most pronounced in the gat, the meat of the raga; the metre takes
over and almost monopolizes the attention welding all the slivers
of sound measures into a composite whole. This is where the
percussion instruments of India come into their own and themselves conspicuously show off all manner of interweavings within
the basic beat of the tala chosen by the singer or instrumentalist.
   A gat consists of a number of differing structures: (a) the sthayi

[1] To be hung around the neck like an auspicious amulet.
[2] The poet's name.
[3] A reference to the placing of a neck-scarf in the hands of the wife as a
tying-together symbol in the marriage ceremony.
[4] The erotic and the spiritual.

which reiterates with rhythm and increased tempo the primary statement of the raga melody first set forth in the alaap; (b) the antara or movement into the register above the upper tonic; (c) tihais, short melodic phrases echoed by parallel rhythmic patterns played three times over and culminating on the sum or main beat; (d) jatis or groupings of notes and beats paralleling each other in fixed patterns:

   (i) tisram: 3 notes or 6 against 4
  (ii) chatusram: 4 or 8 notes against 4
 (iii) khandam: 5 against 4
  (iv) mishram: 7 notes against 4
   (v) sankirnam: 9 against 4;

(e) jhalla, groupings of melodic notes interspersed by plucking special chikara strings on stringed instruments, used to emphasize the rhythmic beat (this is called pat or thonk, meaning staccato notes); and (f) jawāb-sāwal dialogue between instrument or vocalist and percussion concluding in a tremendous climax in the sum.

The matras can be broken down, like the shrutis, into fractional divisions but they can go beyond the srutis, continually dividing themselves according to the abilities of the drummer and the physical limitations of speed in the player's fingers. From the 16-beat Teen tala, a drummer will pass to 32 beats, to 64, to 108, *within* the same cycle of the sum that is being held by the instrumental or vocal music, so compressing and accelerating at a phenomenal rate. The classification of the talas falls into many varieties. For instance, a tala of 10 beats in Hindustani music— Jhaptāl—is a rhythmic cycle of 10 beats for as long as is stipulated in the raga by the desire and the mood of the solo musician, but it can be ordered into innumerable and different changes of accent. Jhaptāl has to be: 2–3–2–3–2–3–2–3, etc.

Hand beat =	×	count		wave	count
(o) = K̄hali = void):	1	2		0	3
Thekā or syllables					
played:	dhi na	dhi dhi na	ti na	dhi dhi na
Counting:	1 2	3 4 5	6 7	8 9 10

Another tala having 10 matras or beats in different divisions means an entirely different tala, such as the tala Shool: 4–2–4.

Hand beat:	×		o		2		3		o	
Thekā or syllables:	dha	dha	dhin	ta	dhin	ta	tita	kata	gadi	ghina
Counting:	1	2	3	4	5	6	7	8	9	10

This may, on the face of it, appear simple. It is certainly not so! Within the rigid discipline of this seemingly straightforward framework, a drummer can ring innumerable fractional changes of emphasis within the continuing pulse; as the raag increases tempo so the breakdown into mathematical fractions of the 10 beats can take place and the mind and the ear are left in a whirr of closely differentiated beats – not blurred, or fused, but crisp and defined, except to the befuddled Westerner who sits gasping, straggling behind the pace of flashing beats, like the weary runner last in the arena in the Olympic marathon!

In all talas, no matter their purely mathematical subdivisions, there are different ways of hitting the drum as illustrated later which make a *qualitative* difference, and there are some accentuated beats which contrarily enough are left up in the air, unaccentuated – counted in the mind but unsounded on the drum. In drum notation, such hinted but 'lost' accents are marked with a small zero (o) under the matra line. In actual play these are not clapped out by a beat of the palm or fingers as is customary in an Indian audience. This is a matter of intriguing interest to anyone who is not native-born. To watch the gentle slap or quick flick of fingers among the Indians around one is to watch an unerring instinct for rhythm at work spontaneously. In fact the word tala itself means 'the clapping of hands' from its root तल (tul) = a palm of the hand. Many of the soloist's *confrères* may be gathered on the platform during a concert and while the musician and his foil, the drummer, are locked in an intense duel of skills, these others will be seen swaying in sympathy, nodding and shaking their heads from side to side in profound approval, letting out gratified exclamations at a particularly well executed passage and keeping time by the clap and wave of their right hands. The unaccentuated beat is passed over by a backward flick of the hand into the air – the result being a total loss of directional sense for the newcomer! Already the Indian audiences are back on the track with the accented beat and another permutation has begun while one is picking up the traces again.

Professional musicians and lay audiences alike seem to possess an electronic capability to pick out the essential threads of beat from the whirring shuttlecocks of sound. Over and over again at the beginning of this encounter there is the painful sense of loss as one's mental processes go wandering astray, and the only sure place to try to start again is at the unmistakable heavy thud of the sum when the melodic paragraph, the drone tonic and the commencement of a new passage for the drum all coincide. The emphatic beat is always at the beginning, never at the end, of a cycle.

Tala is the sentence. Matra is the word within the clauses of the sentence. The paragraph is the over-riding laya. Many waves and rufflings of the surface water can occur as the ground-swell comes in, especially when the drummer gets into his stride and with a nod from the main artist takes over the solo-playing, elaborating increasingly difficult permutations on the regular beat. Part of the zest given to any performance is in the intricate cross-rhythms a drummer deliberately traces across the melodic line. This the instrumentalist will answer in his own turn. These alternating passages are enlivening to any raga performance and arouse the audience to vociferous response.

As the units of rhythm have been said to range from 3 to 108 (there are thought to be over 300 variations of these in use in different parts of India) the mathematical implications can be seen to be vast indeed. What seems a sixth sense electronically in a master-drummer is the result of painful training. In many talks with Alla Rakha, his continual harping back to the years upon years of training, his practice of yoga, the dreary business of exercise and even hanging from the ceiling to strengthen his arm muscles, all reinforced my respect for the Indian discipline which holds that there is no easy road to success in our rapidly commercialized Pop sense. Their training is a gruelling physical torment which our own master ballet dancers would salute in turn, in order to overcome the nerve and muscle barriers and limitations which would otherwise encase such fluid yet crisply articulated shatterings of sound.

Just as the raga has been classified with such care and attention to detail, so also has the tala. Within these talas or time-cycles there have come to be about 20 currently in use in Hindustani music, the talas differing and taking other nomenclature in the

Carnatic system. Robust and powerful rhythms have been sorted out into a language called mnemonics, a kind of spoken shorthand which spells out the way the drum accompaniment should be beaten–the way the palm and fingers should touch the drum for each stroke: either on the rim of the drum, in the centre or slightly off-centre, with the full cushion or side of the palm, or with the fingertips. The subtleties of all this can change the whole inward feel of the drum and its resulting 'talk'.

The two tablas are tuned in unison with each other, the right-hand note of the drum to the tonic (1st note) or its octave in the upper register and the left-hand note to the 5th note, pa, or the predominating note of the raga (perhaps the 4th note). Such a process gives an incredible range and resonance, an inward quality in striking contrast to the more extrovert impression given by Western percussion. This is obvious if one thinks at random of its usage in our own symphonic music. Even in the more emotional field of jazz (for instance in Dave Brubeck's quartet or in the technique of a jazz drummer like Hershey playing Deep in the Heart of Texas) the quality is external, not the inner language of the Indian tabalchis, for they too are concerned in a musical system of yoga, a creative dhyana which in Indian terms always means a meditation of an active rather than a passive kind, hence its continual presence in building up the process rather than its intermittent use as in Western music.

Indians can be said, like Africans, to have speaking drums, and mnemonics is the language made up of an intricate vocabulary of syllables called out aloud in many cases to aid the drummer in passages of extreme complexity. The syllables go towards making the words or bols of this drum language.

One must not think in terms of one line of drum sound. Although the drums are tuned in unison (or two-headed drums likewise) there is a constant interplay of contrasting tones between them, an alternation of sound noticed long ago by Mr Fox-Strangways, so 'incessant and instantaneous that the two notes merge; and they are obviously there for the same reason as they are upon the drone strings of the vina and the tambura, only as enrichment of tone'.

Just to add further confusion, the drummer can switch and vary the accents deliberately to put the solo musician on his mettle, but he must do this within the framework of the tala chosen. These divisions can be compressed and then broken up into smaller and smaller fractions so that at stages they spill over into longer rhythmic cycles – but in the end they must always come together upon the sum. In this way patterns of irregular rhythmic counterpoint are giving yet one more dramatic dimension to the dialogue being carried on at the melodic level with its own intricate weavings in and out of the svaras.

This is indeed the point where the listener absolves himself from the mental processes of registering and cushions himself in meditative oblivion.

But even the most muffled Western ear will be able to pick up the traces as all the running figurations chase one another into the same resting-place on the sum. This harmony of movement gives the raga form. After a long throw of the line the reeling-in to base must occur as surely as for the angler playing out his fishing-line. And no matter how disintegrated the units of beat, especially in the gat where extraordinary feats of skilful and flashing speed occur, the duty of laya is to maintain accurately the uniformity of the span of units in a given time measure.

This pronounced beat, the sum, more often than not commences a new cast of the melodic line, but in virtuoso playing – of the kind heard with Pandit Ravi Shankar and Alla Rakha, or with Ustad Ali Akbar Khan or Vilayat Khan as soloist, with Shanta Prasad, Thirkwa or Faiz Khan at the drums – the melodic variations last several percussive cycles ignoring the sum during this period of time. Then there is set up in the mind a gravitational pull towards this final coming-together which is deliberately bypassed; thus is created further tautness and finally a heightened sense of completion for musician and audience alike.

Once this pulse is recognized, certain other accents can be put into place and they will then be heard to 'articulate' the metre of the singer's melody, giving bones to all that seemingly undifferentiated mass of flesh in the ornamentation of the notes or svaras. Then there is the next step, the challenging possibility of chasing the infinite mathematical isolation of the individual matras. It will certainly be much easier if the player of the tabla, the pakhāwaj, the South Indian mridangam – or whichever the many other varieties of drum that exist in India is being played – continues to stay on the regular beat of the tala cycle. Then there is a chance of picking up the thread, and one is able to feel the tension generated within the rising expectation of that resounding thud upon the drums. Thus the cycle begins again. But should a player of such eminence as Alla Rakha, undoubtedly the most versatile and intellectual tabla maestro in North India today, embark upon an 11-, 13- or 17-beat cycle, a little knowledge is a dangerous acquisition. The total asymmetry of such talas is a rare aesthetic experience to listen to, almost as forbidding as *musique concrète*.

Origins of Tala

One has inevitably to turn back to the beginners of Hinduism and the mythology written around the pantheon of gods to understand the deep and ever-present significance of tala to the Indian. The word is derived from the symbolic syllables 'ta', representing the Lord Shiva, the Dancing Nataraja whose Tandava dance, the Cosmic Dance, infused energy into inert matter and set universal matter in motion, and 'la', derived from the dance of Parvati, his consort.

This concept of the harmonious and ever-recurring elliptical rhythms of the universe, and the delicate but precise balance of all the physical laws that sustain through the principle of dharma not only our galaxy but those within all the many expanding universes, is a basic tenet of all Hindu philosophy and was so long before the physical sciences of the West confirmed such a postulate. Dance is the absolute synonym for the abstruse philosophical idea of such a rhythmic law governing all creation, and music becomes the algebraic formula expressing the even flow of these laws of the cosmos. It is a much more potent concept than our own ideas of dance and is easily assimilated deep within the Indian mind because every aspect of Hindu belief reinforces it and is geared to this integrated wholeness of philosophy, religious belief, and artistic expression of their truths. Science and art have become divorced from the religious channels of our own thought; not so in India, where even the most ignorant bystander somehow feels that the flow of these eternal rhythms and the more specific measurements of time that he hears and sees in music and the dance, are one and the same parts of a gigantic, divine whole.

'The union of the First Principle (Shiva) and his Energy (Parvati or Shakti)' is this tala. 'Shiva and Shakti being its very nature, rhythm or tala, one with life-breath, is meritorious, leads to fame, gives enjoyment and liberation and so is cherished by the yogis.' So runs a Sanskrit text.[1]

Rhythm is the over-riding principle of the universe. We are locked within it upon our planetary orbits. Every single atom is moving in the same immutable process of motion. To an Indian this not only affects him in a profound spiritual sense; it is of aesthetic significance also. Perhaps this accounts for the important part rhythm plays not only emotionally but at such a complex intellectual level in his awareness of the music and the dance. The metaphysics are clearly understood and accepted to this day.

By the time of Sarangadeva's treatise in the thirteenth century, the *Sangeet Ratnakara*, a very elaborate system of the basic idea of tala had evolved from the earliest Vedic hymn-chants to simple time-cycles. One tala, it was said, could reach up to 60 or 70 matras or beats (that busy Hindu mind again having reasoned that a matra or beat was sufficient time for 3 vowels to be sung).

It can be seen that tala works at two levels: the long swell or tempo (=laya) which gives shape to the whole through vilambit (slow), madhya (medium) and drut (fast), and the individual breaking waves or beats (= matras) that awaken our senses with their prestissimo sounds.

DRUMS

In Hindustani music the tabla and pakhāwaj are most commonly used. In Carnatic music, the mridangam comes into its own. South India is the region where drumming is a fine art in itself and the mridangam has been affectionately termed 'the Lord of Sound'. Bengalis also have a saying in Sanskrit: Yantra patir mrdang-, meaning the Lord (Pati-husband) of instrument (yantra = means of holding, i.e. instrument) is the mridangam.

The tabla could be described as the mridangam cut in half. The right-handed part is specifically called the tabla, the left-handed half is the bayan, 'bayan' being Hindustani for left. The tabla is most easily recognized by Mr Fox-Strangways' definition, which likens it to an upright coffee-cup in comparison with the more squat tea-cup shape of the bayan drum. This is the base drum and is the more difficult to play. The least pressure of the palm can create the most resonating sound. To achieve absolute accuracy

[1] Translation from Alain Danielou, *Hindu Polytheism*.

209

drummers have to practise with meticulous and painstaking care.

The pakhāwaj, a large, two-headed drum which is the accompaniment to dhrupad-singing, has a gutteral depth of vibration which is a sensuous delight to the ear. A plunging well of noise emanates from this drum, vibrations which stir at the very bottom of the dark depths where waters lie cool, limpid and echoing.

On nearly all the drums the centre of the drum-head has a circle of black plaster which is made of atta or flour and iron filings hardened into a black pitch. This is a permanent surface on the bayan and tabla skins but is reapplied each time to the mridangam and to one head of the pakhāwaj.

Tala Vadya Kacheri

The force and clarity of Indian drumming upon this hardened surface can make it sound as clackety as if wood were hitting it, so disciplined and hardened are drummers' fingers. The apogee of such artistic delight must surely be the experience of a tala vadya kacheri in South India; there is no more perceptive an audience than one from Madras, where music and dance thrive like commerce in an urban city. To attend such a concert of drums is not only to savour the enjoyment of the most precise dramatic musical form in India, but also to wallow in the sensual assault of the audience; South Indian women come laden with great coils of white jasmin in their jet-black hair, flowers bought fresh daily in the great Madras flower-market. 'Ta-ki-ta ti-ki-ta ton-ki-ta nam-ki-ta ta-di-mi ta-ki-ta tam', chants the cross-legged time-keeper or nattuvanar whose specific job is to sit through the performance talking this language of bols to enable the dancer or drummer to unravel the labyrinthine rhythm.

At such a percussion concert the tabla, the ghatam (an earthenware pot placed with its open neck towards the naked stomach of the player – the fatter the stomach the better the resonating sound!), the kanjira (a one-sided skin drum with small bells attached like a tambourine), and perhaps a violin or veena to take up the melodic line of the raga, are all assembled in a semicircle.

Each instrument improves on the raga, 'talking' the melody, the ghatam for instance possessing a surprising array of soprano sounds as the fingers or knuckles hit the fire-baked pot. There then begins an elaboration of the tones played on the tuned percussion instruments in turn. Sometimes the musical jal tarang (china bowls filled with water) and stringed instruments or flutes are added. These elaborations are held strictly within the limits of the tala chosen so that as each performer comes to rest upon the basic beat or sum the next musician takes off, building up a fantastic edifice, like terraced paddy-fields climbing back and up a parent mountain. The whole effect is reminiscent of the culminating upsurge of Ravel's *Bolero*.

The solo improvisations of each performer become shorter and shorter until all the musicians have, with mounting tension, reached the point where one strike separates their meeting upon a tremendous crescendo of the sum again, and there they join in joyful reunion to play the final passage. It is one of the few times in Indian music when crescendo is used as a technique for dramatic effect.

On one such occasion the wiry South Indian with the typically elongated South Indian name – the late Devakottam Sunderaraja Iyengar – fell on his kanjira like a hawk and so worked himself and all of us in the audience into a frenzy, that his tightly knotted Brahmin bun, worn at the nape of the neck, flung itself loose, shaking in the flood of spiralling sound like a galloping mane, while the tempo of the kacheri advanced and his gold earrings flashed in abandoned enthusiasm. Under his fiery enthusiasm we were all passion spent.

Such complete and utter involvement, a living of vital rhythm by every body muscle, is most apparent in the astounding skill of a man like Palghat Mani Iyer. To see this greatest of all mridangam players is to believe in the unbelievable. On one occasion I had the extreme luck of being called in to an All Indian Radio recording session by a friend of the great Malayalam player.

The studio was full of the sounds of southern Malabar; the language of this beautiful, highly cultured and aristocratic area of India always reminds me of the bubbling gaiety of a Scottish hill stream. We all settled ourselves cross-legged on the studio floor while that man of extravagant girth, a man as large as his – again – singularly long Southern name, Umayalapuram Kothandarama Iyer, organized his earthenware ghatam against his massive belly. This instrument was to keep the thudding beat along with, and in opposition to, the king of all drums, the mridangam.

Then in walked a short man with crew-cut hair and a vitally

alive face. He has in fact been called a benevolent and dusky Yul Brynner. He took up the drum and cut it clean with a crisp sound as though each finger were an engine-driven piston. Palghat Mani Iyer began to play without fuss or ceremony. My whole body was turned into a parade-ground, shaking to the ratchety precision and the pounding rhythm. Every muscle pulled with the impetus of these iron hands, marking the changes in his flickering finger-beats. It was all at shutter-flash speed and beyond my Western comprehension. I could only gasp and marvel that fingers of the human hand, so much bone, flesh and sinew, could hold such piston strength allied to the padded ferocity of the tiger.

First came the ungainly, asymmetric cross-weavings, almost as though he were hobbling over the drum-skin; then the stealthy taps of leopard softness; and finally the chasing, scuttling fingers lost in a swirl of sound, scattered in a unity like the Marcel Duchamp painting of a man walking down the stairs, a movement broken into fragments of a camera exposure yet retaining the unity of the process even in the fragmentation.

With the informality of India, a bare-footed fellow artist slid through the red-lit door to fetch a coca-cola; Mani Iyer tilted it to his lips without the bottle's even touching them and disposed of the drink in proper South Indian fashion, having first thrown away the unwanted straw. What a marriage of East and West! But then great artists often show a healthy irreverence for all the orthodoxies of taste, as did Alla Rakha on one occasion in Paris where, with gay abandon, he tapped out on a shop window-pane as we walked down the Champs Elyseés, a straightforward tala to a current pop song of that day, Calcutta, Calcutta! Cultures meet at all levels.

For the connoisseur there was nothing to equal a performance in which Ariyakudi Ramanuja Iyengar, a great man in the art of singing Carnatic music (for which he received the Presidential Award in 1952), and Mani Iyer balanced each other, complemented each other and inspired and provoked each other to further virtuoso performance. It was as if Yehudi Menuhin and David Oistrakh appeared on the same concert platform. In status, of course, the vocalist is supreme in Indian music but when one had the good fortune to hear these two there was an unusual give and take, each having arrived at that 'lonely peak of eminence' where they matched each other in improvisation and arrogance. It is not easy for such eminent artists to play together in a music which leaves much to the immediate and individual extempore musicianship; there is much jealousy if there is discrepancy in the balance of play and if the instrumentalist or vocalist denies the percussion player a chance to show his mettle. In this respect Ravi Shankar has shown his generosity as a musician in encouraging Alla Rakha to demonstrate his extraordinary virtuosity as a tabla player. The same is so in the younger generation with Ashish Khan and Zakir Husein. Ravi Shankar understood its appeal to Western audiences and has given Alla Rakha pride of place in solo performances during his concerts in the West. But this is certainly not the rule within an Indian concert–some eminent musicians will not allow their drum accompanists to display their prowess at all except when and until the musician nods his head to the drum player to take up the ropes, metaphorically speaking, in play.

Where the normal playing of tala is concerned, with the more commonplace and less complicated beats, members of the audience can follow the practice of Indians who keep the time, not through affectation as some foreigners think, but almost unconsciously because of this instinctive feeling for rhythm with which they are born. This is to be seen most noticeably in little Indian girls taking classes in classical Bharata Natyam. Of this I am particularly aware because our own daughter became a pupil of Indian dance; seeing her beside her Indian friends was like seeing a ramrod placed against new willow branches bending in the breeze.

Sense of flow and the pause of rhythm is theirs from birth. The wave of the hand, the click of the fingers is a constant part of an audience's participation; it also warns the performing artist–who may be way out on a flow of improvisation–not to get lost in it, but to pull himself in fast to the approaching sum.

Take for instance Tintal of 16 beats divided into four even groups of matras:

1 2 3 4	5 6 7 8	9 10 11 12	13 14 15 16
| | | |	| | | |	| | | |	| | | |
X	2	O	3
| dha dhin dhin na	na dhin dhin na	na tin tin na	na dhin dhin na |

Here the sum leads off on the first matra marked 'x'; there is a further emphasis on matras 5 and 13; but what one would expect–

213

a definite pulse on matra 9-goes unaccentuated instead. But even if the complete greenhorn at deciphering such a code should lose this beat on 9, it is an easy enough tala to pick up the beat again with a tap of hand on the 1st, 5th and 13th matras and to count through to 16 in order to meet up with the sum on the next round. The sound written underneath each beat indicates how the fingers and cushion of the palm should hit the drum, so giving a particular bol or word to it.

Tintal can be counted out this way: with the whole right hand on left palm:

  beat-mark out three counts with the fingers
  beat-mark out three counts with the fingers
  throw-with the wrist on unaccentuated beat, count three on
      fingers
  beat-count out three on fingers.

This method aids the mind to keep track while all the other processes are going on. It also helps the listener to follow the counter-rhythms built up by the drummer in the fast tempo of the gat or coda.

A drummer does not stay on this monotonous plane of percussion beating out the regular matras for long. He may stay in the background while a vocalist is elaborating or improvising, especially during cadanzas and taans, or when two instrumentalists are carrying on a dialogue. But then suddenly when an opening appears and the soloist nods, the drummer will launch forth into a mathematical breakdown of this regular 16 beat, dividing it up into many fractions of time, each round dissimilar to the preceding one, like this:

1	2	3	4	**5**	6	7	8	9	10	11	12	**13**	14	15	16
♩	♩	♩	♩	♩	♩	♩	♩	♩	♩	♩	♩	♩	♩	♩	♩
I	I	⊔ I		⊔ ⊔ ⊔ I				I	I	IL	⊔	⊔ ⊔	⊔ ⊔		
⊔ I	I	⊔	⊔ ⊔ LL I		⊔	I· L	I	⊔	0		⊔ ⊔⊔				
I	⊔⊔ ⊔⊔⊔ ⊔		⊔ ⊔ ⊔⊔⊔ ⊔⊔⊔			I	I	I· L		I	I	⊔ I			

These are 'regular' irregularities. The complexity starts when the

bars are dislocated in order to give cross-rhythms. This is brought
to its ultimate in counterpoint in an uneven tala such as a 9- or an
11-beat, tapped out in matras which run like this: 3–2–3–2–1–
3–2–3–2–1

Another tala in regular usage is Jhoomra–or Jhumra–which is
more difficult than Tintal:

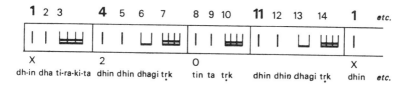

This pattern looks more complicated than it really is. Jhoomra is a
14-beat tala consisting of 14 divisions: 3–4–3–4 or 7–7. In this
example the 3–4–3–4 is broken down again into faster slurring
beats (the tirakita or trk for short) so that a matra the length of a
crotchet is halved again into two matras of a quaver length, and yet
again speeded into four semiquavers. Nevertheless the main
handclap still comes on the beat of 1, 4 and 11. The real difficulty
sets in if the drummer begins to show his prowess and rings the
changes on these main beats. Sometimes the 2nd and the 9th
matras are also left silent so that even when the tala is played in
very slow tempo (as upon the pakhāwaj) one's mind lurches on
expecting the regularity of emphasis–and stumbles when it is
unaccountably absent.

When the ear and the mind have become attuned to these more
straightforward talas, then the adjustment in speed to correspond
with the melodic line can take place. Raga and tala go hand in hand
and what is happening at increasing tempo upon an instrument or
with the voice of the singer also follows suit upon the drums. Both
must in fact end their fixed or extempore passages on that constant,
prevailing sum, the beginning of a new cycle which becomes the
most important anchorage throughout the recital. Without it the
musicians would be lost. If listening to a vocalist singing without
drum accompaniment or an instrument being played solo, watch
the performer's foot. Occasionally it lifts and then taps the floor,
just to remind the musician of his own inbuilt sense of this anchorage which marks the commencement, beat *one*, of another cycle of
melodic development.

All this is not by any means the sum total of what drum-playing is about. The drummer deliberately complicates the issue by building up cross-rhythms to the melodic line, a kind of percussive counterpoint, to show off his own knowledge and technique, to add zest and to spur the instrumentalist on to further improvisation himself. These 'dialogues' overlap for many phrases until that final liberation, the resolution, when the melodic paragraph also uncoils itself and the whole unity is drawn together in the mind, knitted into the clearly manipulated emotions. A tala and its individual bars of matras can switch from regular flow to irregular humps like a ship hitting rough weather, going through great troughs of waves where the flow of the sea is uneven, pitching and tossing the ship in dizzying lurches.

Even a simple irregular tala such as Rupak often leaves me floundering, even to this day, because it runs totally against my inherited Western grain, being a 3/4 time with a 'back-to-front' emphasis.

1	2	3	4	5	6	7	1 _etc._

X   2   3   X

dhin dhā na dhin dhin dhā trik dhin
(ti–ri–ki–ta)

I find myself over and over again returning to the reverse accentuation, 'oom-pah, oom-pah, oom-pa-pa':

1	2	3	4	5	6	7	1 _etc._

X   2   3   X

whereas it should run entirely in reverse, 'heh-di-di, hey-di, hey-di'.

Dhin, na, tirik, it, ta are played by the right hand, Dha, ta are played by the left hand and dhin and dha are played by both hands together.

Rupak tala of the Carnatic system is very different: a more even beat of 2–4–2–4, a clap of the hands and a wave, a clap and counting on fingers of 2,3,4. The bols are also of different nomenclature: ta dimi takitta, tam.

ta = hitting the drum with right-hand first finger on the border of
    the drum
di = hitting the drum with left middle-finger
mi = right middle-finger on middle of drum
ki = as mi
tta = as ta
tam = both hands hitting drum together

Because the matras can be broken down into so many mathematical
equations there is undiminished interest in following, or attempting to sort out, these divisions.

It may appear to be inexplicable chaos, but that is only because
we have not been reared to it. Always in the background and im-
printed upon the Indian mind is that belief in the unity of all
things, suffusing heart, soul and mind. It works in both musician
and audience with a certain and sure magic. And even at moments
of high tension when such tabalchis as Alla Rakha and Jan Thirkwa
are off in their own private world, entangling themselves in the
criss-crossing currents, you will find the great soloists and other
Indians in the audience counting the beat aloud as one; equilibrium
is always eventually reached, no matter how long the evolving
process.

Chapter Six

A WORD FOR THE VOCALIST

'A show of instrumental agility in which words have no importance or hardly any, but which for perfection of speed, neatness and precision of intonation, has perhaps no equal anywhere in the world.'

DR ARNOLD BAKE

Up until recently vocal music was the culminating point of Indian classical music. To be expert in this field was to have reached the apex in the striving after the fullest expression of rasa. Nowadays the young lions of the North, and a few courageous musicians in the South, musicians who have felt the urge to break through into further creative realms where the purists dare not follow, have brought instrumental solo-playing to an increasing degree of popularity with the modern city-dwellers of India, both the intellectuals and even the vast popular audiences who throng the open-air concerts of Bombay, Madras and Calcutta.

Yet to many academics, vocal music is still the summation of all that has evenly flowed through the centuries – the unhurried, uninterrupted stream where the principles appear to remain static, founded upon the rules laid down in the old treatises of well over thirty centuries ago. The Indian theoreticians of those times believed that the human voice was more capable of expressing human emotion, and therefore rasa bhava, than any instrument. It 'could range over the whole gamut of human emotions more explicitly than all instruments', Mr Goswami writes. 'Singing is more than mere music because besides its human appeal, it possesses the power to express the emotional depth of the individual, involving a complete psycho-physical release – thus the svara (sol-fa note) was not just a pitch of sound – it was a pitch of sound plus expression.'

There is no doubt that in experiencing the reality of vocal music in India and becoming part of Indian audiences, one does begin to notice this subtle elevation in status accorded to the great vocalist, a status that attaches itself in the same way to the great singers of

Covent Garden or La Scala. Its appeal is a very heightened and specialized one, directed at those who are educated in the art and sophisticated in their awareness of the principles of the music. But the ordinary Indian whose mood is more immediate and less intellectually rarified finds concerts devoted entirely to vocal music long-winded and boring.

The grammar of the music expounded in these particular sammelans or gatherings has become far more important than its imaginative spirit. Theoretical technique is the foundation-stone of this art, not the searching, tortured spirit of those creative artists attempting to give new expression to old truths. The grammar of the music is absolutely essential for 'right' singing. The melodiousness is not. Dr Narayana Menon has aptly commented that the voice is considered no more of an asset to a vocalist than good handwriting is to a poet.

A vocalist, as he composes instantaneously throughout a performance, is drawing upon all his inherited knowledge as well as that *memoria technica* acquired from centuries of family training. His voice is an instrument, not a vehicle for the lyrics of some composer, be he the equivalent of a Bach of the St Matthew Passion or a Cole Porter with his musicals. 'Words are simply vehicles of tonal expression carrying the melody and therefore should be used at a minimum,' reiterates Mr Goswami.

It is the svara carried on the vocal strings which evokes the aesthetic appeal of the raga being sung – not the bol or word. Svara is pre-eminent. Hence the use of the voice as an instrument. One of the most striking examples of this use of voice is on a well known recording by Kesarbai, the renowned woman vocalist of Hindustani music, singing Jaunpuri. Her voice merges with the stringed sarangi accompanying her and in fact becomes indistinguishable in sound, so that at some points it is quite impossible to tell which is being heard, Kesarbai's voice or the sarangi. The two intertwine, identical in effect.

At this point I must make it clear that Carnatic and Bengali music have a different attitude towards vocal music. Words *are* important as expressions of religious passion: in idealism, in the loving worship of God spilling over to colour the love between human beings, and in the yearning for personal fulfilment in reaching perfection. Many of the songs sung are mystical hymns of supreme literary beauty composed by Jayadeva and Thyāgarāja,

Swati Tirunal and other saint/musicians mentioned before.

It is of interest to read the comments of a South Indian music critic, S. Y. Krishnaswami, on the passing of the great Carnatic vocalist Ariyakudi several years back, in order to appreciate this shift in attitude towards vocal music in the two traditions. Writing in *The Hindu* (the *New York Times* and *Christian Science Monitor* of South India), he had this to say of the legendary vocalist:

'For a period of more than sixty years he preserved the purity of a great tradition, unperturbed by the transient innovations in taste and style, unimpressed by the novelty of new forms, unprepared to sully the chastity of his singing by resort to adventitious vocal effects or arithmetical exercises, and preserving a musical sanity in the face of artistic as well as social temptations ... The achievement of an equilibrium between the two methods [the romantic one of fresh experiment and the classical one of restraint in accepted forms] is a mark of distinction, a marriage between the freedom of the imagination and the shackles of scholarship. This is not a blind balance that is gifted at odd intervals but it is a permanent two-eyed vision that unfailingly sees beauty in its entirety and proportion. This evenness reached its zenith in this music of Ariyakudi. His "graces" were inherent and not imposed and they looked as if they were part of the composition, but they represented the crystallization of previous experiment. Ariyakudi did not parade his romanticism but he gave the public the fruits of it ...

'A distinguished feature of his music was his tempo. It was his exclusive property. There are artists who can shoot from the base of the first to the top of the second octave like greased lightning. There are others who move with the unhurried ponderosity of a temple elephant. There are a third group who have schooled themselves to sing in a facile middle speed. The first is an assault on the ear, the second is dignified in the beginning and funereal at the end, while the third becomes an exercise in single-speed monotony.

'Ariyakudi achieved the best of both worlds. He never went in for the supersonic velocity which startles more than it pleases. Between the slow and the middle tempo he constructed for himself a compromise which may be described as one of middle tempo in detail and slow tempo in movement. The tala looked slow and steady, but the song seemed fairly fast ...

'His sense of values was seen nowhere in greater strength than in the subordination of the grammatical and intellectual aspects of classical music. The singing of svaras in accordance with recondite tala combinations or the exhibition of memorized crescendo to-wards the conclusion of svara-singing or the elaboration of an obscure raga in which there is only one song known to the world, made no appeal to him. He felt that music should take grammar in its stride and that nothing should be done to violate the unity of the raga, the song and the svaras which constituted a combined structure. His grammar was faultless but hidden. His svaras seemed to be an extension of the song. They never entered into a duel with the drummer. They were adequate, and not proliferous ... Long-winded alaps often conceal repetitions that escape the unwary and after the first few moments of music, drift into voice culture at varying speeds. Done well, as in Hindustani music, they have a charm, but Ariyakudi who patterned his exposition on the style of the late Veena Dhanam, scorned any kind of repetition; in fact it was repugnant to him to meander in a sea of sound.'

This can hardly be said of some Hindustani vocalists of the old schools of training where the svaras or notes are still used for vocal gymnastic exercises, where the bols or words and syllables are like so many ropes and bars of the gymnasium, where the voice does not in fact need to possess even a musical timbre in our sense. Instead it is the vocalist who has above all to have a knowledge of the mechanics: of the way the notes should be approached through many different kinds of gamakas, of where and when to use the graph-shaped taans and the alamkaras or melodic figures. Mechan-ics, the grammar of vocal music, are still more important than the technique of voice production to some existing musicians, although, as I have just said, the temper of modern audiences may well change the ennui of these expositions.

On a good many occasions, such a performer is really tracing a mathematical formula in abstract sound. There are few words or meaningful lyrics as we know them: sometimes there are no words at all and the syllabic sounds of the sol-fa notes are used to create effect. Even despite what I have said the hymns or litanies of South India, the kritis, *can* become exercises also in mathematical formula if the singer is second-rate. Only the master-vocalist can give the words of Thyrāgarāja's effusive paeons of praise to God the emotional meaning they carry within their form. Others will just use the words as grammatical equations to carry sounds forwards in the movement and to give a variation in tone-colour. The words then become the abbreviated syllables described earlier and in severely classical singing are chosen only for the way they enable the larynx to emit the sounds.

In Hindustani music there is hardly any regard for the structural logic of words because they are entirely independent of speech rhythms. Nor is there regard for their *meaning* as a method of arousing emotion in the listener. Perhaps one could draw parallels with sweeping oratorios and operas of Western music where the words are too unintelligible for the listener to make sense of them. Without a libretto the words are fused and blurred within the whole sound and become compacted as sound alone. Words are not emotional factors carrying meaning within themselves, especially in an Italian opera incomprehensible in meaning to an English audience. They are really means to an end. In this way the few words of a chosen verse in dhrupad- or khyal-singing are used in similar fashion.

USE OF BOL-TAANS

The one way a vocalist can be tested and judged as a pre-eminent artist or just a pedantic grammarian, is by his use of taans. These are the configurations built up from the very simple graphs of ornamentation; they are not always symmetrical in pattern and develop into very dense and complex streamers of notes, sung at fast tempo.

In treatises on raga systems, authorities such as Pandit Bhat-khande give skeletal patterns of svaras for these taans which are more geometric in design than Western roulades flung out from a linear melody.

Ordinary musicians will labour the techniques; the effect will be strained and full of mannerisms. The resulting sound, in all honesty, resembles nothing more than an unmusical gargle. This is what has alienated a good many Indians as well as foreigners from classical vocal music. But when used by true artists such as Omkar Nath, D. V. Paluskar, Bade Ghulam Ali, the Ali Brothers, Keserbhai, Girija Devi, Hirabhai and Subbulakshmi, they represent a fascinating but intricate process of elaboration and enlargement of the main body of the raga, especially the final section, the gat.

Again improvisation plays a very great part in the artistry within the framework set by convention, tradition, the particular gharana or the particular guru.

As the raga is expounded from the simple graces of the alaap, these graphs are gradually delineated, slowly at first and then in a shower of sound, either in pure abstract taans where the vocal chords are opened to the fullest extent and the singer is emitting a straightforward 'aa-aa' flowing sound, or in bol-taans, which are the sargam syllables of the svaras. The vocalist accelerates dramatically and the drummer increases the momentum of the tala to match this performance.

But no real musician will ever allow the execution of this feat to be a mechanical exercise of grammar. There are moments when the inspirational mood overtakes a vocalist–suddenly even in slow tempo he will release a ripple of fast-ascending phrases rising perhaps two octaves, each phrase in geometric balance with the preceding; or he will swoop up as Abdul Karim Khan used to like a hawk freed at last to perch upon a svara an octave higher; or groups of notes are rolled around like a ball and pounced on staccato fashion, as the older purists such as Mushtaq Hussain Khan and Pandit Ratanjankar were apt to do.

On the other hand, patterns of notes can be held tensely in elongated exhalations of breath, like those which Nazakat and Salamat Ali execute (especially in a recording of Raga Kalvati). A musician such as Bade Ghulam Ali displays these fast runs of svaras in effortless svaristars (meaning the spread out of the svara, weaving patterns in and out), opening them up in fan-like shapes so liquid that one forgets the mathematics behind the technique.

Then there will be a lull in the performance while percussion player and solo instrumentalist take over, 'treading water' so to speak, reverting to the ordinary exposition of the melody. The tabla will take up the regular beat of the tala without showing off in any cross-rhythms while the vocalist relapses into himself, lost in thought.

Then, on the emphatic thud of the sum that lone protaganist will spring to life in a dramatic spurt of precise tones, showering out dazzling cascades of patterned phrases so clear that if even a ma tivra or a pancham is touched upon when unintended the connoisseurs will know and the effect will jar the ear. The various complications of pattern which from a whole body of taans are given in the glossary; they present the listener with an absorbing challenge in deciphering sound of almost molecular density as the singer moves up the ladder or down the different descending avorohi, precisely and correctly. Anyone who has had the good fortune to hear Subbulakshmi will appreciate the validity of this particular form of singing as an art form in itself. I always remember one concert when this South Indian artist gave a rendering of Saroja-dala-netri (lotus-petalled-eyes), a composition in Telegu by the famous composer Shyam Shastri. Although this is a song addressed in meaningful words to the goddess Meenakshi enshrined in the huge temple at Madurai, Subbulakshmi began Raga Shankarabharanam (the Northern Bilawal scale-C major) in abstract vocalizing. There followed a passage of solo violin, then a duet in the upper octave with her voice still outpouring pure sound, and *then* the worded song was sung in Telegu. After this there came the bol-taans in svara syllables and the whole was brought to a climax in percussion with a tala vadya kacheri.

What struck me most was the abstract vocalizing, which can only be likened to non-representational art, perhaps composition in tone-colours. Beautiful patterns floated out of her larynx, eddying, descending in space, spiralling upwards again, then twirling downwards, always followed by the echoing violin repeating every inflection and embellishment, perhaps trailing half a phrase behind, just that little short of unison. Here was melody in staggered tiers, finally to be reinforced by the drum-beats matching the voice pulsations. It was at an even more unsurpassed peak when her daughter finally took up the accompaniment, singing the descant, while mother and daughter used the hand gestures of vocalists to express the pitch and the phrases, gestures as delicate as ballet dancers', almost drawing the fluid run of tones out of the mouth on invisible filament threads.

Although many North Indians do not take kindly to classical vocal music – I have heard even those who care for classical instrumental music calling this form a 'pain in the neck'! – in South India there are musicians who object to contemporary developments in which accompanists such as drummers or violinists overstep their function, which is secondary to the vocalist's. In the delicate subtlety of the true vocalist there is only one player, the singer; all other instruments must play court to the central figure. Nowadays even in South India there are complaints that percussion players

and other instrumentalists merely make time in order to break
through and show off their individual merits while the vocalist is
gathering breath.

I shall always remember one memorable concert of Subbulakshmi in Madras, where she sang some of the Hindi bhajans or
mystic devotional hymns of the famous woman composer Mīra of
North India. One of these, Hari Tuma Haro, was one of Gandhi's
favourite hymns and was recorded by Subbulakshmi in traumatic
anguish the night of his assassination. In this hymn Mīra recounts
the life of Lord Vishnu when he came as an avatar or incarnation
to this world to alleviate the suffering of mankind. The refrain of
the song is:

Oh Lord, take away the pain of mankind.

There are many moving songs of Mīra sung by Abdul Karim
Khan, Mirabai, Hirabhai Barodekar, Manik Varna and Rasoolan
Bai: songs such as Moreto Giridhara, and Hari Avan Ki Avaz,
which Subbulakshmi also has sung to crowded audiences in
California, New York and London; songs addressed to the Lord
Krishna or Vishnu, likening Mīra's devotion to God to the creeper
tended by the waters of her tears, yearning for the love of her Lord;
songs as spiritual in content and as beautiful as any psalm, but
transformed to even yet another level by that particular sentiment
of the warmth of bhakti devotion in which the amours of Krishna
and his teasing pranks and the ecstatic surrender of human love
also take their rightful place as relevant in the loving of
God.

Mīra hears the footsteps of the Lord. It is the monsoon season
when all the birds sing in joyful release. The fields burgeon with
green shoots and new life is breathed into all living things. Thus
should the King come as a shower of rain breathing new life into
Mīra. It has been written by a South Indian 'that musical prowess
is the means to aesthetic beatitude', a religious experience that
transfers itself from the musician performing an immediate
creative art, an unpremeditated composition, to the audience.
Another Indian in a fit of American polysyllabic terminology has
called it 'deconceptionalized egolessness'! Whatever it is, the
power of real vocalizing carries its own emotional electricity, the
voice sparking off the charge, so that a psychological impact certainly

does take place when vocalist, drummer and drone fuse on the heavy thud of the sum. I have myself experienced this 'charge', a coming-together in oneness which is the same psychologically as those rare moments in life when a human personality senses a complete oneness with all creation around it.

The pendulum has swung considerably in the popular response to this pure vocalizing. Too much concentration on its mechanics during the last dying century at the end of the Moghul rule, when dissipation and disillusion set in under the new British dominion, had a ruining effect on the effusiveness and spontaneity of the spirit of true Indian culture. As a result, outer form came to dominate the world of master-musicians; the imagination and the effervescence which we can hear again today, no longer concerned the theoreticians until the liberating spirit of Pandit Bhatkhande brought order and a refreshing irreverence to all the traditional shibboleths. Singing had become arid. Nowadays, drama is demanded, most especially in the duel and duet of jawab-sawal as vocalist and instrumentalist answer each other. Quality and timbre of voice are also reasserting themselves.

The first impression anyone gets on coming to the music from our totally different concepts of musical principles, is this unique characteristic of not hitting the sol-fa notes in the centre. The singer is gliding over fine intervals between the full shuddha notes of the octave, slurring the sharps and the flattened flats in the process. The voice, being much more easy to control than an instrument, can overshoot the 'white' or 'black' notes with meticulous accuracy and then slide back to the central svara tone, so creating all manner of thumming vibrations and echoes which remain in the ear long after the vocalist has moved on to elaborate further around other groups of notes.

This constant overlapping and echoing gives Indian vocal music its strange and unearthly quality, producing for us a slither of sound which we are far from used to hearing. Ananda Coomeraswamy, who spent much time in the West and who has written many books in English interpreting his culture and its artistic attainments to us, has said that this slurring, or grace, must obviously appear to be an unnecessary factor to our ears as we are so attuned to hearing many notes simultaneously through the use of harmony. 'But in India the note, or svara, and the microtonal grace compose a closer unity, for the grace fulfils just that function of adding light and shade which in harmonized music is attained by the varying degrees of assonance'.

The art of the vocalist is certainly a demanding one for us. Sometimes the singer may take half an hour or so to work the voice in, and then continue to expound more fully for at least another couple of hours!

Writing again on Ariyakudi, S. Y. Krishnaswami has mentioned how great singers commence a concert with 'what may be called their "domestic" voice. As the concert proceeds the voice comes round as it were, its abrasiveness disappears and it becomes moist and not dry, pliable and not recalcitrant, and it develops a resonance that functions as an inner drone or "sruti" from within. This is the voice which is eminently suited to the best forms of Carnatic music, capable of giving breadth and volume to the lower octaves and restrained melody at the higher.'

Often it is not until the artist has been singing for hours that he or she begins to show the real range, versatility and ingenuity of his art. And while the singer is extemporizing an infinite variety of embellishment, the violin, or perhaps the sarangi, the flute or the veena, tries to match these improvisations, echoing their patterns and their frequency. Sometimes they run parallel with the singer's melodic line and its ramifications; sometimes they zig-zag across it, playing hide-and-seek until the very end of a long passage of improvisation.

This in turn may be the signal for the drum player to move in and mark out the same pattern in drum language, repeating after the vocalist each new phrase that he is working out in his mind at that immediate moment in time and which he is relaying in sung sound. The mood is heightened and enriched as the melody expands under the influence of his inherent knowledge and reservoir of emotional inspiration. A vocalist must, in fact, be just as sure in his knowledge of rhythm as in melody: it is he who will instigate the dialogue and the duel with the drum player.

So it goes on, a spiralling process of tension; the phrase shortens in length as the tempo increases and the beats come faster until the whole raga gives the impression of exploding into space while the friendly rivalry grips audience and musicians into one integrated whole.

The release at the final consummation is the same as that felt by the practiser of yoga. Having taken the body through one position of tension and muscle-stretching āsana into succeeding phases towards increasingly difficult positions–which in turn could not be so effortlessly reached unless the others had not preceded these culminations–the yogi's set order of discipline is then complete. He unties himself from the interlocked limbs, and falls into a trance of relaxation on the ground–free, effortlessly free. It is as though bone and gristle, obstinate joint and shackling vertebrae have dissolved and the body has taken on the wispy fluidity of ectoplasm. The same effect occurs in the music when the final movement in the gat has been stated, examined, improvised upon and searched in depth. The tension is very strong, moving inwards, not forwards as in our symphonic music. And then comes the relaxation in a spasm of release, at the very end.

But for most people, to start with the vocal music is like plunging into the fugues of Bach at his most erudite and gaunt, shorn of all the sparkling clarity of spring days and dancing sunshine that suffuses many of his gayer airs. It is much more of a challenge to us as Westerners and, unfortunately, not to everyone's taste.

For instance, certain vocalists, who shall remain nameless, can be heard at Sangeet Sammelans expounding a type of singing which can have no other description than 'arithmetical jugglery', that into which dhrupad evolved at the tail-end of the Moghul period. Younger Indians shy away from this.

The verbal acrobatics of the tones and their intervals, lost in a florid display of microtonal grace, become of supreme importance. There are vocalists even to this day who seem in mortal danger of gargling up their epiglottis. My husband and I have (to our chagrin) experienced them and the conspicuous display of their betel-stained teeth.

The great vocalists would be equally capable of rendering these virtuoso performances, if they so wished, but they upset the traditionalists by not conforming to the atrophied doctrinal theory. They sing notes outside a given raga; they do not follow a set order of melodic embellishments; they may not come to rest upon the tonic every time or the dominating note at the end of the melodic and rhythmic cycle; they may even jettison certain required orders of notes. But they lead the audience into realms where the singing melody and the beauty, the loneliness, the yearning after mystic love, the pathos and the light merriment, but above all the drama of interplay between melody and rhythm, all combine into a satisfactory artistic whole-and therefore a spiritual completeness. Those of us who care to listen are taken out of the world of mundane reality into that meditative and serious concern of mind and heart with which Hinduism is so ultimately concerned in its higher reaches of philosophy.

CATEGORIES OF VOCAL SINGING

Indian vocal music can be divided into six categories:

(a) abstract sol-fa singing,

(b) auspicious phrases with strong religious overtones which call to mind the concept behind such short-hand philosophy as 'Tat Svam Asi', or 'Narayana' (the name of God in another form) or 'om',

(c) words in praise of the deity as mentioned in the Mīra bhajans,

(d) rhythmic sounds and calling of the tala or words (see Chapter 5 on tala),

(e) light classical thumris in which refrains of meaningful words are used, and

(f) folk-music similar to our own folk-songs where lyrics convey real meaning.

Because of the nature of Indian instruments and their incapacity to change key with ease, vocalists tend to sing throughout a long concert to the same tonic. They do not change key. On the whole, men tend to sing in the keys of C, C♯, D and D♯, and women vocalists G, G♯, A and B♭. Each singer orders his pitch according to the raga, hence there are no specific altos, sopranos, etc. True pitch is important in melodic music-the interval effect of a note assumes a much greater influence than in harmonic systems, where a number of notes are played simultaneously. Therefore vocalists have to be truly accurate in sur, as it is called, working as they do against the steadying persistency of the drone notes in the background.

On the other hand, the great singers have an astonishing range over the octaves. For instance, if one cares to listen to a collector's item, the recording of Abdul Karim Khan singing Jumuna Keh Teer (The Banks of the Jumna River at Delhi), one would be hard put to distinguish whether the voice was that of a man or a woman. Not until he plunges to the lower register does one realize how remarkably unstrained is his chorister voice in the upper octaves.

FORMS OF VOCAL MUSIC

Many types of vocal music have evolved since its crystallization in Moghul times. Khyals, thumris and bhajans are most likely to be encountered in concerts given by Indians in our own countries. Padams and kirtans would be found in concerts of South Indian musicians and in Bharata Natyam dance recitals. Dhrupad- and darbari-singing are of the most demanding kind in classical music and group-singing of the qawali kind is a special Muslim contribution to Hindustani music.

In the development of vocal music there are three points to be born in mind:

Early Classical Vocal Music

This is dhrupad-singing, pure and severe.

Words in praise of gods and their consorts, Sanskrit prayers and fervent beseeching of God to give of his love to the one who sings of his joyousness, eulogies to rajas and patrons, and songs sung in certain seasons such as the monsoon, are all representative of this Indian classicism, so different in form from Hellenic or Roman classic principles of art forms. Even lyrics in restrained sensuous praise of female beauty are not held to be out of context with such classical music; they are harnessed to a very high level of poetic and mystic philosophy, so being transformed beyond the immediacy of the animality of human sensuality.

Developments in the Middle Moghul Period

During this period of unfolding of the art, baroque elements began to creep in reflecting the abundant richness of the princely courts, the sexual provocativeness of the developing Moghul dance forms taken from Hindu Kathak (so very different in this later development from the content and motivations of Bharata Natyam in the South) and the decadent atmosphere which too much luxury encouraged.

Lighter thumris and khyals, less orthodox in manner and permitting the inclusion of different ragas and folk-themes, became very popular and still remain so. The actual form of the khyal, its scaffolding–of building upon a few vernacular phrases and taking apart the syllables of these words and using them in episodic and abstract decorative phrases ranging sometimes over three octaves – is most factually illustrated by Mr Fox-Strangways in his chapter on form in Hindustani music in his book *The Music of Hindoostan*. For the musician, his notation makes it clear at first sight what edifice is being built up by the vocalization of the music. These songs expressed the spiritual in sensual and lyrical terms. Although Hussain Shah Sharqi is credited with evolving the khyal form in the fifteenth century (the word being of Persian origin, implying imagination), the embodiment of the spiritual in such terms is so basically Hindu that Muslim elaboration served only to magnify its Indianness, that essence which is so perfectly represented in the stylized, erotic sculpture on the Hindu temples of Khajuraho and Bhuveneswar. This is not a Moghul characteristic, although the erotic is very much recognized in Muslim mystic poetry; it emanated from the late Hindu rulers before the Pathan invasions, just before the tenth century. These rulers enjoyed a high standard of living and the many luxuries of a civilized courtly life.

This especial feature of Indian culture demands attention of its own–so much of Indian vocal music being inspired by sringara rasa, or the erotic.

Theme of Unrequited Love

The lover is constantly identified with human longing for union with the Godhead. So the love is never actually consummated because there is never tangible proof of his having attained such absolute identification with the Divine. Unrequited love is therefore inherent in the Indian situation. This romantic urge and search could in a way be likened to the convention of courtly love in the romantic serenades of medieval troubadours who addressed the beloved (who may well have been married to someone else) in a strictly stylized convention. This did not prevent such spiritual eulogies in praise of the loved one being couched in terms of the sensual.

Of course the Indian attitude towards sex is a coherent attitude more comprehensive in its psychology and philosophy than our own. Its expression in vocal music requires explanation, sex being totally alien to the Christian concept, touched as it always has been until this century with an atmosphere of guilt born from the sense of Original Sin. Even now as we in the West attempt to defy this guilt, we still unintentionally display an unconscious awareness of its force. Hindu philosophy, in its comprehension of the unitary aspect of nature, has always accepted an inescapable link between the body, mind and spirit in every department of life. Male and female principles of energy dominate metaphysics with a scientific objectivity, and dance itself is an art form deliberately expressing abstract scientific principles of creation and energy. This led towards a much more balanced and healthy biological acceptance of the place of sex in the human situation; however, this was before stern and militant Muslim rule (under such fanatics as Aurangzeb) and Victorian prudery (introduced by the British and most of all by missionaries) confused the guidelines laid down by the indigenous civilization and society of India. Sadly enough, an imbalance in the Christian ethic which we ourselves are only now arighting, established a sense of prurience and obscenity that is wholly foreign to the very ancient acceptance of sringara rasa as being pre-eminent over the other eight dominant passions. Sringara rasa and the sensual passions it arouses are endemic to all Indian art previous to this latter period.

Rukmini Devi Arundale, exponent of Bharata Natyam, creator of modern ballets and one-time administrator of the Dance Academy at Adiyar, a suburb of Madras, has, through intimate experience of the prejudices of Indian middle class society, written feelingly on this subject in relation to the dance. It applies as much to the music in India. She herself is a dancer, having defied these prejudices in the twenties in order to follow the disciplines of the dance form and the music at a time when it was not considered proper for a girl of her aristocratic background to think of appearing in public in such an activity. She became closely involved with Dr Annie Besant of the Theosophical movement and married an Englishman. This is what she has said: 'The sentiment that gives the greatest scope to the dancer with all its variations and gradations, its refinements and subtleties, is sringara rasa. According to Bhoja, one of the great authorities on Indian rhetoric, sringara is the pre-eminent rasa and all the others arise from it as modifications.

Bhakti or devotion which forms the basic subject matter of most Indian dances is bhava or the portrayal of this emotion, for without bhava, it is not possible to evoke rasa in a cultured audience . . . this enkindling of emotion which results in impersonal delight . . . is totally different from an emotion that is the outcome of a *mere experience of the senses.* In the latter case, the feeling is limited to the individual concerned. In a dance, the emotion portrayed is impersonal and is shared, and has undergone a transmutation so that what a member of the audience feels even when viewing a sorrowful scene is not something unpleasant but is really a delight, an ananda that is aesthetically conveyed through the dancer's superb portrayal . . . the final effect that is left on us is not that of the passion depicted but is an impersonal absorption in the aesthetic mood.'

This capacity to concentrate emotions, so intensifying their impact but also objectifying them, I know from personal experience. Long ago in my initial discoveries of the joys of Indian music I came to a memorable concert in New Delhi. Ravi Shankar and his shy wife Annapurna–a deeply sensitive surbahar player–were appearing in a concert together, a rare and exquisite pleasure. Both are musicians of great artistry and many discerning musicians in India acknowledge Annapurna as having been the more perceptive and finely attuned player, even if she was not the more dramatic and imaginative of the two. Sadly enough she no longer fully continues her art.

Slowly and serenely Annapurna bent over her difficult instrument, almost caressing the notes as she expressed their softness and sweetness. Each musical phrase was built piece by piece in tender meends, those gliding passages of floating, elongated slides and rippling movements where all the notes seem to flow one after the other as running water.

Ravi Shankar, playing his larger surbahar, took up the same movements and phrases, exploiting them each time in a slightly different way and bringing out pathos and rare beauty as he played around the ga, ma^t and pa, emphasizing these predominating notes with lingering care.

To and fro the melodic treatment went, from the one to the other, expanding, distilling the mood of controlled sensual passion, in the dhrupad section, the wild richness always held in check by the spectacular control, as if the emotions which were held within

233

this control would run amok if allowed full rein, as volatile Indian crowds do if their discipline is finally broken.

The execution of Raga Yaman suffused the atmosphere with romantic passion, as if all the love lyrics ever written were being concentrated note by note to stir the heart-beat and tear at the heart-strings. It was further enhanced by the physical effects of the throbbing resonance of the surbahar strings which seemed deliberately and physically to play upon the erogenous areas of the body, demanding orgasmic release.

As Annapurna fingered the notes with the caress of a lover – first thoughtfully, then lingeringly, then shaping each full note as with a potter's touch, enlarging them with those luminous graces and finally sliding luxuriantly down the frets – a sigh breathed over the audience, an audible expression of ecstatic desire. I was startled at first, never having come across such an uninhibited display of emotion in our concert halls! Then it happened again as Ravi Shankar and Ali Akbar played on their instruments in thumri style, moving like a breath of wind soughing through tall pine trees. The whispered need was there and in the playing when, both transcendentally and bodily, orgasmic release came, certainly in the playing and certainly to myself, and I was all the wiser for it.

I suppose it could be said that this is the classical equivalent of teenage pop-music swooning. It was a vocal response and an immediate emotional one to the performers for they seemed to be transported to further flights of musical exploration of very great beauty. The chemical reaction was there as the impulse flowed backwards and forwards between participants on either side of the stage. The adrenalin charge was the same, even if by drawing analogies with ephemeral teenage emotion I might appear to denigrate Indian music in the process. That is indeed very far from my mind. My concern is only to show what integration there is in the whole musical experience of an Indian classical concert; audience and musician are linked by indefinable bonds, swaying and responding and being inevitably drawn towards the coming-together in the emphatic beat. From this platform of the sum both these performers would launch forth into virtuoso improvisation and each time, by some miraculous juxtaposition of notes, the patterns of the gamakas playing around them, the length of the vibrations in the notes, the feeling way they expressed viyoga (which mean the separation of lovers), they stirred the packed hall.

And back came the response each time. A gasp escaped from the listening crowd as at moments of highest tension, or as in the release of sexual consummation.

Here there was no escape. This was the very essence of a distilled and refined emotion, emphasized by the amplification of technique in playing.

To my astonishment afterwards, this was confirmed. Yaman Kalyan has been called 'the gateway of evening melodies'; it expresses the yearning sringara rasa of separated lovers. As so often happens in India, the mind confirmed what the heart already instinctively knew!

LOVE POEMS AND LYRICS

As vocal music developed, especially in North India under the individualistic genius of Muslim musicians, the drive in both Muslim and Hindu forms to express love of God in graphic, human terms, found expression in the lighter classical forms of khyal and thumri and in the folk-songs where vernacular words are used (as in our own music). Thumri, because of the very nature of its romantic mood and appeal, allows much more development of the lyrics than khyal, but always within a strict framework of discipline. The words or bols are succinct and romantically based but much of the vocalizing begins to polarize around a few refrain words, such as this famous thumri of the Punjab taken from the film *Tansen*, which K. L. Saigal sang in the forties. This Punjabi singer achieved tremendous acclaim through films and so reached a much wider public than he would have through the normal musical channels.

Din sunna, suraj binā aur chanda bin rehn

is sung to Deepak Raga, the raga of fire associated with Tansen's legendary remarkable capacity to set fire alight when he sang it.

The day is dismal without the sun
and without the moon, the night;
Without the lamp the house, and
without the light the eyes.
Put the light on (diya jalao); put the bright lights on.

> Oh beautiful (married) woman, just listen
> in your temple (house); look, there is all darkness.
> See that your beloved man may not get cross.
> Therefore, put the lights on
> and bring him back to terms with you.
> Put on the lights; put the bright lights on.

The words 'diya jalao' (put the lights on) occur again and again as a vehicle for the rapid cascade of taans. It is in the use of these refrain words, as in the notes of a raga, that the importance lies. This 'bol-making', as it is called, allows for different patterns of alamkaras and ornamental graces of a wide variety to the *same* word. This changes the mood and the expression of the word in the most subtle of nuances. The best thumri-singing is of a highly romantic order of tenderness, using evocative ragas like Khamboj (Khamaj), Kafi, Bhairavi, Tilak Khamboj, Piloo and Kalyan. They act as lightning-conductors for this intensity of emotion.

Those love poems and lyrics are essentially devoted to the themes of Krishna, the best expositions of which are in the books written on the Radha-Krishna theme by William Archer, one-time curator of the Indian department of the Victoria and Albert Museum, and in the description given by an elderly Indian lady, Raihana Tyabji, in her little book *The Heart of a Gopi*.[1] The interesting thing about her emotional experience of becoming enthralled mentally as a gopi, is that she comes from a well-known Muslim family. Such is the cultural synthesis always at work within the whole of Indian society.

Shaktis or female friends of Radha, the leading gopi, are enlisted to aid in the fulfilment of love in these songs, and the poetic content of the words is heavily laden with the allegory of sensual love in terms of the Divine.

An Indian will, with disarming candour, say to you, 'The ecstasy of love appears to be the best approach to supreme happiness. This is not lust as you would call it, but human love at another remove where each being respects the full, whole personality of the other. We realize it is not total identification with the Absolute; but the joy of the awakening gives us insight into the loving aspects of Godhead.'

It has been said of the Hindu that his discovery that the sexual

---

[1] Published by the Chronicle Press of Delhi.

236

act has a double intent, immediate satisfaction and procreation, has led him to refuse to exalt the one in order to denigrate the other, somewhat different from our theological condemnation of one in order to sanctify the biological processes of generation.

Such a sense of emotional love in warm, bursting, human terms was a necessary revolt, as Mr Goswami says, against the cold intellectualism of Brahmanic philosophy, ascetic discipline, lifeless formalism and ritualism.

It emerged in the Radha-Krishna cult particularly prominent in South Indian dance. The musical verses that intersperse the whole performance in the effusive mood of the padams and varnams, combine into the compelling force of the poetry, the abhinaya mime and the reiteration of the musical passages, the highly-charged, emotional longing of lovers to be reunited.

The *Gita Govinda*, mentioned before, is also saturated with the intense passion which Indians feel on this subject. The Krishna cult formulated this into what is known as bhakti–devotional worship of a vibrant, tender and romantically idealized kind which through full erotic imagery in the poetry is transformed into a love of God completely beyond sensuality. It was typified for me twice in India, in the faith of two old ladies, both times with humbling simplicity.

In the intricate narrow lanes of the Benares brocade bazaar I was buying miniature saris which are woven there for the dressing of devas or gods, the miniature figures which each home keeps on a small altar for personal worship. A bent elderly woman hovered beside me, watching with absorbed interest; in all faith and innocence she came up to me, and with motherly concern asked, 'What Thakuji are you buying for?'

To her, God, known affectionately as Thakuji, was as real and as needing of our combined love, as her own son.

And again in Brindaban itself, after wandering around the many temples where the Bengali widows sit, shaven-headed in their white saris, quietly begging for alms and awaiting death longingly, another elderly women was softly singing the *Gita* in a corner of the garden to some men who had come on pilgrimage. I sat in the shade and listened to the peaceful cadences, so restful in their soft meditativeness. She turned to ask my Indian companion, 'Had I faith?'. It did not matter what faith, so long as I possessed it and believed in the ultimate truth of God. Reverence and love exuded from her whole attitude as she talked of God in real and motherly terms as though he were truly as part of her as a beloved child. This is indeed vaatsayala rasa, beyond sringara.

This sense of bhakti is not the fierce, individual love of Western romanticism, but an expanding emotion searching into the universality of love and finding liberation there.

It is this ubiquitous word–liberation–that immediately comes to mind whenever one considers the principles of Indian music at a distance. It is after all so vividly felt when the resolution finally comes. The sexual implication of this is clearly known to all Indian artists, most of all to those craftsmen who portrayed sexual union of every kind on the walls of the great Indian temples. Somehow it is never pornographic (except in a minority of carvings), being too artistically stylized for that.

Mr Goswami explains this: 'The bhakta sought to establish with his God such a friendship based on the man–woman relationship with himself as the woman in search of her man.

'There is nothing ludicrous or unnatural in men displaying this feminine attitude as modern biology has proved that each individual has genes of the opposite sex.

'The assumption of the feminine passive role solves an inner conflict as well as a social predicament in as much as the sex urge which disturbs the course of emotional life is subdued. In the matter of religion the male desire is projected to God, while the feminine attitude, normally suppressed in life, also finds its fulfilment. Such capacity to accept the opposite sex-attitude seems essential . . . for resolving many of the disharmonies in sexual behaviour.'

The music, especially vocal, because of its specific devotional content is obviously expressive of these subconscious urges in the Indian psyche as well as of those forces that display themselves more externally in Indian culture. This sounds a truism, but it is one that is so often forgotten. We try to put Indian music into our own frame of reference without conceding the fact that culture grows out of environment and the indefinable goals towards which people are striving beyond their mundane daily existence through a sense of identity with either a tradition or a national heritage, as much as from any other influence. Without knowledge of the people who live within the ambit of a certain civilization we are only on the edges of discovery.

Within the raga form, whether it is performed upon instruments or worked out within the more explicit terms of vocal music, the motivation and the execution are clearly Indian. Our music is of us; theirs is of them.

So a unity comes to be comprised from the multiplicity; an adamantine discipline encompasses the root of all emotional and sensual experience; there is the losing of awareness of individuality, of self in communion with the Absolute. Even in the most abstract vocalization the emotional content embodied there is released in such explicit terms that the rasa is very clear indeed. Austere, stylized abstraction, as heard in the art of khyal, and the shorthand words suffused with romantic overtones as used in thumri-singing, can be as intensely evocative to the Indian as the most persuasive and tangible of stimuli can be to our own emotional response.

Rasa generates potency.

Chapter Seven

INFINITE VARIATIONS ON ONE THEME

'Multitudinous disguises evolving in a thousand shapes of the same eternal aspiring theme.'   YEHUDI MENUHIN

If two musicians followed one upon the other at a Sangeet Sammelan, both applying themselves to an exposition of one particular raga, their instantaneous composition would in no way be the same. Why is this?

The formal rules are strict. The grammar is laid down. The principles are developed in dozens of treatises. The intricate scaffolding is there. But just as one scaffolding can be the framework on which a hundred different structures might be built, so the rules, principles and grammar of the ascending and descending scales within which each raga is encased make the framework for a multitude of evanescent forms reflecting that 'one eternal, aspiring theme.'

Freedom so to improvise within certain clearly defined structures is not so easy for Western music. Some musicians are now trying to compose 'open-ended music' with great areas of notation blotted out in an attempt to free the participating instrumentalists and singers from the prison-house of previous regimentation in notation. Ostensibly, the free areas are to enable the musicians to improvise as they progress forwards in time, if not in space. So far the results are not all that encouraging. The means are arbitrary and artificial; one realizes just how deeply embedded are the principles of fixed notation in an unchangeable keyboard scale. There are also layers of subconscious comprehension and reaction for Western audiences when we tamper with this. However, that does not mean that the experiment is not valid and should never be attempted. With that attitude we should be on a par with the most rigid of Indian purists.

The problem is that some of our experimenters seem to be con-

centrating so self-consciously on breaking down the previous structure, that all musicality has fled their present one. A London music
critic, commenting on an *avant garde* concert in which four
musicians 'on four superb Steinway grands spent nearly half an
hour dispatching with no small refinement the doodlings on four
notes called for by Terry Riley's Keyboard Studies', voiced an
extreme reaction to an extreme swing of the musical pendulum.
'Then four minutes to relieve the cramps by pounding up and down
the keyboard for an Earle Brown piece before a complete marathon
performance of John Cage's Music for Piano, many if not all of
whose notes were indeterminately determined (by Cage) by spot-
ting imperfections in his MS paper . . .' He went on: 'In the early
fifties Cage, Brown and Feldman set out to free music from all
formal relationships. This of course is like trying to free the apple
from gravity. Behind the brave words of liberation, the excitement
of the "neck-breaking game at the edge of impossibility" are, in my
view, inferior musical minds who have not got what it takes
to be real composers and who hope to avoid acid comparisons
by proclaiming their weakness as their surest source of
strength.

'To escape the traditions to which they are the dissolute heirs
they have placed themselves beyond criticism by cultivating osmo-
tic growths in a stagnant pool, which is given out as being a well of
life (as opposed to art). Here is no end and certainly no beginning,
but a purgatorial limbo.'

In fact, these modern Western musicians are doing no more than
their 'minimal art' colleagues of painting. But the shattering of
tradition and principle also seems to have an adverse effect on the
sense of wholeness in the music and one has the nagging feeling
that the baby is as usual, *in extremis,* being thrown out with the
bathwater. Somehow it needs to be seen that principles and traditions do not necessarily limit freedom and flexibility. This is where
we can learn from the example of India's classical music. It may be
more creatively worthwhile for our musicians to turn to these
sources of logical, mathematical, functioning principles rather than
to turn our own, created from an entirely different rationale, inside
out.

We accept a Beethoven symphony, a Tchaikovsky sonata, a
Brahms violin concerto, knowing full well that it will be the same
today as it was when composed. The notation is fixed and per-

manent, written down by the original composer centuries ago for all to see, for all to comprehend. Short of its re-creation under the personal idiosyncracies of the conductor of an orchestra and the various sections of the orchestra, the actual piece to be played is already fully determined.

There are of course subtle inflections and different types of emphasis, as anyone can decipher from listening to Sir Thomas Beecham or Leonard Bernstein or Stravinsky himself conducting. But nevertheless the framework is there, notated in scrupulous and finalized detail.

But Hindustani and Carnatic music have open-ended possibilities of interpretation. An Indian or Pakistani musician has the very wide scope, therefore, to make of the few rigid principles and fixed notations what he will. Through his imagination the whole spectrum of a raga can be changed by his inventiveness and his control of the voice and the scale of the raga, the range of talas to be chosen and the shifting dialogue between him and the percussion player.

Within the set pattern of exposition–the alaap, jor, jhalla and gat–these must follow in prescribed order. The arohi and the avorohi order of notes is fixed. The special phrases or pakad are there and the vadi note which has to be set before the listener's ear. The taans are delineated in embryonic form. But after this 'programming' of the musician, just as after a computer is fed the basic information in cybernetics, the principles of serendipity allow a number of interpretations happily to emanate forth.

Each section of the raga can be as developed–and as lengthened–as an individual musician wishes. Vilayat Khan and Ameer Khan, for instance, will spend far longer elaborating a meditative alaap than Ravi Shankar, who may pass very quickly to the gat if the mood of drama is upon him so that he can shine in the fast taans and meends. The choice of tala also presents a variety of changes to one raga because then there is a change of emphasis between soloist and drummer. A musician can further subdivide the presentation with explorations concentrated on the singing of the bols at any given instant. He can let the percussion player take over for some time, highlighting the cross-rhythms in the beat rather than in the melody. He can even choose to remain silent while drone and drummer ease the tension. Then he can plunge in with a nod of the head, to vary the rhythm at the melodic level in as many dramatic ways as he cares to display once the gat has commenced. The pitch and the tonic from which the two scales derive their being, are his to decide.

There are in fact limitless possibilities. Just as the galaxies remain fixed within the certain laws of their ellipses and planetary revolutions *within* an expanding universe, so also the rules of structure in a raga remain constant but can be expanded within their right ratio.

And even then, one musician will never play the same raga in exactly the same way from performance to performance. How much more so then will two separate musicians differ in their renditions?

There is, of course, one more component that influences this outcome. I have mentioned it many times already, but unless one has experienced the rapport of an Indian audience with the musicians it is difficult to imagine how active an agent such corporate participation is.

A musician of acknowledged standing will in fact be improvising into eighty or ninety per cent of the construction, and his exploration of the raga chosen may last anything from fifteen minutes for the recording of an LP disc to an hour or two hours, depending upon his creative imagination at that particular time of performance and the responsiveness of his audience. The musician is intimately concerned with this reflection of his emotive artistry, as if from a sounding-board within each listener's personality. Response is an active agent in the chemistry of Indian music. All the separate responses – the ecstatic sighs after a delicious glissade, the tapping of the beat by individuals, the exclamations of 'vaa vaa' (bravo) after a well executed taan or a delicately drawn-out meend – are the electrical impulses which spark alive the vivid rapport that sets a raga apart from its re-creation on another occasion.

I have known a concert in the warm, red-stone fort of Delhi when we were all saturated with the splendour of the musical interpretation. As hour upon hour slid by until the final culmination, the entire audience was in a high state of intoxication, letting escape gasps of astonishment as each new phrase was created by one artist in reply to the other, intuitively conjured out of the mind and heart of the exposition a few minutes beforehand. Shouts of exultation came when the great Ustad Allauddin Khan, his son Ali Akbar, his son-in-law Ravi Shankar and the ebullient tabla player Chatur Lal,

243

all took up the challenge thrown down by the predominant rhythm. Each kept within the circumscribed skeletal frame of the raga, but each was weaving a rich fabric of the most intricate hue until we all were dizzy.

Then the tension became too much as each time the sum was delayed with yet another division into fractional mathematics and voluptuous beauty. I found myself longing for the resolution on that final accentuated beat. Such was the see-saw of emotion that Ravi Shankar had to break into the full swing of the playing of the raga while he laughingly expostulated with the audience whose joy and explosive enthusiasm had become too much of an interference with the intensity of concentration needed for proper dialogue between the performers.

Strung taut like their strings and drums, we too were caught up in the tremendous battle as Chatur Lal scuttled on in his improvisations, trying to keep up with the changes rung by sarod and the sitar in turn. When Ali Akbar completed an extempore passage, Ravi Shankar took up the inspirational theme; each derived zest from the other's playing, with the tabla acting as foil to both, until we all were swaying, tapping our hands and feet to the marked beats. And then we all burst forth with a terrific emotional release as the point of fusion finally came when all the players achieved rest on the one peak, the great predominating sama or summit, the tautness gone, all passion spent.

Naturally enough a raga which undergoes such rarified treatment is not ever going to be quite the same again, when played in more tranquil conditions. Even if it were possible to transcribe it in black and white the same intrinsic changes would occur.

The second major variant is that of creative genius at work compared with pedantic technique. In Sanskrit there is a word which has come to symbolize wholeness; this word is 'dhyana'. Its actual meaning is active meditation which in effect implies for the Indian a 'causing to be'—in fact, creating. To each raga an individual musician will bring his individual view of life and 'cause to be' a very different arrangement of the same prescribed notes and their microtonal graces. This depends on his own personality, his state of mind at the time of playing, his temperament, the acuteness of understanding of the nature of the raga among those who sit listening, and his long-learned skill. This is in essence the spiritual process (in its widest sense) that every artist feels. The Indian artist takes it one step further by exploring inwards into the complex inner world of human personality.

On the other hand there are some musicians who are masters of technique, who know the way to order the alamkaras and to make the grace notes play around the proper full tones, who can sing the right pakad or groups of notes that constitute a certain raga – but who stop there. Their compositions are external ones, technical ragas which do not speak to the heart as do the same ragas played by musicians such as Ali Akbar Khan with his meditative genius, Bismillah with his incomparable shehnai, and Ameer Khan with his expressive softness of voice. Masters such as these, and there are many others who ought to be known in the West, will charge a raga with an insight, a spiritual dhyana born of their own especial divinations and intuition. They are composers and executants and in their improvization right at the moment of play the raga is shaped and re-created each time.

In some ragas, of course, expected orders and graphs of notes have to be followed, just as varying kinds of note formations are prohibited. In Darbari, Mālkauns and Piloo, for instance, the pakad, the group of notes which give rise to a recognizable phrase, is awaited by a knowledgeable audience. The corresponding loss to us would be if the restatement in any symphonic work were dropped from a movement. The point to remember in Indian music is that expectancy is aroused by the freedom of spontaneous play by the artist – and the audience never quite knows when the delights are to be served up.

The following well recognized pakad from Darbari illustrates this. It consists of the ga^k, reh – reh, sa; dha^k, ni^k, sa (all in lower octave), reh, sa. The vadi is reh. Because it is such a major raga many recordings have been made of it and it is now possible to compare how leading musicians approach it with differing emphasis.

There is a shake upon the ga^k and dha^k and these notes are intended to be sung with a light touch and not in a ponderous manner. If they are, this would change the raga into another closely related mode. Below is a characteristic phrase of the Darbari. If it were whistled, an Indian who knew his Hindustani music would be able to say that Darbari was intended, but this is not to say that the phrase has to remain moulded in this form whenever touched upon. It can be broken up and expanded in turn, but the ratio of note to note (the dha ni reh sa, or the pa sa ni dha) will come somewhere along the melodic line just to remind the audience in which raga they are participating.

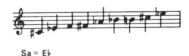

Sa = E♭

and the special pakad is:

N S N S N S R S D N S R G M R S   G M R S

To see how one raga can be given different treatment it is worth listening to Ghulam Ali and Ameer Khan who have both recorded the same. For one thing they use different motive words and different talas for the same melodic scale. Ameer Khan is conspicuously more meditative and inward-searching in the timbre of his voice. This gives an entirely different charisma to the whole raga: Bade Ghulam Ali is more forceful and affirmative.

What happens in technical terms is more elusive to us than to Indians. We can, however, recognize that Ameer Khan is pitching his voice in a lower register than Bade Ghulam Ali. His tonic sa is E♭, whereas Bade Ghulam Ali uses D♮ as sa. This means with transposition that we can listen to it in two different Western scales while it still remains in a fixed ascending and descending pattern within the Indian scale. The lower register brings out the regal, contemplative character of the raga. An Indian friend once explained to me his own feelings about this raga: 'It should have a very special type of performance reflecting a mixture of profound emotion, of happiness of the true inner kind, in the way that you say "all is well with the world", and a flowing dignity. This is a raga of the late evening when all is settling and there are no pent-up emotions.' He felt this in his bones. As soon as Darbari is mentioned an image flickers in the Indian's mind recalling the many times that he has heard it before; it is as popular with their audiences as Beethoven's Emperor Concerto is with our audiences.

To clarify the finer details which help distinguish the one vocalist from the other needs much greater familiarity than most of us will ever possess. But for Indians who are versed in their own music (the disillusioning discovery is to find so many Western-orientated Indians who are not) it will be easy for them to disentangle the elements immediately a new singer shifts the approach to a raga.

In the decorative motifs and the elaborations, Ameer Khan uses fewer taans than Bade Ghulam Ali, whose voice ripples through them like shimmering rivulets. He keeps returning to the phrase dha .. ni .. sa and then coming to rest in the middle of the upper phrase on ga^k. Ameer Khan more often comes to rest at the end of the phrase, upon the dominant note of reh itself–the vadi.

Those who play by ear rather than by sight are at a distinct advantage when dealing with this music. An acute sense of differentiation between fractional tones is of great help in heightening one's appreciation of the pressures and elongations of such notes as the reh in Darbari, the fall downwards from ma^t in Kafi, or the inflection of Mālkauns.

It is also interesting to note how two musicians will concentrate their attentions on different sections of the tetrachord, even though the notes remain unchanged. Take an example, a raga at its simplest:

This is the skeletal form of Raga Bilahari, a very sweet melody not found in the North. It is frequently used at times of marriage when the nadaswarams, the South Indians' large equivalent of the shehnai, blare forth.

One musician may well stay the lower side of the vadi note–pa or G in this instance–elaborating down to the particular turn of phrase in lower dha > middle sa lowering to ni (only in the descent) and again to dha. Another musician may well move into the upper half of the tetrachord above the vadi, using the dha > upper sa, ni, dha to come to rest upon the vadi note pa–eventually. One singer will linger on the sa; another may fix his attention upon the vadi and its satellites, and the twisted pakad of dha, sa, ni, dha, using them almost as a whispered refrain of infinite delicacy, hardly touched upon at all. If a song is put to the notes and it is a gay and lively air, concentration will be on certain notes; if it is of a more reflective nature the axis will be shifted to the lower register and more *appogiaturos* or grace leading to a predominant note may be employed, so delaying the substantive note and making it seem more dominant and luminous.

Ali Akbar has commented that a good musician spends years learning other peoples' idiosyncratic phraseology in a certain gharana – and then beyond all this is territory of his own where he can explore interpretations other than the accepted and orthodox ordering of the notes and the graces. The way a musician attacks these notes can shift the entire mood of the raga and accentuate angles of the surface melody as seen from different viewpoints. T. K. Jayaram Iyer put it to me in his own explicit imagery:

'A singer will linger on some notes more than others. It is like a boy skipping downstairs. The notes are in the particular order like the steps of the staircase, but one boy will run, or even slide down; another boy will hop; another go the whole way glissando down the banisters. It will still be exactly the same staircase.

'Or suppose I am going along the road. I will stop in some houses longer than in others. I will say: "Is this your house? I know you and you will not mind if I stay for a while and talk." But the lady next door might object because she does not know me and she may be more formal, so I will quickly go to my South Indian friend at the end of the road. That may be way at the bottom – in a lower register. But the other man, the other singer, might not know you so well and will call in at some other house on the way where I will only look at the garden and go away again. It is the same road with the same number of houses but we will have done different things. So it will be with the same raga, but with different singers.'

Again, with the increasing number of LP recordings of Indian music one can take yet another major raga, such as Todi (Toree). This is the raga that called Gregorian chant to the mind of our old friend T.K. It exudes an atmosphere of serene devotion, so expressive of individual Hindus at worship. This is its basic scale:

Ali Akbar plays it straightforwardly on his sarod, giving a slow exposition to the serious prelude. Bismillah Khan gives it many decorative flourishes and swinging, syncopated graces on the shehnai. The luxuriantly modulated voice of Bade Ghulam Ali ripples over the many taans of its minor scale and the 'black' notes of its descending scale, the dha^k, ma^t, ga^k and reh^k. Even playing the ascent and descent of Raga Todi on the limited range of the piano gives an indication of its mellow and solemn melodiousness and of the many rich variations which could be extracted from these notes.

There are so many ways that changes can be rung on the one melodic line of the raga. Improvisations on these set notes can be in any number of permutations of the intervals, with different qualities and approaches to them. The graces can be used in any manner of variation barring the few that may be disallowed for a certain raga. A throb, a slur, a staccato group, a swift meend, or a melting-away can be favoured and perfected by one musician, whereas another will prefer a different approach to create the full relish of the raga.

Full substantive notes can be joined together with long glissandos or accentuated on a level (asthayi), as Abdul Karim Khan often does in his vocalizing. An example of this repetitive emphasis within a very narrow range appears at the beginning and end of this short passage of notation by John Barham from the recording of Sindh Bhairavi by Ali Akbar Khan.

One singer may care to arouse continual tension by coming to rest at the end of a slide just short of the tonic or dominating vadi note, or may suddenly sway and swing upward to the corresponding note in the upper octave (this too is a favourite device of Ali Akbar Khan when he slides along the flexible wire of his sarod which may then cause the note to slur up the chromatic scale).

The free run of improvisation which a musician can employ (the more he masters the intricacies of the techniques at this service), reminds one of recent geometric art: the play with patterns of lines and circles within the rigid, unchanging perimeter of a shape or the circumference of a circle. The outer limits remain constant. The inner design presents all manner of possibilities.

A raga is not a horizontal plane packed with dense chords travelling sideways, but moves forwards and backwards within a cone, endlessly in tension due to its own centrifugal pull.

In addition to all these tonal patterns, their combinations have to be married to the many different talas chosen by the soloist. At different levels these spur him on with rhythmic challenges to create further shapes out of the svaras.

The fascination in Indian music is that, as audience, one is present at the birth of this entity, following the musician as he explores mentally and musically the interrelationship of the intervals chosen and their contrasting sound and the resultant mood. And all the time the fixed tonic is persistently being reiterated on the drone instrument. The way these notes fall into place with this static harmony of the drone strings is very important and is the test of the musician's calibre as a craftsman. The audience awaits any slip which may prove he has not as much mastery of the raga as a preceding musician.

After a deliberately lengthy passage of improvisation which may involve many accidentals – accidentals which create a dissonant juxtaposition with other notes – there is always the danger for inexpert musicians of losing the tonic to which they must, in the end, return. A certain pattern of notes may start a new train of thought and cause this straying-away. This can result in the creation of an entirely different raga and is not to be expected of a worthwhile musician. No matter how far an artist may wander in his exposition of the raga, he must always bear in mind its essential unity.

It is unity, unity, unity, a force and urge, that stirs every level of the mind in Indian thinking. Each musician as he approaches one and the same raga, is bringing to it his own uniquely individual concept of this unity, echoed in these very words at an introduction to a Festival of Indian Arts in London in 1970. The Indian High Commissioner, Apa B. Pant, said exactly this: 'Through sound and through rhythm the separate I-consciousness is extinguished–and unity is achieved.'

So there are many possibilities; the edifice is never quite the same no matter how often the raga is played. The style of Milton is very different from that of the poet Shelley despite the fact that they may use exactly the same words of the English language. Just so a master-musician will differ in style from another. Grace notes linger in all their emotive quality when Vilayat Khan approaches the alaap; with Ravi Shankar they are merged at tremendous speed. The one brings out the singular detail; the other the excitement of precision in acceleration. Both are valid.

Ali Akbar Khan will shape the gat in a different way from Sharan Mathur, the woman sarod player, or from Ashish Khan, his son. His knowledge of grace and melodic movements is obviously more extensive, and the dexterity of his masculine hands can accomplish more of the electrifying crescendos and intricate pluck-ings and slides along the fingerboard, so that his own rendition of the srutis will be that much more complex and commanding.

So also musicians like Pannala Gosh and Mahalingam with his South Indian flute can range over scales, notes and grace tones in octaves incapable of being covered fully by the ordinary flute. Thus a given raga expands to further edges of exploration under inspiration such as this.

A raga sung by a vocalist of the old school, such as Ustad Mushtaq Hussain Khan who has been a court musician for nearly half a century, will be very different from the lyrical and 'feeling' exposition given by Bhimsen Joshi. This singer's voice is softly modulated and he takes a passage of notes (ranging over three octaves) without seeming to pause for breath as he slides through the patterns and figures that highlight the raga. This is grammar with a poetic content, very different from that of Mushtaq Hussain Khan. Such treatment can, of course, happen in our own operatic arias; it sets apart Maria Callas from the third-rate singers applying themselves to exactly the same notes. The latter may be technically correct, but the result will be Callas without the fire.

No art form, however, can remain static. This is a real problem in a land like India which is so deeply embedded in a traditional, rural society where the aesthetics of art form tend to make for passivity and a state of creative immobility. This arouses the despair of Western theoreticians who marked these matters out (since the Greeks) with clarity of logic and a tendency to separate artistic principles from philosophy, which in its turn parted company with religion. But the Indian has through his history set his whole being against watertight compartments.

He is artist, philosopher, theoretician, composer, creator, religious adherent, practiser and meditative sannyasi, *all* at the same time. Many Westerners are flabbergasted by this. Rather they become infuriated by the all-embracing, excessively universal nature of the Indian temperament. It is, to coin a terrible phrase, un-get-holdable-of.

Indian theoreticians on music had already accepted the hypothesis of their philosophic works. In the Sanskrit it is written: 'Rasa brahm sahodre asti' (rasa and Brahm are born from the same place). This has meant all along that music is not only art, but within its form carries religious and spiritual implications – if a musician could touch the right note, perform the correct nritya, of dance, and evoke the right flavour of mood, the rasa, he was preparing himself for true salvation and the joys of paradise, according to the texts which are not seen as pedantic even today. They are living potent forces in cultural life.

The artistic search through feeling out the sādhana of the musical art is, as a result, inward and contemplative. It is the exact opposite of the thrusting experimentation of Picasso, Pollock and those young artists trying out sculptural painting and kinetic art forms. So far, no-one has experimented with two Indian musicians singing the same raga to the same tala but in a different tonic or pitch. Certainly two drones tuned to differing tonics would create difficulties in playing together. Vocalists would be entirely thrown, in keeping absolute pitch.

Indian music, being entirely melodic, has always been conceived in terms of the human voice; that is perhaps why its instruments have evolved into such sensitive purveyors of the intonations and feel of the human voice. But as Dr Narayana Menon has very recently pointed out, contemporary times demand the emancipation of Indian instruments from this subservience to the human voice.

With orchestration as the next real experiment he feels that

Indian musicians could 'evolve a harmonic style (orchestration being an adjunct of harmony) which will be in keeping with the genius of our own music–and without losing our identity or cramping our national spontaneous expression. Rules of harmony came after the music is created and not before, just as grammar comes after a language has been formed . . .', but it should 'strike out along new paths, and not get marooned in little islands of orthodoxy'.

'The moment we put thirty instruments together', he has gone on to say, 'they will cry out for new kinds of discipline, create new types of sonority, new nuances. The melodic line will change and with it its rhythmic basis. Orchestration will mean the beginning of part-playing, then of counterpoint, then perhaps of full harmonic writing.'

Many Indian musicians would perish this thought for fear that the gigantic body of traditional music might be irretrievably corrupted; but such a search for new statements of old truths should not mean an alternative in the form of a challenge to the old classical music–it has such a vital force, not only for its native land, but also for ourselves. It should mean a release of other energies. I often heretically feel that it could be our own younger generation (who are genuinely forcing the pace in the best forms of popular music) who could achieve the breakthrough if only they could get together with traditionally taught young Indians like Amjad Ali and Ashish Khan. Groups such as Quintessence (with whom John Barham has been composing) and individuals of the integrity of George Harrison, who have this particular empathy with India and Indian thought processes, have already injected sacred chants and Indian instruments and rhythm into Western processes–in recordings such as Dive Deep (LP Island Records 9143 Stereo) which is a really exciting new music with an ability to move from Indian to Western idiom and back with refreshing fluency, and the deeply moving My Sweet Lord by Harrison, virtually a hymn in contemporary terms. It needs a further serious step forward, made with honesty and willingness to analyse all hypotheses, to create a proper emancipation of both systems. In certain aspects these groups appear to be more susceptible to new theories and more capable of making them aesthetically joyful than are strictly classical musicians–although the arbitrary and snobbish division becomes increasingly irrelevant today.

One point that must not go unnoticed is that the youngest generation of serious Western musicians has begun to approach Indian music with a positive sense of humility and with earnest study, which means ironically that they know more of the Eastern system than their counterparts in India do of the Western. It is therefore with a heartening sense of expectation that at this very moment in writing I discover that John Barham, who long ago began to study Indian music when I first began to write this book, is now collaborating with Ashish Khan, attempting yet another serious work of marrying the two systems.

John Barham has used the piano as if it were a santoor, adding harmony through chordal-type clusters, together with the sarod; while Ashish Khan, with a similar welcome humility towards Western music, has also began a dialogue with stringed instruments, working closely with John Barham, in a string quartet for sarod. The melody he has created with different part-writing and tantalizing Indian rhythmic dialogue between sarod and the stringed instruments, must surely be fruitful. It is young musicians of this calibre who can cast aside the fears of an older generation and meet to good effect, despite all the preconceived attitudes which have built blinkers into the aesthetic views taken by musicians at work here and in India.

The Indian has to be convinced though of the worthwhile nature of experimentation, because all through his history he has not been concerned with wayward and restless innovation but rather with exuberance blended in totally with severe mathematical balance—that classical ideal of the Greek temple and its well defined laws of space versus solidity that the Parthenon holds within its architecture. And to this severity of construction in his music he brings the integral ornament of grace, which gives as marvellous effect of shadowy edge as the chiaroscuro of a Masaccio painting.

Here is a music evolved, refined and sifted through 20 centuries of theorizing, 30 centuries of tradition, and 40 centuries of philosophical searching—*so* old and yet so vitally in our midst today, speaking to us even in the West across vast historical and geographical distance, speaking with a universal appeal. This is its growing strength: it has no need to fear the young who wish to change it, so creating a new range and body of dynamics, because in its essential core there is still the replenishing ever-green spirit of the Indian genius.

It is this ability to hold this harmony – a fundamental mathematical law in the svaras, the srutis and their complex ordering, combined with a spirit to breathe – which brings huge audiences, not only Indian, to such a remarkable pitch of fusion. It is for all men and women a religious experience in the Wordsworthian sense:

> . . . sensations sweet,
> Felt in the blood, and felt along the heart;
> And passing even into my purer mind,
> With tranquil restoration . . .
> While with an eye made quiet by the power
> Of harmony, and the deep power of joy,
> We see into the life of things.

INDIAN INSTRUMENTS

STRINGED INSTRUMENTS

SITAR

*The sitar is the most popular stringed instrument in North India, and has existed in its present form for roughly 700 years, having evolved from a modification of the tri-tantra veena. Sehtar is the Persian name for this instrument–a 3-stringed instrument perfected by Amir Khusru who settled in India in the twelfth century.

*It is made from seasoned gourd, ivory inlay and teakwood. The track along the elongated, wooden stem consists of 20 movable frets of curved brass, easily adjusted to suit the different scales of the ragas to be played.

*There are 6 or 7 main playing strings above these brass bridges and 19 sympathetic strings for resonance below. These sympathetic strings provide the characteristic twanging in *perpetuum mobile* during the entire performance as they respond to the playing of the other strings. These are plucked with the little finger of the right hand, which can be bleeding at the end of a long performance.

*The main strings are played with a wire plectrum worn on the index finger of the right hand. This plectrum is a piece of wire twisted three-dimensionally to facilitate the intricate motions of the finger.

*The first wire on the left is so flexible that by pulling it gradually 4 or 5 notes can be played in a meend or ligato.

*The sitar can cover 4 octaves and most masters of the sitar bear the marks of its demanding play in their scabbed and calloused finger-knuckles which are bitten into by the wires with the force of play.

SAROD

*The sarod is a stringed instrument smaller than the sitar and with more of a mandolin sound than the veena overtones of the sitar.

*It is plucked with a piece of coconut shell.

*The large, gourd-style sound-box covered in skin is made of wood. Over it run the 25 strings. The smaller sound-box below the wooden end where the main string-pegs are positioned is made of metal and adds the haunting resonance of this instrument.

*Of these strings, 10 are played with the coconut plectrum on the right hand: 4 carry the melody; 2 serve to accentuate the percussion; and 4 are tuned to the dominant note of the scale chosen.

*The other 15 strings are for sympathetic resonance and are placed below the main strings. They are not played by the plectrum but in fact respond to the playing of the main strings; they resonate continually during play, so reinforcing the drone strings either on the similarly tuned tampura, or on the integral drone strings of the sarod.

*The left hand develops a vibrato along the metal fingerboard throughout play.

SURBAHAR

*The surbahar is a more majestic instrument than the sitar. It has a pitch $\frac{1}{5}$ lower, 6 metal strings for melody and drone, and 13 sympathetic strings plucked by a wire plectrum.

*It was invented by Gulam Mohammed Khan whose son, Sajjad Mohammed, was a great exponent of this instrument, a passion later to be carried on by Emdad Khan, the grandfather of Vilayat and Imrat Khan.

*It differs from the sitar as the 'cello does from the violin.

*Whereas the sitar plays at fast speeds and in higher octaves, the surbahar is more suitable for slower tempos and lower octaves. It is in fact tuned an octave lower than the sitar and is capable of being played two octaves lower still because of the addition of 2 extra brass strings – tuned to the octave below the 2nd and 4th strings.

*It is suited for passages of slower movement and compositions of a sombre vein.

*The technique of pulling the strings across the frets at right angles to the neck increases the tension and raises the pitch. This is a speciality of the Gayaki style of playing perfected by Vilayat and Imrat Khan his brother. Because of the large nature of the instrument, extra duration of sound is achieved also.

SARANGI

*The sarangi is the most popular accompanying stringed instrument of the North. It is especially used as accompaniment for vocal-singing because of its capacity to echo the voice. It has a wide range of sound: sometimes like an Irish jig, sometimes deeply mellow like the violin.

*It is shaped like a squashed guitar and is made from one block of hollowed-out wood with a parchment cover.

*The 3 or 4 main strings are bowed, not plucked. These are made of gut with one of brass for low pitch. Under them runs a variable number of sympathetic strings, 13–35 in number.

*No pressure is applied to these strings but the finger-nails slide down the *side* of the strings, which are never touched by the bow. They reverberate with the sound coming from the gut strings. The vibration communicates between the upper layer of played strings and this lower level, either in unison or an octave apart. The amazing vibration is caused by the adhesive power of the bow pulling against the strings. The friction so caused has hardly died down when the bow has commenced the return movement.

DILRUBA

*It is slightly smaller than a sitar, with 4 main strings and 19–22 sympathetic strings. Is played with a bow over movable frets.
*Unlike the sitar, it has a belly instead of a bowl for resonating the sound. This is covered with sheep parchment.
*In a more primitive form it is commonly used by wandering minstrels.

EKTARA

*The ektara is an instrument of 1 string, commonly used by villagers to accompany their folk-songs or for the rendering of simple, evocatively plaintive airs.
*It consist of a hollow gourd or simple clay bowl, covered on one side with thin animal skin, goat-skin for instance.

VEENA

*To be able to play this doyen of all Indian instruments is to be able to play any instrument. This is the South Indian instrument *par excellence* and it occupies a most important place, not only as the vital accompaniment to all Carnatic vocalists, but also as an instrument for solo play.
*It has been said by Yajnavalkya, the ancient Indian writer and philosopher: 'He who knows the art of veena-playing and sruti shastra can attain God easily.'
*The veena is so delicate in its nuances and nicety of true intonation that the slightest difference in pressure from the fingers, or the distance in the frets can almost indefinably change the true tone. Of all instrumental sound, that of the veena is said most closely to resemble the sound of the human voice.
*Its lineage is so ancient that it is said to have evolved from the Egyptian lute (called a vena) 4000 years ago. It is certainly mentioned in the Vedic index of instruments along with cymbals, wooden drums, vāna, a lute of 100 strings and a reed flute. Many scholars assume the swaradhae veena (svara = note adi = beginning or the first in Sanskrit) mentioned in these ancient treatises to be much more primitive than the present, sophisticated form–perhaps there were no more than 12 frets for the octave.

INDIAN INSTRUMENTS

*The modern veena has 24 *movable* frets, comprising 2 octaves, fixed in wax on a hollow, wooden base. This fingerboard rests on 2 hollow gourds, one larger than the other. The player can easily reset them by moving the wax very slightly, so changing the pitch fractionally.

*The 7 strings are placed over an ivory bridge which stands high above the frets.

*Of the 7 strings, 4 are for playing and 3 are placed at the side of the fingerboard for rhythm and as a kind of drone accompaniment. These are made of steel, the others of brass and silver.

*The veena is played either completely horizontal, resting on both gourds – with a plectrum or with a glass egg that slides up and down the strings leaving behind an extraordinary mellow oscillation – or it can be played with one of the sounding-gourds resting on the left knee of the cross-legged player. Sometimes this is placed over the left shoulder more like a tampura.

*The two gourds are of natural wood from the jack-tree and the strings are of wire stretched over the flat top of the bowl, which is approximately 1 foot in diameter. In early times the gut of animals or certain kinds of strong grass were used when wire was not known.

*The veena is a popular household instrument in South India and is most often played by women.

VICHITRA VEENA

*This is played in the same way as the North Indian been, but always rested horizontally.

*It stands on 2 equally large gourds over a foot in diameter.

*Each finger can wear a plectrum, sometimes made from fish-scale and fastened on by strings or with cotton thread.

GOTU-VADYAM

*This South Indian instrument is played like the veena (carnatic) but looks like the been.

BEEN (NORTH INDIAN VEENA)

*The been differs from the South Indian veena in having 2 bridges, one of which is chiselled ivory to increase the resonating effect of the strings.

*This instrument also looks different from the South Indian veena. The 2 gourds are large and equally sized. They are attached to a long bamboo or wooden piece bearing fixed wooden frets on wax (with metal on top, but nowadays movable frets are in vogue).

*The playing position also is different – it is compared with wearing the sacred thread. The instrument is placed diagonally, that is across the torso of the musician, with one gourd on the left shoulder and the other on the floor next to the right thigh on which the right forearm rests. The right hand plucks, wearing plectrums on two fingers–the index and the middle.

TAMPURA

*The tampura is a 4-wired drone instrument with a big gourd at the bottom of a long, narrow, jack-wood neck. The four wires are carried over this by 2 bridges and are adjusted by pegs at the top. Wool or silk is inserted between the wires and lower bridges to emphasize the vibrations of the notes.

*Because it is the most common instrument in North India where it is essential for any singer, it comes in a variety of carvings. Ravi Shankar carries a miniature one on his world-wide tours.

*In shape it looks a little like the veena but with an integral gourd and minus the carved headpiece.

*The bowl is large, sometimes 10 inches wide, hollowed out of the jack-tree. Cheaper ones use an ordinary natural gourd.

*Of the strings, 3 are of metal and 1 is brass. These are most often tuned to pa, sa, sa and lower sa.

*The tampura is always held upright, resting on the lap or crooked leg of the musician. It is played by a mechanical, rhythmic, continual flow of the four fingers of the right hand from highest to lowest note.

RABAB

*The rabab is a multi-stringed instrument played flat on the lap. It has a wide shallow bowl of wood covered with parchment.

*It is strung with gut strings and has no frets. One string may be of brass. The fingers of the left hand stop the strings on the fingerboard while the right hand plays with a horn plectrum held between the thumb and index finger.

*This ancient Central Asian instrument is much used in the music of Kashmir. Its modern version is the sur-sringara which has a double belly of wood and is a bit longer than the rabab.

SANTOOR

*The santoor also is of Kashmiri origin. It has many strings and is played by striking 2 sticks against the strings which are stretched over 2 longitudinal, pegged bridges. It has a sound rather like a xylophone mixed with a harpsichord, but is much more complex. In the hands of a master-player such as Shivkumar Sharma it takes on an intricate range of subtle harmonies not so distant from Western melodies.

SVARA MANDOLA

*The svara mandola is a Southern instrument (originally called sata-tantri veena of 100 strings), standing on legs. It can be played with a shell moved to and fro or struck with 2 sticks like a xylophone.

WIND INSTRUMENTS

SHEHNAI

*This is a wind instrument of North India, its Southern equivalent being the more strident nadaswaram. Its origins are said to lie in Persia where the meaning of the word is 'the flute of royalty'.

*It is of the double-reed oboe type, fixed to a short metal staple, but unlike the oboe it has no keys on the staff. Instead there are 7, 8 or 9 holes (as on a recorder) which are stopped by the fingers while the player blows into the mouthpiece. The upper 7 holes are for playing. The others are stopped with wax or kept open and used for tuning.

*It is capable of producing long, sustained notes and therefore needs strong breath control. In the upper octaves it has great versatility and can be played in extremely fast tempo, especially by one who is incomparably its master – Bismillah Khan.

*It is always accompanied by another shehnai as drone. This shehnai sustains the tonic without moving from it during the whole performance – again a feat of strong breath control.

*Shehnais are most often used in the temples of North India. Therefore, because of its auspicious quality it is an intimate part of wedding ceremonies in the North, and during the times of month when astro-logers consider the planets to be in their most favourable conjunction, shehnais can be heard in the big towns welcoming guests and celebrat-ing the religious ceremony in the home.

*Because of this association with times of marriage, the shehnai has provided inspiration for innumerable love lyrics and has an emotive value that no other North Indian instrument possesses.

NADASWARAM

*The nadaswaram has a much harsher sound than the shehnai, and is played in a higher pitch which carries long distances over temple courtyards. It is used in South Indian wedding processions.

*It is a $2\frac{1}{2}$-foot reed instrument of conical shape, made of wood and sometimes silver, with 12 holes: 6 for fingering, 6 for regulating pitch.

BANSARI

*This is the poor man's musical instrument, be it only the simple bansari made of bamboo, a hollowed sugar cane or a metal tube. In North or South India it is universally played by the villagers, and in the spring one can hear all the little shepherd boys in the surrounding open plains of the Punjab fluting their simple, haunting melodies. It is associated with the Lord Krishna who claimed the gopis with it.

*The bansari is limited in range to 1 note less than 2 octaves. Only Pannalal Gosh and South Indians like Mahalingam have evolved truly classical flutes capable of carrying the full range of a complicated raga. Pannalal Gosh's bamboo flutes were sometimes over 3 feet in length.

*The flute was used as a drone by the Aryans before they adopted stringed instruments like the tampura from the rural tribes which they absorbed.

*The South Indian flute is played with more syncopation and the sound has an entirely different 'feel' when compared with the pathos and the sweet melancholy of the Northern bansari.

VENU

*The South Indian flute is 10–12 inches long with one end closed, and is played from the side through a hole made near the end. There are 8 finger-holes and for the subtleties of grace in Carnatic classical music it demands a very high standard of play as it is extremely difficult to control the finger-stoppings.

VIOLIN

*Our familiar stringed instrument has, in the last 300 years, become a very popular and favourite accompanying instrument for the vocalist in South India, and popular even in percussion ensembles performing a tala vadya kacheri.

*It is played upside down between the crossed legs of the musician.

PERCUSSION

Indian drums are as old as Indian history and Indian culture. They are mentioned in the *Samaveda* and the *Athaaveda*. They are to be seen depicted in all ancient sculptured reliefs – many nearly 2000 years old. Earliest drum music was, of course, made by beating the stomach.

Some of the drums, particularly ones which accompany classical music, can be tuned to a desired pitch; others have the pitch fixed when they are made. Some are played with sticks; others with the bare hand or with hand and stick.

Variations of sound are achieved by alternately using the cushion of the palms of the hand, the fingers for a clipped, light touch, and the base of the thumb for heavy resonance. A wet drum-skin gives a muffled sound. The lacings of the skin are tightened or loosened to produce different tones or pitches.

A paste of iron filings and atta (flour) is applied to the centre of the skin stretched over the drum-head. This is permanent on the tabla drums. For the mridangam it has to be freshly done for each performance. The paste is a reminder of past days when war drums were smeared with the blood of animals to bring strength in battle.

In some tribes elaborate ceremonial is attached to the making of a new skin for a drum. A bull is sacrificed to the tribal god and the old drum-head is made to touch the new one fashioned from the skin of this sacrificial beast. In Vedic times drums were beaten on the occasion of sacrificial offerings – at the time of the Das Ashwamedha horse sacrifice when warriors worshipped them, for instance. They are still used in North India on auspicious occasions and in South India they accompany the nadaswaram when the deities of the temples are taken for their morning procession or for their 'bath'. Drums are also beaten at time of marriages.

TABLA

*The full name is tabla-bayan. Tabla refers to the right-hand wooden drum, bayan to the left-hand metal drum. There is controversy about its origin, some authorities saying it is the pakhāwaj split in two. It is the most popular drum in use in North India, introduced into India during Moghul times.

*The right-hand drum is tuned to the tonic, dominant or subdominant, and can be retuned during a performance with the tuning hammer as the heat of overhead lights and concert hall often throws the tuning out.

*The bayan acts as the bass drum and is a very subtle instrument to play. It needs long years of practice to achieve the intricate tone-colours.

*It can be played at tremendous speed without ever losing its crystal-clear clarity.

PAKHAWAJ

*This is another North Indian drum, bigger than the mridangam but like it in shape. It is played most often as accompaniment to the classical style of singing known as dhrupad. Nowadays it is more often made of wood, instead of burnt clay, in the shape of a fat-waisted barrel $2\frac{1}{2}$ feet long. Both heads are covered with parchment. A thick paste of boiled rice, manganese dust and tamarind juice is applied to one head, and a paste made of wheat to the other, so producing the bass pitch. These are removed after each play.

*The pakhāwaj produces a rich, deep sound.

*The original name for this drum was mridanga, not to be mistaken for the South Indian mridangam.

DHOLAK

*The dholak is much used to accompany folk-musicians who travel from village to village.
*It is 20 inches long and made from a solid piece of wood bored right through. Its pitch is variable. The skin over the heads is stretched into hoops and fastened by interlaced leather thonging. It has no paste on the drum-heads.
*It is played by hand.
*It is very popular in the Punjab and UP, and during village wedding ceremonies girls sit around it, one playing and another keeping time on its wooden body with a ring, while all of them sing a chorus.

MRIDANGAM

*This is the counterpart of the tabla in Carnatic music. The word comes from the Sanskrit 'mrit–anga' meaning a clay body. It is the most ancient indigenous drum of India, depicted on many Hindu temple walls in the South.
*It has a remarkably crisp, well defined sound, and is indispensable to a classical dance concert of Bharata Natyam, when the drum-beat is essential to the dancers, maintaining acute precision and rhythm.
*It is a 2-headed, barrel-shaped drum, more elongated than the pakhāwaj of the North. Nowadays, instead of being made of burnt clay it is carved out of a single piece of jack-wood.
*The right head is the larger and has to be very carefully prepared, for tuning purposes. This side is covered with 3 layers and 3 kinds of hide. A permanent black crust covers the head which is tuned to sa–the crust increases the pitch of this tonic note. Bare parchment is left around it.
*The left-hand side is the bass. It is covered with 2 layers of skin and treated with boiled rice and water, and manganese filings in the centre.
*It is played with dexterous movements of the whole hand, wrists and fingers.

CHENDA

*The chenda is another drum of the South, from the west-coast Malabar area where it is the principal accompaniment to the mime dance-drama of Kathakali.
*The quality of its sound is ear-splitting and harsh.
*It is a 2-headed membrane drum played with sticks.

DUMRU

*The dumru is the hour-glass-shaped, tiny drum with a leather thong
attached to the narrow waist. This thong is flicked to hit each side of the
parchment-skin heads.
*Shiva in his Dance of Creation – the Tandava Nrittya – plays the dumru
as symbol of sound and revelation of creation. Now it is to be seen most
in use by the monkey wallahs beating out the simple beat for their
monkey charges to dance to.

KANJIRA

*This is a small, tambourine-like drum with copper or bronze discs
dangling on the frame. The single skin used on the drum-head is that of
the sand lizard.

DHOL

*The dhol is a big drum played with a stick.
*It is popular in tribal areas and villages.

GHARRA

*The gharra is an earthenware pot used in the North.
*It is often played with brass 'knuckle-dusters' attached to the hands of
the drum player.
*It is used as an accompaniment in Kashmiri music.

GHATAM

*This is a larger earthenware pot of symmetrical shape used in South
Indian music.
*It is beaten with the finger-tips and palms of the hand.
*It is cleverly designed to produce the tonic of the singer in question.
Ghatam players carry a whole range of these pots to suit vocalists using
different pitches. Their great asset to improve the quality of the thrum-
ming, resonating sound is a large stomach; against this the mouth of the
pot is manipulated to let air in and squeeze it out.

GLOSSARY OF TERMS

Abhang. Maharashtrian religious song.

Abhoga. Finale of the entire movement of a raag – a summing-up of the musical idea developed in sthayi, antara and sanchari.

Akbar (1556-1607). Moghul emperor who with Ashoka (268–27 BC) and Harsha (AD 606–47) achieved territorial unity over the major land area of the subcontinent from the NW frontier provinces (now part of West Pakistan) down to the southern Deccan and the Tamilnad plateau, leaving southern Hindu culture virtually untouched by Muslim influence.

Akbar was a political contemporary of Elizabeth I (1533–1603), Shakespeare (1564–1616) and the Dutch and British arrivals in North America (1609–10 onwards). He encouraged discourse among the intellectuals of his court, between persons from many other cultures, and with believers of other faiths – and did himself try to found a universal religion comprising aspects from all religions. Every branch of art flourished under his reign. He married a Hindu princess and encouraged the synthesis of the two civilizations, Hindu and Muslim.

Aksara or Akshara. A time measure in a tala, constituted of several matras or subdivisions of a percussive beat, just as a semibreve is made up of 2 minims, 4 crotchets or 8 quavers.

Alaap, Alapa or Alapana. Introductory slow movement of a raga, in which attention is given to particular notes, their order, usage and emphasis. In the alaap the dominating note is placed clearly before the listener. There is no rhythmic accompaniment. In Hindustani music the elaboration of the alaap is an indication of depth (and virtuosity in the technical sense) of musicianship, whereas in the Carnatic it is often curtailed for the main body – the gat – of the raga. The alaap is the invocation to the raga, calling forth its mood or rasa.

Alamkara. Ornamental movements or flourishes combining several melodic phrases which form into a disciplined pattern of graph-like figurations – although not in a mechanical, over-regulated sense.

Alvar. Tamil composer (c. sixth–eighth century) of hymns extolling Lord Vishnu and Shiva. These melodies are heard in temples and concerts in South India to this day.

Amsa or Amsha. 'Chief part' in Sanskrit. The most important note in a raga, used as a pivotal note to be returned to again and again. In its quality and emphasis and the way it is lingered over it creates the soul of the raga. The note upon which the musician most often comes to rest at the end of a long passage or range of alamkaras when the

cycle of rhythm returns to the first beat, the emphatic sama (sum).
Also known as the vadi note – the predominating sonant note.

Anudruta.   The time duration of one handclap. The druta is one
handclap plus a sideways flip of the hand, written thus in drum
notation ⌊ .

Anuvadi.   'Followers' that support the vadi and samavadi (the
secondary note in consonance with the vadi note).

Arohi or **Arohana.**   The complete ascending scale of a raga (pronounced 'aroharrn' with the 'r' rolled like the French but deeper in
the larynx and difficult for English people to feel as a sound).

Astapadis.   Composition of Jayadeva's *Gita Govinda* comprising
songs in asta (eight) pada (feet).

Asthayi.   Cf. **Sthayi.**

Atikomal.   A double flat note.

Atitivra.   A double sharp note.

Avasama.   The sama (sum) or first beat of the rhythmic cycle of the
tala.

Avorohi.   The descent of the gamut, invariably slightly changed by
one or two modified notes from the ascending scale.

Barhaat.   To proceed gradually in the musical composition.

Bauls.   Bengali folk-musicians who wander on foot from village to
village singing songs of mystic significance using commonplace words
and phrases to imply double meanings at a spiritual level. There have
been bauls of both the Hindu and Muslim faith, equally accepted and
singing in a similar religious vein.

Been or **Bin.**   North Indian name for the veena.

Bhajan.   Popular religious song (there are many well known ones
associated with Gandhi) with a fixed tune, accompanied by percussion
and often sung in mixed ragas. Essentially Hindu, expressing bhakti –
a warm emotional faith in a personal God which is expressed in
adoring and passionate human terms. Bhajans are often devoted to
the Krishna theme of the loving God. A bhajan is similar to the
kirtan of Bengal and the kriti of South India, but whereas the musical
element is uppermost in kriti, words and emotional content are
stressed in bhajan.

Bharata.   A person of mythological and historical significance, being
the originator of the *Bharata Natya Shastra*, the treatise of principles
concerning all the arts of drama, dance and music. This treatise is of
questionable date (*c.* second century BC to fourth century AD) because
in the Hindu religious view Bharata learnt all the aesthetic principles
of the arts directly from the Lord Shiva himself when he performed
the Cosmic Dance, so beautifully represented in sculptural terms at
the vast temple of Chidambaram, south of Madras.

The form of the major scales, the existence of the shrutis and an embryonic concept of moods (the nava rasa) conditioned by each note of the scale, were formulated in his time. These elementary compositions were known as jatis – songs with fixed narrow musical outlines from which the more comprehensive raga form grew. Scholars have now established that his original scale was in the D mode and not in the C mode.

Bhava. A mood with deep spiritual connotations. In music, bhava is the aura of devotional worship conjured up by specific sounds and is the portrayal of bhakti. It is to be distinguished from emotion that is the result of a mere experience of the senses. Emotion, even erotic emotion, must always be harnessed to sterner disciplines to make it reach out to the cosmic level.

Bistar. The meditative section of a fixed musical composition or gat.

Bol. 'Word' (Hindustani); bolnaa = to speak.

Bols. The syllabic words called out aloud to denote which kind of strike is to be made upon the drums, e.g. tri-ki-ta.

Bol-taans. Musical phrases, like arpeggios, interlinked with words, to be found especially in thumri-singing. A line of verse is sung in such a way that isolated words are used in a variety of ways to express different shades of emotion.

Charanam or **Carana.** Carnatic name for the section of raga where the first and second movements are developed and intermixed. There is also a wider deployment of grace notes as the melody interweaves the straight line of the alaap with more variations.

Cheez or **Cheeza.** A song often figuring in the classical vocal art of khyal. It consists of four parts:
  (a) the statement or asthayi beginning with the first line of the lyric and using syllabic sound;
  (b) slow development of the asthayi in an alaap with svara and words or bols;
  (c) a movement into the upper section or antara of the scale of the raga in question, the upper tetrachord;
  (d) the use of increasing tempo and bol-taans.

Deshi. Popular tunes sung by different tribes and rural people throughout India. Desh means land or country.

Dhammar. A style of vocal music similar to dhrupad but without its austerity or tonal restrictions. It uses more grace notes than dhrupad. Krishna legends are its subject and therefore its songs are sung predominantly at times of the Holi festival in the spring.

Dhrupad. This particular kind of vocal music with its long sustained notes has been called India's most 'massive and sublime' music. Developed at the beginning of this millenium from the singing of Sanskrit stanzas, prabhandas, around the eleventh and twelfth centuries. In the thirteenth century a saint/musician called Baija

268

Baora created dhruva geet during the reign of Allaudin Khilji, Pathan ruler of Delhi. This singing (geet) of dhruva (fixed) became known as dhruvapada (a fixed text). During this development the context of dhrupad changed from the temple devotion in Sanskrit – which, like recent liturgical Latin, was not understood by the mass of worshippers – into the vernacular. Emphasis has always been placed on the sahitya or thoughtful meaning behind the symbolic words used, but with the spread of Moghul rule dhrupad took on more ornamental improvisations. It still is sung in Brijbasha.

Its form is, however, strictly prescribed to follow a fixed pattern: the sthayi, antara, sanchari and abhoga with prescribed notes, words, and limited majestic talas.

Gradually through the richness of court life under the Moghul Emperors its severe classicism softened into the darbari style of vocal court music and its devotional roots were severed. Eventually it became stereotyped – an artifice in fact – with the decadence of the eighteenth century.

Dhrupad is still sung at connoisseur musical concerts in slow time, usually with a bass voice and few extempore passages in the fixed text.

Dhun. Dhvani = a sound. This is a light air, or a mixture of sweet melodies free from the formal disciplines of a raag. The musician has much more freedom to improvise and to syncopate the rhythms, returning again and again to the first line of the theme after improvising on many folk-melodies.

Drone. An accompanying instrument such as the tambura or sarangi or violin in the South, on which the tonic, its lower register and the dominant note (sometimes its consonant note) are played continuously throughout the raga. If a musician has to play without this accompaniment he can incorporate these drone notes in the chikari strings of his own instrument. The drone serves to reinforce the melody played or sung by the soloist and because of its 'permanent invariable' quality it also helps to mark out the relationship between the successive notes of the raga's melodic line and their individual relationship with the tonic.

Drut or **Dhrut.** Fast playing in the rhythmic beat of the tala.

Gamaka or **Gamaak.** Grace note.

Gat. The gat follows the alaap in the movements of the raag. It is a well defined composition (or of well structured bols in vocalized music) played first in slow tempo, then twice in double tempo and four times in quadruple tempo with short phrases or tihais played rapidly three times in a row, ending on the sum.

One could liken it to the coda of Western music. A coda is a peroration, a distinct and separate section structurally, a working-out of all that has preceded it, with ever-increasing acceleration and virtuosity. This is different from a rondo, which is a separate finale returning to an initial theme but with different episodes between. In the gat, phrases are dramatically presented which have already been placed before the ear in the alaap, and a dramatic duel in the form of statement and echoing statement can take place between melodic and rhythmic line.

Gayaki. A certain type of singing depending on what school or tradition (gharana) a musician belongs.

Gharana. A family of musicians in the medieval guild pattern – now meaning a school of music – in which knowledge of the especial handling of notes is passed on directly by aural tradition from relative to relative, rather than through theory written in books.

Gharanas flourished in North India under the numerous Hindu rajas and Muslim nawabs. These gharanas became more and more isolated from the main body of Indian culture during the alien rule of the British Raj. In their isolation they grew arrogant towards other musical styles which deviated from their own, as well as towards the mass of the people beyond the confines of the court. Licentiousness set in among musicians and dancers and music fell into disrepute. Now these gharanas have been revived, some well known ones being Gwalior, Rampur, Lucknow, Baroda and Patiala. Bade Ghulam Ali belonged to the latter gharana; Abdul Karim Khan belonged to another, Kirana, tracing its ancestry back to the Beenkar gharana of Tansen's daughter.

Each school is famous for certain characteristics of singing or playing. Kirana school, for instance, concentrated on the major serious ragas in slow tempo with long elaborations or vistars. Gwalior gharana was responsible for developing khyal to the summit of its artistic achievement. D. V. Paluskar was an exponent of this school.

Ghazal. A love lyric of Persian Muslim origin. There is no alaap. The music goes straight to the middle section of the raga and sings a simple melody. Begum Akhtar is a popular vocalist of these devotional songs. They are similar to Hindu bhajans.

Guru. A teacher in both the secular and the religious sense. It is said in the Hindu scriptures: 'Guru Brahma, Guru Vishnu, Guru Devo Maheshvaraha, Guru Sakshat, Param-Brahma, Tasmai Shree Guru-ve namam.' This means: 'I bow down therefore in homage to my guru who not only represents the Trimurti (the three images of the Trinity – Brahma, Vishnu and Shiva), but also the whole universe (Param-Brahma) incarnate.'

This explains the tremendous reverence given to one's guru throughout life. The guru is not only teacher in our sense but the guide for a person's development of spirit, and Indians seek out their gurus not only in respect and love, but out of dharma or dutiful action during their whole life's span, returning again and again to that same person for encouragement and advice.

Guru-shishya-paramparya. The especially Indian sense of handing down knowledge in the intimacy of close-knit family teaching-circles, in intense and almost secretive knowledge. This whole system of teacher-pupil relationship was originally used to transmit the entire Sanskrit literature, philosophy, legal codes and religious ritual in long quatrains or slokas by word of mouth and learnt by heart. In the principles of music so much depends on this person-to-person tradition where factual knowledge cannot possibly fully interpret the subtle nuances of individual teaching.

Jati. An elementary form of music which preceded the raga development. Jati is used as a specific term for the ordering of notes into meaningful sequences in the *Bharata Natya Shastra* (second century BC–second century AD).

Jatis. Used in South Indian rhythmic cycles of the dance, each jati is named after the variations within the 7 talas used in Carnatic music, e.g. tisra jati is 3 beats in a 4-division tala: |ı ı ı|ı ı ı|ı ı ı|ı ı ı|.

Jāvali. South Indian tune, light and gay both in spirit and melody, like the dhun of the North.

Jawab-sawal. Dialogue between two instruments or a vocalist and accompanying instrument. It heightens the tension and the corresponding release through the repetition of phrases, changes of tempo and even the speaking bols that Alla Rakha is so master of, replying to Ravi Shankar's virtuoso playing at high speed.

Jawari. That quality of voice which is husky and seductive. 'Soz' is also used in Urdu for this depth of resonance and timbre.

Jayadeva. Bengali poet-composer-musician who lived about the end of the twelfth century. Best known for his remarkable Sanskrit love poem *Gita Govinda* depicting the yearnings and frustrations of the love of Radha for the God Krishna. It is no ordinary love poem, but rather an interweaving of song, narration, recitative, and philosophical passages of the most mystical kind, with descriptive verses rich in pictorial imagery. It could be said to be a folk-religious-opera – the last flowering of Sanskrit literature before the process of synthesis began to combine Hindu and Muslim cultures into one art form.

Jhalla. Final section and climax of the alaap introducing the element of pulse, although not at this stage the percussion instruments. Its special form lies in the melody notes' being continuously interwoven with a pattern of level drone notes plucked on the sarod, sitar, veena or sarangi.

Jiva. 'Life' in Sanskrit.

Jor or **Jod.** The second section of the alaap. Numerous melodic patterns begin to build up, along with a slight increase in tempo.

Khali. The wave of the hand to keep the beat of the tala on an unaccented note. Differentiated from the beat of the accented matras marked out by a clap of the hand or a flick of the fingers of the right hand.

Khusro or **Khusru, Amir.** A formative musician of the late twelfth century who modified the three-stringed tritantra veena and named it the sehtar (which means three-stringed in Persian). He was also a forceful Muslim innovator who created the qawali style of singing, devotional songs in chorus which are still popular among the Muslim community. He also put meaningless syllables such as 'tum', 'der' and 'dani' to music, adding Persian words suggestive of abstract ideas, and so created what is now called the tarana style of singing.

Khyal. An Urdu word literally meaning 'imagination' or 'creative thought'. It is applied to a particular classical type of Hindustani singing. Khyal is spiritual music 'in sensuous and lyrical terms', less rigid and formal than dhrupad-singing. It came to full development in the baroque period of the Moghul courts, drawing material from secular music for its decorative motifs rather than from temple dhrupad with its austere devotional aspects.

In technique, notes are used clear-cut rather than run together at high speed as in the thumri. There is simplification in the embroidery, with straightforward ascending and descending ornamentation in the trills, graces and taans. Khyal can be in any time measure, unlike dhrupad with its ponderous tempo. It can be sung by baritone or tenor and has a much wider emotional range. As dhrupad is to khyal so khyal is to thumri.

It is not necessarily a style peculiar to vocal art. The musician Pannalal Gosh used to play in lyrical khyal style on his three-foot flute, systematically and fluently developing each note of the raga perhaps more clearly to the Western ear than could be done on any other Indian instrument.

Kirana. A gharana founded by Bande Ali Khan a century ago with descendants of the Beenkar school of Tansen's daughter which used the veena.

Kirtana. More austere compositions of the South in praise of God. Somewhat akin to the khyal-singing of the North but of a much more disciplined musical form, Carnatic music being less ornate in the use of grace, trills and arabesques.

Kirtans. The devotional songs of Bengal and Brindaban, a group of Krishna temples near Mathura in the UP. It is the legendary stories of this very human god which are the source of inspiration for kirtan. Kirtans do not strictly adhere to the raga scale and they incorporate a chorus led by a leader. Much of the musical value is subordinated to the sentimental emotion expressed in the words of the song in the highly charged atmosphere of Bengali emotion, which is a law unto itself.

Kirtans were introduced at the time of Chaitanya who inspired the great period of bhakti worship.

Komal. A modified, flattened note.

Kriti. The name by which a set composition in Carnatic music is known. This is the dhrupad of the South. The constituent parts are pāllavi, anupāllavi and carana. Very devotional in nature, often in the Telegu language of Tamilnad and Andhraa, and composed by saint-musicians in effusive praise of God. Thyagaraja and Swati Tirunal were exponents of kritis.

Krṣna. The actual transliteration of the anglicized spelling of the God Krishna – pronounced 'Kersh-nn' – the avatar or reincarnation of Vishnu, the Deity of Preservation in the Trinity of Brahma, Shiva and Vishnu.

Laghu. The term for a length of beat in a tala: the duration of two hand-beats and a flip of the hand sideways. The laghu can be counted also by a hand-clap and two or more quick finger-counts (made using the thumb against successive fingers or against the joints of the inside of one finger).

Laya. The overall tempo of the raag as differentiated from the more specific beats of the tala.

Laya kiri. 'Playing with the laya'. A skilful weaving by the percussion of intricate patterns of time measure into and out of each other. (Kishen Maharaj of the Benares school of tabla-playing is noted for this style).

Linam. A type of grace of a very delicate nature in which the slide passes through intermediate prime notes, linking them all together and almost absorbing them. This is different from the meend which is a slide between two primes and can be clearly heard linking them.

Madya drut. Medium fast tempo.

Marga. 'The sought' in Sanskrit. In musical terms *Marga Sangeet* was one primary stage of development beyond the earliest Vedic music of chanting mantras or magical incantations of symbolic sound. Marga combined elements of the early folk-music and harvesting-songs into the ritual music.

Matra. The specific beat within the rhythmic bar or cycle of the tala.

Meend. A smooth-gliding fast-moving descent, executed by deflecting the strings to 'elongate' the note plucked, or by 'squeezing' it on flute and shehnai. On a modern sitar some wires are so flexible that 4 or 5 notes can be played in a meend with one pull of the string. In a 2-octave sitar, notes can be produced up to $3\frac{1}{2}$ octaves in this way.

Mirh. A glide or slur, characteristic of instruments which either have movable frets or do not have frets at all.

Mnemonics. The drum language of syllables used and called out aloud for the many complex and subdivided beats on percussion instruments.

In Bharata Natyam performances in South India, the nattuvanar or dance teacher/conductor sits at the side of the stage and calls out the bols that make up mnemonics in order to help the dancer weave her way through the zig-zagging interweavings of rhythm. This sometimes sounds like an auctioneer at full tilt and can be heard very clearly on the UNESCO recording of Alain Danielou's Indian Music series (record 2) in which Venkatarama Iyer in the pallavi section calls out the vowel sounds and Gopalachari calls the mnemonics, so providing a fascinating molecular structure which only a computer perhaps could analyse into a mathematical design.

Mridangam. Mrit = clay, ang = body (Sanskrit). South Indian, two-headed drum.

Murchhana. Murchhit = unconsciousness (Sanskrit), implying the intangible quality of a note which is created by the actual change in difference in vibrations, so literally meaning extension or gradation. The word has been variously used:

(a) It is the ancient name for the early modes in Indian music before the raga system emerged.

(b) According to Popley's book, *The Music of India*,[1] murchhana in South India refers to ascending and descending varna or graph-like grace movements.

(c) According to Tagore the murchhana is the extending of the note 'to another in the ascending as well as the descending scale (like an *appogiatura*) without any intermediate break in the disposition of the srutis in the interval'.

Naad or **Nada.** Literally 'resonant sound', but like most Sanskrit words its overtones are more than the literal and precise English. It is much more complex, implying 'vital power'.

According to Sir John Woodruffe who wrote *The Serpent Power*:[2] '... the universe of immovable and movable things is linked together and pervaded by this shakti (female energy as seen in a universal and biological sense) which is called by such names as naad, prana, etc.'. In another book, the *Sangeet Sar*, it is put this way: 'Without naad there is no sangeet, without naad there is no knowledge of the universe and without naad there is no existence of the Lord Shiva. In fact the whole universe is illumined by naad, the divine energy.'

Lord Shiva symbolizes this energy, expressing it visually in the

[1] Now in reprint; p. 85.
[2] To be reprinted 1972; Published by the Ganesh Press, Madras.

274

Cosmic Dance – the source of all classical dancing – hence the spiritual overtones to dance and music in even modern India.

Nada Brahma. Na = praña = life breath; da = agni = fire; Brahma = omnipotent, absolute, male manifestation of Brahman, the neuter creative energy that motivates the whole entire cosmos.

According to the *Yoga Shastra*, nada is the source of music inseparably connected with the kundalini or vagus nerve. The *Sangeet Ratnakara* of Sarangadeva gives profound metaphysical connotations to these Hindu and musical concepts: vocal music is considered pure, primary sound, different from instrumental sound which is struck sound. Vocal music emanates from the internal spirit of man. It wells up from the soul and floats out through the vocal chords – which explains the particular Hindu attachment in supersensory or magical terms to the chanting of certain word patterns in Sanskrit mantras, for example the evocative sound 'OM'.

'The notion that the power of music, especially the intoned word, can influence the course of human destiny and even the order of the universe, goes back to the very oldest surviving form of Indian music, namely the music of the Vedas. The intoned formula is the pivot of the whole elaborate structure of Vedic offerings and sacrifice. It is the power of words, enunciated with the correct intonation, that determines the efficacy of the rites; a mistake may destroy everything.'[1]

One can see from this how vocal music became supreme as an art form in India and how important was the accurate use of, and approach to, a given note.

Nattuvanar. South Indian music teacher and guru of the dancer. He recites the songs and the mnemonics of the tala.

Nava rasa. The theory of the nine principal emotional moods which are aroused in all the various spheres of Indian art. (Referred to in Chapters 2 and 4 above).

Padam. South Indian love lyric, set to music, usually of slow tempo. Integral to classical Bharata Natyam dance. Concerned with the romances of the gods, most especially with the amorous adventures of the flute-playing god Krishna and the infatuated milk-maids or gopis.

Padams demand a very dramatized technique of mime gesture and facial expression known as abhinaya, and often the dancer joins in the singing at this point to express the pain and anguish of longing for the beloved.

Pakad. The characteristic phrases of a raag. To these grouping of notes the musician repeatedly returns as to an anchorage after the many extempore passages of free improvisation.

Pakhāwaj. Pucca = pure; āwaj = sound. North Indian drum

[1] Dr Arnold Bake, 'Music in India' in *The New Oxford History of Music*, Vol. I, *Ancient and Oriental Music*.

primarily used to accompany dhrupad/dhammar-style music. First used for accompanying mantra-chanting.

Pāllavi. First section of Carnatic raag, the asthayi, in which the emphatic note is established and displayed. Also the refrain in a set composition in the codal summing-up. Anupallavi is the second section or antara, concentrating on the consonant note and moving slowly up the octave.

Pāllavi is one of the most difficult forms for a South Indian musician to negotiate and is a carefully constructed motif or theme following the short alaap of Carnatic music when melodic variations are allowed to develop. It is sometimes translated as 'chorus'.

Pandit. 'Learned one' (Hindi). A teacher of a subject with rank equivalent to a doctorate. Urdu and Persian 'ustad' also means the same thing, a master musician.

Paran. The name given to the syllables corresponding to the different numbers of the strokes of a tala.

Patiala gharana. School of music originating in the one-time princely state of Patiala which was famous for its patronage of music. Bade Ghulam Ali is its most famous contemporary exponent.

Pentatonic raga. A melodic scale consisting of only five prime notes.

Pitch. The level of the keynote or tonic note chosen by a vocalist or instrumentalist as the base for the scale of the raag. All these scales are now shown for the convenience of Western audiences as commencing from middle C, but they can easily be transposed if the Indian pitch is raised so that C♯ or D♮ or any other note corresponds to the tonic sa of the Indian scale or mode. Sa is only fixed in relation to the intervals between sa and the other notes: reh, ga, ma, pa, dha and ni. Male vocalists usually choose C, C♯, D or D♯ for the commencing sa; women vocalists G, G♯, A or B♭.

Prabhandas. An antique word for musical pieces, including all songs, as used in old texts such as the *Sangeet Ratnakara* (thirteenth century).

Praña. Cf. Nada = life breath = divine energy, the prime cause of life through the divine energy in the air molecules that each person imbibes even without reflection. The very air that one breathes is scientifically the very life force of the universe, a fact which even the most convinced atheist cannot deny in biochemical terms. The Hindu in fact says that by the very nature of our breathing, so philosophically recognized in the science of yoga, we deny atheism. There is in fact no word for this concept in Sanskrit – to deny God would be to deny the creative processes which we have to recognize by our very intake of air/atmosphere/ether, which is called by so many names in Sanskrit.

Qanoon. Instrument like a tambura for vocalists but flat-shaped, wooden, stringed instrument (like a rabab) as used by Bade Ghulam Ali when he was alive.

Qawali-singing. A kind of musical competition in verse-making exclusive to the Muslim community. It is accompanied by rhythmic clapping. This form of Hindustani music was created by Amir Khusro nearly 650 years ago to pay homage to his great guide, Nizamuddin. Every summer large gatherings were held in Delhi by Hindu and Muslim communities alike to celebrate the Urs of Nizamuddin at his tomb (now in present South Delhi). Qawalis are sung – not only devotional in character but also charged with human, sensous emotion, so much so that whole audiences join in the swinging rhythms like contemporary young audiences listening to 'rock' bands.

Raag or **Raga.** Ranj = to colour or tinge with emotional colour.
Historical development:

Grama was the earliest name given to a collection of notes definitely related to one another by certain measurable intervals not of a haphazard nature.

Murchhanas then developed with seven notes strung together, but not necessarily on one octave as we know them today.

Jatis were the next stage when murchhanas became disciplined into a harmonious relationship which projected consonance of certain fixed entities, i.e. one note fixed as sa or tonic or drone note, one as final note, a predominant note which had a good deal of emphasis, and one relating to it in tonality.

Ragas developed as an arrangement of intervals so that seven notes are in a certain relationship with each other and thus define a melody.

(a) There are several hundred common ragas in existence now which have become the foundation for the two classical systems of India.

(b) A raga gives a melodic structure in which a comprehensive ethos is presented.

(c) A note of warning: Pandit Ravi Shankar has said: 'For simplification, it is necessary to know the notes that constitute a raga – but for classifying them according to constructional affinities *it is imperative* to know not only the notes used but also *how they are used!*

(d) Mixed ragas can combine various ideas, so setting contrasting moods side by side as the raga is expounded. This cannot be done to every raga; only certain ones less serious and contemplative are appropriate for such treatment.

(e) Matanga (*c.* seventh–eighth century AD) wrote this definition of the raga: 'a kind of sound composition, consisting of melodic movements, which has the effect of colouring the hearts of men'.

Raag numbers. There are 72 heptatonic (7-note) primary ragas–

melakartas as they are properly called. In all these the 5th note (pa) is constant and never modified. In 36 the 4th note (ma) remains a true substantive note also, whereas in the other 36 it becomes augmented, i.e. in the Western scale F > F♯. There are derivative ragas from these using, in permutation, first 5 notes in ascent, then 6 notes, with 7 in descent, etc., so that in all, from these mathematical combinations there are about 400 in actual use.

Raas or **Rasa.** The emotional and aesthetic relish or flavour of the raag. The very sounding, for instance, of two or three tones in juxtaposition – such as ni^k sa reh^k, or dha^k pa ma^t of Kamavardhani Raag and Bhairavi Raag – immediately sets up an electric response, and therefore a chemical one as well, in the adrenalin of the listener. The fluctuations of constant play through the rasa has a powerful effect on the practised Indian audience.

Rabindra Sangeet. Bengali poems composed by Rabindranath Tagore at the turn of this century, set to music by him and abounding in great lyrical charm easily assimilated by the Western ear.

Riyaz. 'Practice' (Persian word) = abhyas in Hindi. It applies to long years of assiduous practice and discipline for the musician. It also applies to ordinary music practice in home and school.

Sādhana. The word has peculiar Hindu connotations, meaning dedication in the complete spiritual sense of losing one's identity through a single-minded concentration = absorption (in the yogic sense) in the potent energy and mind of the universe.

Sama or **Sum.** Literally, 'composure after agitation' or 'equal balance'. The sama is the anchor of all melodic line and tala. It is the leading beat at the beginning of each rhythmic cycle, not a final beat such as Western music tends to employ.

Sama Veda or **Saam-veda.** The book of the saman chant – simple melodies like Gregorian chant, used for Vedic religious ceremonies at least 4000 years ago. They were melodies for which words were found later, rather as the poet Tagore admitted when he wrote that he often thought of the music first and the lyrics after.

Sammelan. A gathering or festival (Sangeet Sammelan being a music festival).

Sampoorna. A complete raag consisting of all seven notes, unlike some ragas which omit certain notes of the octave.

Sampradāyā. A tradition of music handed down through centuries of experience and research by vidwans or teachers.

Samvadi. The concordant note, second in importance after the vadi.

Samvaditya. The principle of consonance in the specific ordering of notes in the raga scale so that all is harmonious and not jagged or dissonant, with emphasis on the concord between vadi and samvadi note.

Sanchari. 'Mixed'. It is a movement in the development of the melodic line combining both the sthayi level of the middle octave and the antara section moving up the register. Sanchari begins at the upper tonic note and moves up and down over three octaves.

Sangeet. Variously spelled in English: samgita, sangita, sangeeta, or shortened to geet. In the Hindu shastras or books of principles and codifications, this word not only covered the whole area of musical principles but also those of dancing and the theatre. There are three categories in fact: geet or vocal music; vadya or instrumental music; and nrittya or dancing.

The definition of the word also includes the poetry which provides the texts for the songs accompanying the dance and music.

Sarangi. A stringed instrument used much in Hindustani music, sometimes as the drone, sometimes as the main instrument.

Sargam. The shorthand for the sol-fa notes: sa, reh, ga, ma, pa, dah and ni, and the name given to the method of singing these notes in syllabic form to convey abstract sound, a method very different from the Western use of words to convey meaning in music.

Sarod. A stringed instrument of Persian origin, of great sophistication with beautiful liquid sounds.

Shādava. Hexatonic raag consisting of six notes.

Shadja. The keynote or beginning note equivalent to the Western doh.

Shehnai. A wind instrument of the North.

Shruti or **Sruti.** 'To hear' (Sanskrit). A microtonal interval of which there are twenty-two in the Indian octave.

Shuddha. A pure note, the sol-fa notes of the octave.

Sitar. A stringed instrument of infinite complexity much played in North India nowadays.

Sloka or **Shloka.** A Sanskrit verse or quatrain without time measure, used in music, dance and verse dramas as a sung improvisation invariably devotional or philosophic in character and addressed to God.

Sparsha or **Spursh.** A technique of vocalizing or playing an instrument so that an adjacent note is very slightly touched, thus arousing resonance, slurs and overtones of grace notes.

Sthayi. Any matter or thing that is repetitively persistent or permanent, such as the musical phrases reiterated throughout the alaap of a raag.

Svara. A full tone or note.

Svara-dhyana. The devotional attitude of concentration and dedication brought to the music by meditation on the feel of the notes.

Svarakshara. Note-syllables, sa, reh, ga, ma, pa, dha and ni, sung as if they were words; a rapid passage similar to our cadenza in which the singer breaks from the words of the lyric in our sense to sing a rapid passage of sol-fa notes as a *tour de force* of abstract sound patterns.

Svara-sahitya. A portion of the gat which is presented by the singing of the sol-fa notes, giving a 'thought' content to the music.

Svara-varta. Cf. **Sargam.**

Svara-vistara. Improvisation or elaboration upon the notes, a pulling-out and extending of one passage, or motif.

Taan. 'To spread'. This word comprises a good many musical devices which enlarge on the prime notes of a raag scale. Taans creep into the alaap as it extends into the sanchari section as musical figurations in vilambit, madhya or drut tempo. Other kinds of taan consist of a rapid succession of tones branching from the main melodic line of the raag as a shower of sound to expand and spread the basic melody.

The sol-fa syllables are not pronounced as separate entities but only as vowels 'aa' ,'ee' and 'oo', created by the muscular contractions of the throat, so giving flourishes which are to the music as arabesques are to architecture. Amazing virtuoso performances can be given by artists proficient in this art of taan display, but the difficulty is to keep a right equilibrium between showing off one's technical prowess and the desired aesthetic balance of the whole development of the raag.

Taans could be said to be mathematical devices in musical art which use the mechanics of the vocal chords as though the throat was an instrument in itself, a thought related to Vedic belief in the magic potency of pure sound as having spiritual influence over people. These devices can be graphically illustrated:

Choot taan: swinging rise and fall.

Gamak taan: swinging taan, sometimes given a quivering impression by using notes twice over, e.g. sa sa, ga ga, ma ma, etc.

Jabra or **Kampana** taan: a trembling or shaking sound which creates the characteristic Indian gutteral 'gargle'.

Kut taan: a crooked use of notes, a zig-zag which is difficult to execute flawlessly and precisely, when a vocalist compresses a taan into the last section of a tala at great speed. The maximum number of notes are squeezed into the shortest space of time, e.g. Teen tala.

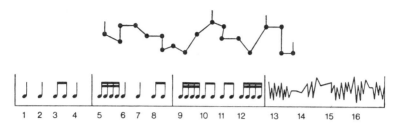

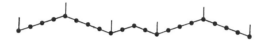

| 1 | 2 | 3 | 4 | 5 | 6 | 7 | 8 | 9 | 10 | 11 | 12 | 13 | 14 | 15 | 16 |

Sanat taan: a rise and fall in equal measure.

Tabla.   North Indian two-piece drum.

Tala or **Taal.**   The root 'ta' stems from tandava = the Cosmic Dance of Shiva; and 'la' from Lassya = the dance of Parvati, the female Principle of the universe. It means a palm of the hand in Sanskrit, indicating the clapping of hands to keep the strict beat and time measure.

(a) Tala is the basic connection between the three constituents of sangeet: vocal music, instrumental music and dance. It comprises the metric patterns, the actual beat of the music rather than the inherent pulse or laya. The origin of the word is connected with the Hindu metaphysical belief in the all-embracing, comprehensive rhythm of the universe as personified in Shiva.

(b) From an original group of 7 main talas, 35 were derived and made popular by the compositions of Purandaradasa (AD 1494–1564). These still remain basic to Carnatic music whereas North Indian tals have come under further influence. These originals are:—

Ek tala	of	4 beats
Rupak tala	2 + 4 =	6
Jhapa tala	4 + 1 + 2 =	7
Triputa tala	4 + 2 + 2 =	8
Mathya tala	4 + 2 + 4 =	10
Atha tala	4 + 4 + 2 + 2 = 12
Dhruva tala	4 + 2 + 4 + 4 = 14

In the North a larger grouping on a different basis is prevalent today. Most authorities agree to the figure of 108 main talas but

281

those most often played now are listed below. Also, many extremely difficult and asymmetric ones are becoming known through the work of Alla Rakha who is capable of playing an irregular tala such as this $5\frac{1}{2}$-beat one divided fractionally and logarithmically into three divisions: $1:833$, $1:833$, $1:833 = 5:499$!

(c) The basic talas used in Hindustani music are these:

 Dadra: a rhythmic cycle of 6 beats divided $3 - 3$
  generally in fast tempo for light music
 Rupak ....7.................$3 - 2 - 2$
  in slow tempo for serious music
 Deepchandi: as for Rupak tala.
 Adi ....8.................$4 - 2 - 2$
  in fast tempo with a beat and three
  counts, a beat and throw, a beat and
  throw.
 Kehrvaa ....8.................$4 - 4$
 Chandrakada ....9.................$5 - 4$
  divided irregularly and subdivided.

X X X THROW

 with emphasis on beats 1, 3 and 5.
 Jhaptāl ....10.................$2 - 3 - 2 - 3$
 Mandari ....11.................$3 - 2 - 3 - 3$
  divided irregularly.
 Ektal ....12.................$4 - 4 - 2 - 2$
  for slow tempo and serious music.
 Jaital ....13............. $9 - 2 - 2$
  divided irregularly.
 Adachautal ....14.................$2 - 4 - 4 - 4$
  for slow tempo and serious music.
 Jhumra ....14.................$3 - 4 - 3 - 4$
  for slow tempo.
 Gaja Jhampa ....15.................$4 - 4 - 4 - 3$
  divided irregularly.
 Teentaal ....16.................$4 - 4 - 4 - 4$
  a very common tala much used in fast tempo.

Tala vadya kacheri. Kacheri = mixture; tal vadya = percussion instruments. A concert of percussion instruments, especially in South India, usually consisting of a mridangam, dholak, tabla, kanjira, ghatam and flute. Each instrument takes up the motifs of the alaap in turn, gradually shortening the phrases and accelerating the beat until the final coda when all come together in unison with the melodic line and a final crescendo on the last sum, when the ghatam player will throw his pot up in the air with a flourish and catch it exactly upon this vital beat. Sometimes the rivalry is so intense that drum players are upon their knees defying each other to surpass the latest improvization.

Tambura. Drone instruments, four-stringed, sounding the tonic, its octave note and the emphasized note.

Tanam. South Indian alaap in medium tempo; a pulse is present but no definite tala.

Tansen (1508-89). India's most famous musician who is buried in Gwalior and who was referred to as one of the Nine Gems in Akbar's court.

Tappa. Muslim love song of the North, so richly ornamented with flourishes and gamakas that the melody is almost submerged. A swinging rhythm accompanies the songs. They were introduced to Lucknow, the seat of Muslim culture, in the nineteenth century by a well known singer, Shouri Mian. Tappas originally were the rough songs sung by camel-drivers in the Punjab until Shouri Mian reconstructed and refined them. They are long recitatives of the love tragedy of Hir and Ranjha, folk-hero and heroine of the Punjab.

Tarāna or **Tillāna.** A fast-moving popular melody often used by bullock and camel-drivers singing the drum-bols as sounds attached to the music because of the rhythm inherent in their syllables, e.g. tillālai, tillālo, lai, lo. A song will run like this:

> Dha ra nāma, dha dha nita,
> Ta dingina tem, tillalai lai lo.

Tata. Stringed instruments, from the root word 'taan' = to stretch.

Tetrachord. The two sections of an octave, the lower half comprising two whole tones and one semitone such as the notes $D\flat > E > F > G$ of the Western $D\flat$ scale.

Thaat. The ten regular primary scales of Hindustani music.

Thēka. The regular drum phrase, the *memoria technica* for a particular tala, e.g. dhin dha na; dhin dhin; dhā ti-ri-ka-ta; dhin ... The variants to these thekas are called parans.

Thumri. Popular light classical romantic lyric, usually based upon sringara rasa (erotic) and karma rasa (pathos). Thumri thrived in North Indian Muslim society in the eighteenth–nineteenth centuries, especially around Lucknow and Benares. Bol-taan, the art of singing certain words and working out as many musical variations of them as possible, is characteristic of thumri.

Thyāgarāja (1800-50). One of the most famous South Indian saint/ musician/composers.

Tirvat. 'Singing' the melody or putting mnemonic sounds used in rhythm to the notes of the raga.

Ustad. Persian and Urdu word for master-musician.

Vadi. In Sanskrit this word means a speaker or dictator, hence the predominant note of the scale, the salient note upon which the musician dwells lovingly, giving it prominence by coming to rest on it. The vadi can be anywhere in the octave in use; it may even be the keynote, although this is rare. The vadi is really the pivotal note of the scale.

Vadya. Instrument.

Vakra. A turning note, such as B♭ in this line: C D E♭ F G A♭ B♭ A♭ B♭ C B♭ A♭ B♭ A♭ G F E♭ D.

Varjit swara. An enemy note which is not to be touched on in a raga.

Varna. Variations on a melodic theme within the specific notes of the raga, so carrying the movement forwards in recognizable 'movements'.

Varnam. The most complex item in Bharat Natyam dance performances, and not to be confused with varna. Varnam begins with precise and pure dance sequences (abstract and geometrical) followed by interpretation through gestures of the words of the song. It compresses the sol-fa syllables of the svaras together with the sahitya words of the song, or poetic text, alternating them with the refrain of the melody in a type of rondo form.

Vidya. 'Knowledge' (Sanskrit). A guru imparts his vidya to his shishya.

Vikamp. Vibrations which change the intervals between notes. Vikar = deformation (Sanskrit).

Vikrit. A note which is 'deformed', i.e. slightly modified in the playing of the raga and touched very delicately as a sharpened sharp or a flattened flat. It does not occur regularly but is used for an especially heightened effect which sensitive ears can perceive (as in Ragas Multani, Pahari and Bhairavi). Vikr = a slight twist or turn.

Vikritatwa. Modification of notes, but not in the sense of the Western scales. Because the notes are not fixed on the keyboard the degree of augmentation or diminution depends on the relationship of one note to another.

Vikr raag. A raag in which the descending scale twists and turns slightly from the shuddha ascending scale and therefore makes it a different raga from the primary one – such as in derivatives of Yaman thaat where ga is omitted in descent and the flow of music moves from pa to reh. Some ragas obey this rule of flexibility even in the ascent (Gaur Sarang).

Vilambit. Slow tempo.

Vistar. Elaborations in vocalization. In Sanskrit it means 'to give length', i.e. development, through taans for instance.

Vivadi. A note that 'quarrels' with a vadi, such as G (pa) in relation to B (ni). These are to be sparingly used as they may influence the vocalist to shift his ground and tonic into another related raga.

Vrinda. A multitude or group.

BIBLIOGRAPHY

A Classical Dictionary of Hindu Mythology, John Dowson (ed.), Routledge and Kegan Paul, London, 1961.

A Treatise on the Music of India, N. Augustus Willard, Nabajiban Press, Calcutta, 1834, reprinted 1962.

An Introduction to Asian Music, William Purcell, Asia Society Pamphlet, New York, 1966.

Classical Dance and Costume of India, Kay Ambrose, Adam and Charles Black, London, 1950.

Gitanjali, Rabindranath Tagore, Macmillan and Co., London, 1953.

Hindu Polytheism, Alain Danielou, Routledge and Kegan Paul, London, 1964.

Hindustani Sangeet Paddhati, N. V. Bhatkhande, Sangeet Karyalaya, Hathras, UP.

India, Madeline Biardeau, trans. from French by F. Carter, Vista Books, Viking Press, New York, 1960.

Indian Dancing, Ram Gopal and Serozh Dadachanji, Phoenix House Ltd., London, 1951.

Indian Music, Shahinda (Begum Fyzee Rahamin), William Marchant and Co., London, 1914 (out of print).

Introduction to Indian Art, Ananda Coomaraswamy, Vasanta Press, Adiyar Press, Madras, 1956.

Music and Dance in Indian Art, Philip Rawson, Edinburgh Festival brochure, 1963.

Music and Musical Modes of the Hindus, Sir William Jones, Nabajiban Press, Calcutta, 1793, reprinted 1962.

My Music, My Life, Pandit Ravi Shankar, Jonathan Cape, London, 1969.

Northern Indian Music, Vols 1 and 2, Alain Danielou, Halycon Press, London, 1949, under auspices of UNESCO.

Oriental Music in European Notation, Chinnaswami Mudalyar, 1892 (out of print).

Pelican History of Music, A. Robertson and D. Stevens (eds.), *Non-Western Music*, Peter Crossley-Holland (ed.), Penguin Books, London, 1960.

Ragas and Raginis, 2 vols, O. C. Gangoly, Calcutta, 1935 (out of print).

Sanskrit-English Dictionary, 1st edition, Sir Monier Monier-Williams, Oxford University Press, 1899.

Sources of Indian Tradition, Vols 1 and 2, William Theodore de Bary (ed.), Introduction to Oriental Civilisations, Columbia University Press, New York and London, 1958.

The Beginnings of Indian Philosophy, Franklin Edgerton, George Allen and Unwin, London, and Harvard University Press, New York, 1965.

The Bhagavadgita, Dr Sarvepalli Radhakrishnan, George Allen and Unwin, London, 1967 (8th impression).

The Dance in India, Faubion Bowers, Columbia University Press, New York, 1953.

The Mirror of the Sky, Deben Bhattacharya, George Allen and Unwin, London, 1969.

The Music of Hindoostan, A. H. Fox-Strangways, Clarendon Press, Oxford, 1965 reprint.

The Music of India, Prof. D. P. Mukherji (out of print).

The Music of India, Herbert A. Popley, Oxford University Press, 1921.

The New Oxford History of Music, Vol. 1, *Ancient and Oriental Music*, Egon Wellesz (ed.), Oxford University Press, 1957.

The Ragas of Hindustan, 3 vols, K. V. Deval, Calcutta, 1918–23 (out of print).

The Ragas of Northern Indian Music, Alain Danielou, Barrie and Rockliff, The Cresset Press, London.

The Story of Indian Music, O. Goswami, Asia Publishing House, London, 1959.

Theory of Indian Music, Bishan Swarup, Swarup Brothers, Allahabad, UP.

Understanding Indian Music, Baburao Joshi, Asia Publishing House, New York.

Index

Abhoga (last section of movement), 96

Abstract syllables (use of in music), 231

Akarsh (ether), 43

Alaap (alapana), 57, 58, 132, 174 (Carnatic), 105

Alamkara (decoration), 131, 157, 245

Amsa (pivotal note or vadi), 181

Antara (second section of movement), 94, 188, 203

Arohana (ascending scale), 56

Arrangements of intervals and their importance, 153, 250

Audience, effect of, 66, 172, 204, 227, 234, 243

Avarohana (descending scale), 56

Baul singers, 36, 48, 50, 100

Bengali music, 99–100

Bhakti (devotional worship), 36, 80, 99, 233, 237–8

Bharata (the sage), 74

Bharata Natya Shastra, 74

Bhāva (innermost sense of realization), 75, 158, 233

Bindu (symbolic point), 48

Bol (drum word), 206, 213, 215, 216, 229, 242

Bol-taans (rapid syllabic patterns), 222, 224, 236

Brahm (Brahman, neuter gender scientific principle of creation), 40

Brahma (masculine personification of above), 41

Brahmin (uppermost caste, religious and secular teachers), 38

Carnatic music (difference in temperament from North Indian system), 103–7, 237

Carnatic music (Karnatakam), 64–84

Coda, 132

Counterpoint in Indian music, elementary, 148 possibility of, 252–3

Dammar (style of music), 268

Darbari, 96, 116

Dharma (innate laws and moral duty), 39

Dhrupad (vocal music), 91–96

Dhyāna (meditation), 244–5

Drone, function of, 130, 148, 176–81, 250

Feeling in Indian music, 143, 234

Gamaka (grace), 131, 133, 135, 138, 186, 194–6, 226, 245

Gat (final summing up of raag), 57, 132, 198, 202–3

Gharana (school of music), 90

Harmony (Western and Indian), 149

Hindu thought, 38–40

Image (the deity of the raag), 173

Improvization and extempore play, 13, 151, 155, 181, 196, 227, 240–3, 245–8, 250

Jati (ancient ordering of scales), 73, 103

jati (grouping of notes), 203

jawāb-sāwāl (dialogue), 203, 226

Jayadeva (Bengali poet/composer), 80

Jhalla (section of alaap), 57, 132, 203

Jor (section of alaap), 57, 132

288